# The Hummingbird Defenders
## By
## Greg Karas

Dear Nicky & Natalie,

Hello from the North Pole! We are, as always, busier than beavers. The toy factory Elves are working around the clock! Chelf & Relf say hello. Last week Chelf took an expedition into the wilderness to track down that pesky Ice-Monster. Forty of the roughest Elf lads went with him. They carried fire brands with them (as they hoped to melt the Rascal). Well, they tracked him all the way to his cave; but the scoundrel dove into a deep crevasse and escaped! Welf, our expert with a crossbow, lit an arrow on fire & shot at the wicked Creature as he descended into the fissure. Most of the Elves there, thought that arrow missed the mark. Some could swear they heard a long wail. Welf remains silent.

The upshot is: We're behind! God Bless You! Pray to Him & thank Him for the Greatest Gift: His Son.

Love,
Saint Nick!

* * * * * * *

# Table of Contents

## Fish and Nuclear War



## Inspiring People



## Kiwanis Stories



## Authors and Books

## Things to Think About



## Poetry



## Baseball

# The Hummingbird Defenders

**The Hummingbird Defenders**
**Stories, Essays, and Poems**

* * * * * * *

By Greg Karas

**This book is dedicated to
Barbara Pedersen.**

## "Milk"

Having a strong long-term memory is a double-edged sword. I can vividly recall things which happened long, long ago which were either delightful or humiliating (depending on whether the Angel or the Devil was sitting at the Control Panel when the Activation Button got pushed). I'm sure that some of my memories have been erased by the filter which we all have that allows us to maintain a semblance of dignity. Some things however, just won't go away…

I remember once in first grade there was a boy sitting behind me in Mrs. Ketchum's class who was apparently hard of hearing. We were having a spelling test and word number 6, was 'Milk'. Mrs. Ketchum (think about the teacher – Mrs. Shields - in **"A Christmas Story"** you know, the film starring Ralphie, and you'll have a pretty good image of Mrs. Ketchum) gave the word, 'Milk'. And then, in accordance with United Nations Guidelines which were in force then as well as now, she used it in a sentence. "We have *milk* with our afternoon snack." Claude, the little rascal sitting behind me, piped up, "Huh?"

Mrs. Ketchum repeated the word (with a stylish variation of the sentence), "Milk. *Milk* tastes especially delicious with hot apple pie." Claude's canals were still clogged. "What?" he groaned.

Mrs. K. didn't bat an eye, but she did clear her throat and those lips did press together ever so slightly. "Ahem, Milk. The farmer gets up to ***milk*** his cows at 6:00 a.m. each morning." Years later, the little smart alec in me might have pointed out that the first two sentences used 'milk' as a noun and now, in this third rendition it had become a verb. But, at the time, the clue-meter was stuck at zero.

While Mrs. Ketchum had a seemingly inexhaustible supply of patience, our gang of five and six year olds certainly did not. With each succeeding "Claudism" we groaned a bit louder. Now, the question became whether or not Claude was grandstanding or was actually having trouble hearing what the word was. "I can't hear you, Mrs. Ketchum," he pleaded and then he stuck out his bottom lip in a bad imitation of Niagra Falls.

I for one, had had enough. I stood up, spun around, and shouted at the top of my lungs, "Claude, the word is ***MILK!"*** I proceeded then, to do the unthinkable. Instead of leaving well enough alone, I let my tirade go on, "A Bridge too Far". I screamed out, "**MILK. M – I – L – K**! Milk, the cold, wet, white stuff in the big glass bottles, you ***moron***!" I had done the unthinkable. I had spelled a word out loud during the spelling test. And, I had called Claude a moron in front of 30 first graders, Mrs. Ketchum, and the Lord Almighty.

There was a pause and a noticeable whooshing of air as the entire classroom gasped. It was probably going to be only a matter of seconds before the principal, the cops, and Roy Rogers on Trigger came bursting through the doorway to haul me off to the East Chicago Public School dungeons.

Now, I can probably blame Moe Howard of the "Three Stooges" for the moron tagline. But, the out loud Spelling of a word from the test caused me to quote Linus from 'Peanuts' at that moment; "I'm doomed." Mrs. Ketchum looked at the flabbergasted children, Claude (who I think knew what the word was ***now)***, and me. I waited for the sword of Damocles to fall…

She spoke (to my everlasting wonder, gratitude, and dismay), “Why, thank you Gregory. Number 7 is *sword.* Robin Hood used a *sword* to fight the Sheriff of Nottingham.”

* * * * * * *

## "The Pen"

I stood in Mrs. Jan Kulka's 3rd grade classroom with my right hand twitching. On the counter next to the window sat a wooden "Lost and Found" box. In it were a pair of scissors, a half filled bottle of Elmer's Glue, a couple of erasers, four crayons (a midnight blue one, a brown one, a broken yellow one, and a violet). Someone had (both jokingly and defiantly) placed a "Bazooka Joe" comic (complete with fortune) from a piece of Bubble Gum in the box as well. There was also a space age looking pen. If I remember correctly it had three separate spring depressor devices, each of which caused a different ball point to descend through the opening in the tip. One plastic tube was filled with green ink, the second one dispensed red, and the third was a bright shade of blue. It was by all accounts, a very worthy pen.

I looked around the room with a guilty expression. The year was 1962. The rest of the class had just stepped outside for recess. That was where I was supposed to be as well. I reached into the box and took the pen. I slipped it into my pocket and headed out on the "Battlefield" to play football with the other grubby third grade boys. The pen felt heavy and awkward in my pocket. I wondered how much it had cost. I wondered which of the other third graders actually owned it. The face of the Greek Priest floated into my mind and I saw the words from last week's Sunday School lesson flash before my eyes. The lesson was about Moses going up onto the mountain and coming back down with the Ten Commandments. "THOU SHALT NOT STEAL!" reverberated round and round my mind as though it were a vast echo chamber. During the football game I got tackled (we were only supposed to play *touch* football) and the pen gouged through my pocket into my right thigh.

After recess I went back to class and spent the remainder of the school day feeling like the character in the Edgar Allan Poe story, "The Tell Tale Heart". When Mrs. Kulka used the phrase "livestock pen" in a Social Studies lesson, I nearly wet my pants and almost began screaming, "I did it, I did it!" The time from lunch until three o'clock seemed to take about a thousand years.

Could I sneak back up to the box and put the pen in without anyone seeing me? No, I was too clumsy and stupid to pull that off. Mrs. Kulka's eagle eyes would spot me heading over in that direction and stop me before I could get anywhere close. Why did stuff like this always happen? If the stupid kid who owned the pen had just kept it inside his or her desk, this problem would have never arisen! That idiot had turned me into a criminal.

On the way home I hatched a new plan for lessening my crushing guilt. I would simply give the pen away. That way, I would no longer be in possession of stolen merchandise. On the sidewalk which ran parallel to White Oak Ave. I saw my brother, Tom. He was walking with Jim Eidam and Mark Berey 40 yards ahead. These were fifth graders. My brother was cool and consequently someone I was either always fighting with or trying to impress. I ran up to the older boys and announced, "Hey Tom. Here's a pen. You can have it."

He looked at the pen and at me and said, "Where did you get that?" I then did what all thieves eventually find themselves doing; I lied. "Uh, I found it on the floor in the classroom." He just looked at me with disgust and said, "You stole it, and when Mom finds out, you're gonna be dead, you little moron."

As soon as we got home he told my mother that I had stolen a pen at school. My mother grabbed her purse and car keys and said instantly, "Get in the car." On the ride back to Elliott School she had me show her the pen. As we marched up the sidewalk into the building I could feel the excruciating pressure that her thumb and her first two fingers were applying to my right ear lobe (Mom is left handed). We walked into school and I could hear my Mom's heels clicking along the shiny tile floor. Mrs. Kulka was still at her desk grading papers. My mom had yet to let go of my ear. I looked at Mrs. Kulka sitting there with her teacher glasses on. She kept track of them with a stylish pearled string device which allowed her to wear them as a necklace when she wasn't using them as a vision aid. My mother said tersely, "Go tell Mrs. Kulka what you did."

I walked up to her desk and said, "Mrs. Kulka, I took a pen out of the Lost and Found box that wasn't mine."

I will allow you to imagine how the story ends from this point. You can speculate about the way in which Mrs. Kulka responded. You can guess what happened in the car on the way home between my Mom and me. You can use your intuitive powers to guess what happened when the Old Man got home that evening from the "Royal Cleaners". All of these are memories which I have spent years attempting to suppress. There is no real reason to bring them up at this hour of the day (or any day, as far as I can discern).

Suffice it to say that that pretty much ended my career as an International Pen Thief. And, after teaching for 32 years I can only say that I wish more parents nowadays used those four little magical words that my Mom did when she caught me messing up my life: "Get in the car."

* * * * * * *

## "The Board of Education"

The year was 1968. The place was Freshman English Discussion class in an almost brand new Munster High School. The teacher was Mrs. Homco. Class was ready to begin. However, my best friend James (actually known as Terry) Lavery and I were not. I was turned around and "Lave" and I were earnestly discussing (I would imagine) the Schley twins, Jenny Treder (you may remember her from the "Martin Homan" Christmas episode), or Lynn Erickson. Rest assured, these young ladies were all worthy topics of conversation. However, the philosophical differences between Mrs. Homco's view of the situation and ours, undoubtedly revolved around the fact that we would be discussing ***them*** during lunch, on the way home from school, and all summer long at the Munster Pool. ***She*** was ready to begin analyzing "A Midsummer Night's Dream". She was getting paid to teach. It was time for business.

"Excuse me, James, Gregory. We're ready to begin class now. Turn around and stop talking please." These were the simple words Mrs. Homco uttered. Now, there were lots of intelligent things I might have done. I might have immediately turned around and shut my overzealous trap. I might have offered up a "Yes, Ma'am. I'm sorry." I could have nodded a "Catch you later" to my buddy Lave. However, adolescence being what it is, I did none of these sensible things. It was as though there were a dozen large diamonds scattered on the ground in front of me with one steaming array of Doberman droppings mixed in among them. Do you understand which item I reached for? Do you understand why?

"Keep your shirt on, Sister. We'll be done in a minute." Now, as soon as I said those words, I knew that the goose had been fully, irrevocably, and disastrously roasted. The entire room did one of those "Whooooosh" moments, when absolutely everything else comes to a screeching halt. Mrs. Homco, who by the way was a wonderful teacher, simply uttered the single shocked and disappointed word, "Gregory!" I turned around and immediately began contemplating what form my doom would take. The rest of the class proceeded without incident.

English class was divided up into two portions. Discussion class had around twenty five students. Immediately following discussion, several classes would proceed to the lecture hall. At that point, another teacher took the helm (with maybe 80 to 100 students present) and other issues relating to the learning of the English language would be addressed. The teacher in English Lecture class was Mr. Robertson. Mr. Robertson was also one of the football coaches. He was "No-Nonsense" personified.

The lecture halls of Munster High School were beautiful and cavernous places. Long curved rows of tables climbed from the front to the back of the room. The lighting system in these rooms allowed the teachers to tweak the mood with reo-stats. There was a wonderfully modern sound system which caused the teacher's voice to resonate richly throughout the space. As I recall the moment when English Lecture was set to begin, Mr. Roberston stood beneath a single spotlight. The rest of the room was shrouded in near darkness. I was sitting far up in the back, perhaps at the 6th row of tables. Mr. Robertson wore a white, short sleeve shirt, buttoned down at the collar with a dark, striped tie. He had on dark trousers and black shiny shoes. He was a physically vigorous and imposing man with a southern drawl, a balding pate, and piercing eyes. I would also describe his forearms as "Popeye-esque". Those forearms were about to become very important to my development as a human being.

He leaned into the microphone as the class settled into their seats. "Karas!" He growled into the microphone and said the name as if I had just sold military secrets to the nearest Russian KGB agent. "Get down here!" I left my seat and walked to the end of the aisle. Then, I slowly descended the wide, broad stairs down to the front of the lecture hall. I could imagine "The Requiem" playing as I marched.

I stood before the podium and faced my judge. "Karas!" He was still talking into the microphone and I heard my name reverberating around the walls of the lecture hall. I had the good sense now to answer with nothing but a, "Yes, Sir?"

"Were you rude to Mrs. Homco today in English Discussion class?"

"Yes, Sir."

"Bend over. Grab your ankles."

Note the brevity of the proceedings. Note the fact that my feelings, my family background, my socio-economic status, my ethnic or cultural heritage, or my psychological problems played no part in the development of the action. It was simply, "Were you rude to Mrs. Homco?" Since the answer was yes, the punishment was immediate and severe. Had I lied, I have no doubt that the sentence would have been even worse. As things worked out, it was bad enough.

My daughter graduated from law school recently and somewhere during the last year I know I have heard the phrase, "Justice delayed is justice denied." Mr. Robertson was all too familiar with this legal principle and he had no intention of delaying anything in regard to my boorish behavior.

I bent over as directed and grabbed my ankles. Mr. Robertson picked up the curved back of a wooden chair which had somehow come loose from it's moorings. It was a hefty piece of lumber with a shiny veneer. He held onto the wood with both hands and spun into his backswing. As he came to the apex of his swing I could see the faces of some of my 90 or so classmates. Their eyes became wide. Their fists clenched. Both boys and girls watched with the same intensity. He spun forward and caused the aged oak to address my hind quarters swiftly, solidly, and squarely. A thwacking noise echoed throughout the lecture hall. Searing, intense pain filled my backside. My field of vision turned red. My recollection is that my feet were momentarily lifted from the ground. Seldom have I felt quite so close to nature. As cotton, wood, and human flesh were pressed together in a manner I imagined to be similar to a nuclear reaction, the clarity of Mr. Robertson's message immediately imprinted itself upon my mind (and elsewhere).

"Karas!"

"Yes, Sir." My eyes were involuntary watering now.

"Bend over, again! Grab your ankles. One isn't enough!"

I bent over again and he walloped me again. The pain was equally as intense the second time around. Maybe even a bit worse.

"Do you plan to ***ever*** be rude to Mrs. Homco again?" I wish everyone in the world could have heard the emphasis he put on the word "ever". Mr. Robertson was a poet and a thespian.

"No, Sir."

"Good! See that you don't."

As I walked back up to my seat (and let me assure you, every set of eyes in that room followed my every step) about twenty years seemed to pass. I had time to think of every aspect of the experience. My rudeness to Mrs. Homco. How embarrassing and humiliating it was being "swatted" in public. The swiftness of the justice that had been meted out. The idiocy with which I had landed myself in this awful predicament in the first place.

Now, everyone reading this story will see it from a slightly different perspective. Some people will note that the punishment was performed publicly. Often, in those corporal punishment days, students were taken into the office or out into the hall to have their hides tanned. Some people will think that it was cruel or uncalled for and would consider what Mr. Robertson did to be "child abuse". The child of today would probably read it as a form of science fiction or fantasy which of course could never really have happened because adults just don't do things like that to children in school.

Here is my take on the situation. I was rude to Mrs. Homco ***once*** in my entire lifetime. Mr. Robertson administered a form of justice which was so clear, so swift, and so absolute that I never thought of doing any such thing again. Mr. Robertson has since passed away, but from my perspective that was one of the best lessons I ever learned. If I am fortunate enough to meet him on the other side of the Bridge, I shall have only admiration and gratitude for what he and the "Board of Education" did for me that day. The point (I can say with complete and utter confidence) was well taken.

* * * * * * *

## "August 16th, 1977"

In 1976 I graduated from Valparaiso University with a degree in teaching. Imagine my surprise (after more than a year had elapsed) that the Nobel Prize Committee had not yet called to ask for my Social Security Number. During that uncertain era, I was holding down two part time jobs. The first one was as a warehouse forklift driver at Wickes Furniture. The second, as a substitute teacher had gone pretty well except for the very first day I did it. You see, on that day I taught Health at Liberty Middle School in Chesterton and I botched things up so badly, that I wondered if I'd *ever* get a classroom of my own.

As my first class of the day began I told the kids to take out their health textbooks and turn to page 127. A large, surly, and disgruntled youngster looked up at me with disdain and said, "You ain't my teacher. I ain't gonna do it!" Aside from thinking that this child could be spending a bit more time in English class, I recognized that his challenge to my authority had to be met head on, or the entire day would turn out to be a disaster.

"Well, I'm your substitute teacher, and your regular teacher has left these plans for all of us, so that's what we're going to do."

"You can't make me."

"I know I can't make you cooperate. However, there are 25 other people in this room and their education is much more important than your misbehavior. So, either pipe down and open up that book, or you and I will be taking a walk to the office."

Burly (I can't remember his real name so that will have to do) was adamant. He folded his arms and repeated his 7th grade mantra of defiance, "I ain't gonna do it."

I walked up and grabbed Burly by the arm (something which nowadays I would only do if jet planes were streaking toward the building) and lifted him bodily out of his chair. Burly was surprised. I don't think he'd ever encountered a Sub before with my level of determination or recklessness. I marched down the hall with Burly in tow until we came to the office doors. They were swinging doors and I remember that holding onto Burly made it impossible for me to open them with my hands. I had been watching some Kung Fu movies back then, so I kicked the doors open with a flourish.

The secretaries glanced up with a "What the heck?" look on their faces. I noticed a couch against the wall and I (gently, yet firmly) spun Burly around by deftly holding onto his hooded sweatshirt. He pirouetted (against his will) down onto the couch. The Assistant Principal, a tall, distinguished looking young fellow by the name of Paul Knauff stepped out of his office with an inquiring look on his intelligent and placid face.

"Excuse me, Mr. Knauff. This young man is being disruptive in my class and I won't have it. His bad behavior is keeping the other students from starting their lesson and learning what they need to know."

Mr. Knauff, in his efficient and elegant style walked toward Burly and said, "Thank you, Mr. Karas. We'll take care of it from here. You can go back and attend to your class."

As I walked back down to the health classroom I notched off the number of mistakes I had just made:

A. Leaving the other 25 students alone in the class for 2 or 3 minutes. (For all I knew they could be raiding the Science lab and mixing Nitroglycerin).

B. Physically grabbing and holding onto Burly and spinning him down onto the couch (Burly didn't smell that great either).

C. Kicking open the swinging office doors. (Bruce Lee was about a thousand times cooler than I was).

D. Not having the skill (within the first two minutes of my first official class) to handle a difficult situation on my own. (The phrase, "Inept Schmutz" occurred to me at the time).

So, the school year went on. I continued to sub (not, as I recall very much at Liberty Middle School), but mostly at elementary schools around Chesterton. The school year ended. 1977 wore on. August came. I had been out of school for over a year and it didn't look like I was *ever* going to get a real teaching job.

I spent a lot of time at the beach, swimming in the cool waters of Lake Michigan and ogling beautiful young women who'd never go on a date with me because I didn't have a real job.

One day, in the middle of August, the phone rang. It was Paul Knauff. He had left his position in Chesterton and had become the K – 12 Principal of Morgan Township School. He told me that one of his teachers had taken another job (with only about 2 weeks until the school year was set to begin) and he was seeking a 4th grade teacher. He told me that he had remembered me because of the confident way in which I'd handled the "Burly Discipline situation."

My jaw dropped and I realized right then, that I had been assigned a very forgiving Guardian Angel. You see, I assumed that I had totally botched the Burly Challenge. I guess the moral of the story is, "If you *act* like you know what you're doing, people might really believe you know what you're doing!" Because I had acted quickly and decisively my actions had impressed the leader (and he was generous enough to ignore all the other mistakes I'd made). Now, he wanted to interview me for a job. I guess in Mr. Knauff's mind, a novice asking for help in a difficult situation was exactly the *right thing* to do.

I was staying with my parents in Munster and my car (a 1967 Pontiac Star Chief Executive) was sick. I asked my Mom if I could take their aged Cadillac to the interview. She said certainly and wished me well. I quickly shaved, took a shower, plastered down my hair, got dressed, stole one of my Dad's ties, and did what I could to make my beach bum self look presentable. It wasn't much.

I headed south toward Route 30 on Indianapolis Boulevard. Right near one of the car dealerships on that busy road I felt a sickening thumpa, thumpa, thumpa, and the car got a flat tire. It was at that moment that I realized that I'd never changed a flat in my entire life. I got out of the Green Caddy and stood staring stupidly at the left rear tire. Before I had time to really panic (I think my plan was to seek out a pay phone and call my Dad for help) I heard a car crunching to a stop on the gravelly shoulder of the road behind me.

It was a blue, battered Station Wagon with two adults in the front and 7 kids distributed evenly throughout all the remaining seats. A smiling man with sandy blonde hair climbed out of the driver's seat, approached me, and stuck out his hand to shake mine. "Hello, Son. My name is Pastor Richard T. Walker and I'm a Minister of the Word of God. The Lord has told me not only to preach His Word but to live it. Looks as though you don't know how to change a tire, do ya?"

"No, Sir. You're right. I don't."

"Well, don't worry about a thing young man because the Lord Jesus has set me in the middle of your path today. I'm going to change that tire for you. Say, by the way you're dressed, I'm surmising that you're on your way someplace pretty important, aren't you?"

"Yes, sir. Job interview. I'm trying to be a teacher."

"Well, that's fine. Let's get this fixed so that you can get back on the road and get that job."

As he deftly changed the tire I looked back at the station wagon. His kids were all blonde and incredibly well behaved and cute. His pretty wife sat smiling in the passenger seat. My assumption was that the Pastor made several of these stops. Nobody was impatient. Everybody watched their skillful Dad (or husband) carry out that part of the Lord's plan for the day by changing the deflated tire (which had a huge nail sticking right in it). He did the whole job in less than 5 minutes (even with all the futile "help" I attempted to render which no doubt slowed his progress considerably).

As he finished I reached into my wallet and took out a ten dollar bill. "Sir, I don't have more than this, but I really don't know how to thank you for bailing me out today!"

The Pastor looked at me with a smile. "Son, put that money away. Here's what I want you to do. I want you to get in this car and go get that job. Then, when the Lord shows you somebody in trouble, I want you to use the gifts that **you** have to help **them**. That's it. That's why we're here. To walk in His Path, to do His Work, to show His Love. Can you do that Son?"

"Yes, Sir. I believe I can."

"And Son?"

"Yes, Sir?"

"Learn how to change a tire. It'll come in handy."

"Yes, Sir. I will."

Now comes the part of the story which probably only a select number of readers will believe. I walked to the driver's door of the Caddy, opened it up, tossed my wallet inside, and then turned around to thank the Pastor one more time. He had not had time to get back in his car, let alone start it up, put on a seat belt, and pull around me back onto Indianapolis Boulevard. Nevertheless, he, his seven kids, his wife, and his beat up Station Wagon were gone. I don't mean that I saw them pulling away down the road. I mean, they were gone!

I went to the interview (and as you might guess) I got that job. I had to smile when Mr. Knauff told me again that he called me because he remembered the way I'd handled the "Burly Situation" at Liberty. As I climbed back into the old green Cadillac with another big smile on my face, the thought occurred to me, "Hey, I'm an adult now. I've got a real job."

I reached over to turn on the radio to celebrate as I headed back toward Lake County from Morgan Township. The song "You ain't Nothin' but a Hound Dog," by Elvis was blasting out of the speakers. I started singing along, "You ain't never caught a rabbit, and you ain't no friend of mine…"

The DJ's voice came on at the conclusion of the record. "Once again, ladies and gentlemen, we are sorry to inform you that today, August 16th, 1977, Elvis Presley, the undisputed King of Rock and Roll, has been found dead inside his Graceland Mansion."

Is there a moral to this story? Probably lots of them. Do I owe my entire career to an ill behaved buffoon who decided to see what I was made of in the first five minutes of class? Maybe. If Paul Knauff had not called, would I still be body surfing along the shore of Lake Michigan waiting for some other Principal to give me a shot? Who knows?

Was Pastor Richard T. Walker an angel, a magician, a former stock car driver who really knew how to make fast getaways, or just a genuine Man of God? I think I know. Why did Elvis check out of the Universe on the same day I was allowed to become a grownup? Maybe I'll find out after I cross the Finish Line.

The bottom line is, none of us make it through this

obstacle course alone. Individuals and events are set in our paths (in the words of Pastor Richard T.) for a variety of reasons. Then, because we are creatures of free will, we're supposed to figure out what to do with, for, or because of them. That day, August 16th, 1977, just happened to have lots of things on the agenda. I won't be forgetting it any time soon.

* * * * * * *

## "On Top of Mount Baldy"

You know the old saying, "A picture is worth a thousand words."* This picture will take a little more than that to do the job, but it is a story which might be of interest to some. I can't remember who took the picture, but I'd like to thank whoever it was.

My son Nick is an adult now. When he was in Kindergarten he came home one day with a permission slip and asked me to help chaperone his class Field Trip to Mount Baldy and the Michigan City Zoo. If you don't happen to live around here and you're reading this, Mount Baldy is a huge sand dune near Lake Michigan in Northern Indiana and the Michigan City Zoo is a WPA era institution with beautiful stone lined walkways and animal enclosures which are a little bit behind the times. However, it is a zoo, so 5 year old kids like it just the same.

Nick's teacher, Becky Clover, planned this fun trip so that it ended up being a combination bus ride, train ride, and hike. I can't remember the exact order of events, but I know that it was very enjoyable and I know that that particular day changed my life.

At the time I was teaching at Morgan Township School. Because of the way the Special Education system is set up in our county, I'd had very little experience with kids who have special needs. Let me tell you right away why I don't like the term "Handicapped". A special education teacher explained to me once where they got that word. When people returned from the war with their legs blown off, they would often sit on the sidewalk or in a wheelchair with a cap in their hands, hoping that others would fill those caps up with money. Thus the word, "Handicapped" (Cap in the Hand) seems to indicate that a person whose body does not operate in the "normal" fashion would have to rely on the charity of others to make it through this world.

So, I'm more likely to say something like "Physically Challenged". Probably, the best thing to do is to just call all people, people, whether they are on crutches, in a wheelchair, or shuffling around on two feet. I mean, think about it for a moment. Suppose the hostess at the restaurant said, "Oh, let's seat that **Old** fellow with the **Grey** Hair and **Bulging** Love Handles – I just feel so sorry for him."

Anyway, on this particular trip there were two children who fit the category discussed above. Angie M. was a cute little girl with dark hair and glasses who'd been born with Cerebral Palsy. Jimmy S. (who happens to be the little guy in the picture) had his life made more challenging by Spinal Bifida. When the busses pulled up to Mount Baldy that day all the kids and chaperones bailed out and listened to Mrs. Clover's instructions.

She announced that everyone would climb to the top of Mount Baldy, wait until the whole group decided to come down, and then everyone would return to their own bus. I glanced over at Jimmy, who was sitting patiently in his chair. I think he had already figured out that this was one thing that his classmates could do (like running, jumping, and skipping) that just wasn't gonna happen for him. Mrs. Clover is as sweet and caring a Kindergarten Teacher as there is on the planet. If she thought the busses could have got a running start and clawed up that sand dune, I think she would have asked the drivers to do that. But, she really couldn't see any way around it. Mrs. Clover said that Jimmy and Angie could wait with the bus drivers at the bottom while the others made the arduous climb up the mountain of sand.

Well, since I stuck the picture at the beginning of the story, you know what happened. I think I carried Angie up first. I probably said something like, "Ladies First". Now, I'm not going to lie to you. I am very glad that I was 32 (instead of 53) when I decided to serve as Sand Dune escalator for those two wonderful kids. Angie was actually a bit heavier. I got her to the top, dropped her off with Mrs. Clover and the rest of the gang, then trotted down to get Jimmy.

Now, as I helped Jimmy and Angie up that hill, I also saw my own son (who would one day go on to be a Division I Cross Country Runner at Butler University) joyfully stride to the top with his Kindergarten buddies. It crossed my mind that his life had been (and was going to be) substantially easier (and so consequently was mine) because he did not have to deal with the physical limitations which were staring little Angie and Jimmy in the face.

I cannot remember the exact conversation that we had as we climbed up Mount Baldy. But, look for a minute at Jimmy's face in the photo. Do you see how he's "Looking up"? That's what I remember about Jimmy. He was "Up". He was positive. He was polite. I remember him thanking me (a bunch of times) for carrying him up that hill. I wondered if I could have had that same patience, acceptance, and loving spirit if I'd been dealt a similar hand in life.

Mrs. Clover (and a couple of the other chaperone Moms on that trip) were saying what a nice guy I was to carry those two kids up the hill. Well, at the time, the movie "Schindler's List" had not come out yet. But, if it had come out, I would have reacted the way Oskar Schindler did at the end of the film when he glanced down at his ring and his car. Someone (I think Sir Ben Kingsley) was praising Schindler for saving hundreds of Jews from almost certain torture and death. But, all he could think about was how many more he might have saved if he had sold that car and that ring. Really, I was wishing that it had been Clark Kent instead of me, and that he could fly right up past the top of Mount Baldy and transport Angie and Jimmy to the Moon, to let them see what that looked like. Again, I saw my son Nick and lots of other Kindergarteners sprinting, tumbling, and hurtling down the hill.

<>

Now, I know what a genius Thomas Jefferson was, but there are a couple of things about him that have always bugged me:

1. He owned slaves as he wrote the words "Life, *Liberty,* and the Pursuit of Happiness" in the "Declaration of Independence". One of the British writers (Samuel Johnson) had this to say about that: "It is very interesting that we hear the loudest yelps for Liberty from amongst the drivers of the Negro slaves."

2. He also notes that, "All Men are Created Equal". They aren't. It's not even close, and it would be a boring world if they were.

I also am smart enough to know that God is way smarter than Thomas Jefferson, or you, or me, and that he knows why all men (and women, and little boys, and girls) aren't created equal. One day, I believe we get to find out the answer to that and other puzzling mysteries. Just not yet. But, in the meantime, on that day way back when I was younger and stronger and my knees and back weren't sore much of the time, it was pretty clear what my job was as it related to those two little kids. I thought that it would be a great thing to work in a school with kids like Jimmy and Angie, so that I could help out more often. I thought that it would be a good way to show how thankful I was for my own two strong and healthy kids… I still think that today.

So, that's what happened on the Field Trip. We went up and down Mount Baldy. We went to see the tigers and bears at the zoo. We rode the South Shore train. We had a nice picnic lunch with the little people. Then, we came home. It was a most satisfactory day indeed.

The story also has a pretty nice happy ending. After Nick and I got home the phone rang. A man's voice said, "This is Doug Hollar, Principal of Parkview School. Mrs. Clover told me that you really helped out at the Field Trip to Mount Baldy. We've got an opening coming up next year in 4th Grade. How'd you like to come in for a job interview?"

* This story actually had 1,466 words, not one thousand.

* * * * * * *

## "End of an Era"

I suppose (now that I sit down to think about it) that many thousands of people retire each day in America. Do you know what it would be fun to do? It would be fun to go back through time and watch imminent retirees we've known at all the different stages of life. In your mind, scan back 55 years to the time when your (about to retire) co-worker, or boss was starting his or her first day of Kindergarten. Imagine that you could watch that person go through that day. How many of the little mannerisms and personality traits which you've come to know would be evident at that early date? If you've ever seen the wonderful Albert Brooks film, "Defending Your Life", you'll know where I got this idea.

I remember reading in a biography of the great cartoonist Charles Schulz, that his Kindergarten teacher saw a drawing Charles had done and said, "Why Charles, you're going to be an artist someday." Schulz commented that he never forgot what his teacher had said to him. I read similar stories about how two Presidents (oddly enough, they were Carter and Nixon) were encouraged by their first grade teachers. Both men remarked that things their teachers had said or done had inspired them throughout their entire lives. I couldn't help but wonder just what Richard Nixon's teacher had said to him. Perhaps the people whose lives we were taking a look at had similar experiences. Maybe not.

As we followed these people throughout their lives we would see bike riding lessons, birthday parties, high school dances, ball games, graduations, moves, marriages, their own children being born and raised, in some cases divorces, tragedies, anniversaries, perhaps the arrival of grandchildren, new homes, vacations, and of course the world of work.

Some people are fun to work for and with. But, I have found throughout my long and many faceted career (as a drycleaner's assistant, cast iron bath tub deliverer, storm tile and sump pump dirt digger, King of the Munster Pool, Furniture Warehouseman, Substitute Teacher, Summer Camp Program Director, High school and Junior high coach, and for the past 29 years, elementary school teacher) that the best kind of boss to work for is ***one who knows what in the world he or she is supposed to be doing***. If fun enters in later, that is a bonus. But, the Captain of the Ship who plows into the iceberg, doesn't have time to go see how the shuffleboard games are getting along.

For the past 18 years I have worked for a man who knows what to do each day. For those of you who think the running of a 325 student elementary school is an easy task, let me enlighten you right now. There are whacked out parents, misbehaving students, disgruntled staff members, leaky water fountains, late busses, mixed up milk orders, and a whole myriad of other issues just waiting to take a big chomp out of any Principal's derriere each and every day of the school year. Our Principal, Douglas Eugene Hollar, handled all of those problems (and bigger ones like the shooting death of a student's parent, on more than one occasion) with grace and dignity. I don't know how many times I have said, "That's why you get the big bucks," as I walked out of the office, happy in the knowledge that ***he*** would be dealing with a problem that day that I would not want to touch with a ten foot eraser. Really, a Principal of a school is like the busiest fireman in town. As soon as one conflagration is put out in one corner of the building, another inferno can flare up right down the hall.

Mr. Hollar is probably the most organized man I have ever met. I can truly appreciate that because I am the least organized man that I have ever met. If you go to him and say, "Do you think you have my grades from 1996? A former student is doing some research and he had some questions." He will find those grades in less than 3 minutes. I lose my keys up to 4 times a day. In addition to being well organized, Doug is smart. He was Salutatorian of his high school graduating class in Warsaw, Indiana. He can also tell you exactly what the Valedictorian does for a living (she's an author). When a situation arises at school which requires an elegant and rapid solution, you can almost hear the well oiled wheels spinning in his mind. And, he won't let it go until he's figured it out.

Doug is also a quintessential family man. His lovely wife Judy works at Thomas Jefferson Middle School in the English Department and plans to follow him into retirement after next year. His son David is a well respected attorney in the Federal Prosecutor's Office. His daughter Julie is a successful journalist. Recently, when Doug's mom passed away, we saw the entire family at her visitation.

In this day and age, keeping a family together through all the storms which assail it is no easy task. When Doug's offspring warmly greeted the contingent of teachers and aides who had come to pay their respects, we knew that he and Judy had done a wonderful job of raising their kids.

Doug is also a perfectionist. There is debate in the modern world about whether or not this is a good thing. Everyone knows that perfection (outside of the realm of God) is unattainable. The perfectionist can make himself ill trying to achieve the unachievable. Doug has. Friends and family have often pleaded with him to ease up. As he has gone through life he has figured out that it is not worth sacrificing one's health to see that some project or other is perfectly executed. But, it took him time to figure this out. I would argue that he pushed himself so hard because he cared so much. In today's world, on the other hand, we see so many people just "getting by". Doug never just "got by". And, since that was the case, our school ended up being a better place. Doug got personally mangled on many different occasions, but the institution got better. Is that a good thing or a bad thing? What do you think?

Earlier in this story I mentioned that a Principal's job is loaded with potential pitfalls. That is true. However, it is also filled with wonderful miracles. Like a magician, a principal who works in an elementary school puts funny looking little kids into a silk top hat and then reaches in to pull out successful and accomplished young adults only a few years later. Just recently, Valparaiso High School Senior Alex Costakis invited Mr. Hollar to the Banquet which honors the highest achieving graduates. Each graduate is asked to invite an educator who has made a lasting impression on that individual as he or she was growing as a learner. Doug was genuinely touched by this invitation.

I hope Alex knows the importance of his gesture. Doug has taken great pride in the achievements of the thousands of students he has shepherded through the early years of their learning. To be asked to celebrate the accomplishments of one of those students served as a symbolic reminder of all those other kids he has helped along the path of life. To come in his last months at the helm was absolutely perfect timing. It was a wonderful move on Alex's part which allowed Doug to celebrate and reflect simultaneously.

I also mentioned fun. Since Doug knew what he was doing (remember that thing about avoiding the icebergs?), he was able to create a climate where both kids and adults in his building could have fun. I wish that all the people in town who have never stopped into Parkview School during the Friday each May that we call "Friday Night Live", could somehow see Doug as he delights the students by portraying the villain at this annual reading event. This year for instance, he portrayed "Destructo Ex Libris", a book hating nasty with a flowing cape, spiked blonde hair, and a snarly demeanor who interrupted the kids reading sessions to sing the following the ditty (sung to the tune of "Iron Man"):

I am Destructo,
In my world all books must go.
I don't have to read,
Food and TV's all I need!
I don't want to think,
Got no use for page with ink.
Don't mess with your mind.
Hope for an Ignorant Mankind.
If you kids all read,
That will mean you will succeed...
Don't want no bookstores!
Burn all the Libraries too!
(Doodle lup, Doodle lup, Doodle lup too)
World without Deep Thoughts,
That's what I think we will do!

It's just something that you have to see with your own eyes to believe it is happening. In this insane world where politicians have virtually sucked the joy out of every aspect of education, it is a wonderful thing to witness. Doug let this (and other fun events) happen in his building because he had enough wisdom to see how much happiness it gave the kids.

Now, he gets to rest and enjoy the remainder of his life. Doug's nephew, Steve Hollar, played the character "Rade" in the classic film, "Hoosiers". One of my favorite scenes in that movie is when Gene Hackman is standing in the huddle with his team before the State Championship game.

He looks them all in the eye and says, "I love you guys." You can see in the players' eyes that the feeling is mutual. I think when we're in our final teachers' meeting I can see a similar scene taking place. When I first arrived at Parkview, I thought it was kind of corny that Doug referred to all the people in the school as the "Parkview Family". I was wrong. That is exactly what he has created. When you see him around town in the weeks to come (and we're throwing a big party for him on June 1st at the school), let him know that you appreciate all that he has done over the last three decades for the students, parents, and staff of Parkview Elementary. He has done a lot. He will be missed. It is indeed the end of an era.

* * * * * * *

## "Fireball Joe Crowley"

Sometimes in life success looks like failure. But you just might have to hang out for a few years to see it become success. I want to tell you the ballad of "Fireball" Joe Crowley. When I first came to teach in Valparaiso there was a bright little kid in my class named Joe. Joe was a good student, but he was an even better person. He was the last of a long line of kids from a good Catholic family, many of whom were several years older than Joe. He was used to talking to adults and sometimes you'd even forget that Joe was a kid. He was very perceptive and able to maintain a mature conversation when he was nine better than some people I know now who are 39.

Joe was into athletics, but I think he realized early on that he didn't have the size or speed to be a big time player. That didn't matter to Joe. He loved sports and liked to be where the athletic action was. When he hit high school Joe was the manager for the baseball team & for the famous basketball team led by Tim Bishop and Bryce Drew to the state finals. He tells a great story about using a mild swear word in front of Bryce (Joe was an underclassman and Bryce was a Senior) and getting a stern and swift rebuke from the future college star and NBA guard. When Joe went to college he became the manager for the Indiana State Sycamores Men's Basketball program.

During Joe's fourth grade year we were doing reports on people, events, and places which have made Indiana famous. Joe chose the Indianapolis 500. His dad had worked at the oval for years and Joe knew a LOT about the race track and the sport of auto racing. He had constructed a replica of the track in his basement using Legos. This was no small model. Joe had used many many thousands of the little colored blocks to reconstruct the "Brickyard".

He brought it into school a few years later when our "Friday Night Live" theme was auto racing. Everyone who saw that model said the same thing, "Ooooooh! That's cool." And it was cool. Really cool. And really big.

Here's where the failure part comes in. Every year for several years I applied for a summer grant from the Lilly Endowment people in Indianapolis. One of our Kiwanis members, Gary Gross, was awarded one of these grants to study Franklin Roosevelt's life (you might remember Gary's FDR talk at our club before he became a member). The art teacher at our school, Mary Austin, has also been awarded the grant and it earned her a trip to Europe. Sometimes I feel like every teacher in the state (except me) has earned one of these grants. But every time I have applied, I get the "We are sorry to inform you" letter.

One of the times I had applied I used photos from Joe's Indy 500 model as part of my plan. The idea was to construct similar models to help children learn about the history of the state of Indiana and to use Joe's model as the flagship.

Well, to make a long story short, the brilliant professors who judge the proposals once again thought mine had the ability to imitate a brand new Hoover Vacuum cleaner. I got the dreaded letter. And I felt like a failure once again.

At the time of this failure, Joe was a middle school student. I wrote to him telling him about my cockamamie scheme & the fact that I had failed. I said that my plan had been (if I had been successful) to give him $500 dollars (one, I said, for each mile of the race) for the use of his model and his great idea. I closed the letter by saying that I knew that one day he *would* be rewarded for his creative ideas.

Fast forward again several years to Joe's Senior year of college. Something else special I forgot to mention. Joe is loyal. He has come back to see his old teachers every year without fail since he left elementary school. This definitely puts him in the minority. So, one day during his Senior year I was not really surprised to see him stop in and visit me. He had something folded up in his hand. He said, "Hey, I wanted to show you something." It seems that he had kept that letter tacked up on his bulletin board all through high school and college. He came in to show it to me and to tell me that he had been selected for an internship at the Indy 500 in the media department. He has since parlayed that internship into a full time position. Joe is now gainfully employed as the Media Coordinator for the Indy 500. He flies throughout the world, makes contacts with major news organizations, and is on a first name basis with the most renowned drivers and owners in the world.

So you see, even though my scheme to make a quick buck off some grant money didn't pan out, something much more important did. On top of that - Joe is still the great guy I knew as a 9 year old!

When we take the fifth graders from our school on a two day field trip to Indy, Joe meets us at the track. He talks to the kids about following their dreams, he gives them a little die cast metal Indy racing car, and he gives me a smile about as wide as the Grand Canyon. So, in this case (as in others I'm sure you can recall) success was there all along, it just took a little longer to show its beautiful face. I guess that right there is why I teach little kids! Because they don't stay little forever, and some of them never forget where they came from!

(Update: Joe currently works for the Tony Stewart Racing Team.)

* * * * * * *

## "Mr. Douglass and the Future of Mankind"

If you are spending time worrying about the future because you read and see lots of negative things about America's youth, I'd like you to sit still for a moment and take a deep breath. Everything is going to be okay. Here's why:

I have known Anthony (Tony) Douglass since he was a 4th grade student at Parkview Elementary School in Valparaiso, Indiana eight years ago. The Douglass family is universally admired and respected by the staff at Parkview. Tony's brother (Tim) and sister (Samantha) also attended our school. Additionally, Tony's mom (Deb) has been one of our school's cooks for several years. Everybody in the Douglass family is a positive member of society. They are all hard workers. They are all polite. They are all considerate of others.

I have been fortunate during the 2007 – 2008 school year because Tony has been an Assistant Teacher in my classroom. Four days a week from 8:00 a.m. until 10:00, Tony comes in and works with students in a self contained 4th grade setting. I cannot begin to express what a wonderful opportunity this has been for the students and myself.

I've been a classroom teacher for 31 years and frankly speaking, sometimes having a student teacher is more of a burden than an asset. That is because some young people (even some of college age) don't fully understand what role they should fulfill when they walk through a classroom door. With some individuals in their teens, poor appearance, problems with punctuality, weak language skills, and failure to serve as an appropriate role model are all typical concerns.

With Tony, none of those issues have arisen. He shows up

on time, with a terrifically positive attitude, well dressed and totally prepared for the day. Then, he immediately goes to work.

When I think about how self absorbed many high school Seniors are, and then reflect on Tony's attitude, I am frankly amazed. He is truly an individual who thinks more about others than himself.

He starts each day by making sure the 4th graders have some challenging morning work. "Mr. D." spends lots of his free time designing fun and challenging learning activities to engage the children. He teaches whole group lessons, helps with the lunch count, runs off papers, assists the Kindergarten teacher when our class has Music or Gym, works with students one on one, and generally does whatever he is asked in order to make our classroom a place where everybody is encouraged to strive for and experience success. He's even written an excellent letter to parents, introducing himself and laying out what he hopes to accomplish by working with their children.

In February, Tony designed an excellent "Word Search Puzzle" to get the kids' Valentine celebration off to a good start. I asked him how long it took to design the activity. It took two hours. Tony was not assigned to create this particular activity. He did it because he knew the kids would enjoy and be challenged by the work. Showing that kind of initiative is just one of the reasons we need to feel a bit less trepidation about the future of this land.

On many days Tony takes small groups to work on projects and assignments in the library. He has also designed seating charts, volunteered to help chaperone field trips (he's going with us to Camp Tecumseh in about a week), developed special projects for the 4th graders, and brought in extra treats as well.

He has instituted a wonderful journal program in which students record thoughts and ideas throughout the week. He takes the time to personally respond (in writing) to every students' journal!

All the children really enjoy working with "Mr. D." because they can sense that he truly cares about them as individuals. His commitment to the kids and his work ethic are outstanding.

All of the things mentioned above are even more amazing when one considers the fact that as a young person, Tony was challenged by certain aspects of the school experience. He has *worked* to make himself into a successful individual. I also think that he understands and has patience with students who have trouble tackling certain academic tasks, because he can recall what that is like.

Every aspect of Tony's character and work ethic are beyond reproach. His enthusiasm and great ideas have made our classroom a more vibrant and exciting place in which to learn. As he moves on to the next phase of his life I am certain that he will be an individual who will experience tremendous success. That is because Tony Douglass cares.

So, if you are worried about America and our future, you need to remember that the coin always has two sides. There may be teen-aged, meth-addled, narcissistic, lunatic, gun toting gang members running through American cities and towns. And you and I may have very little power to change that. But, there is also Tony Douglass. He is a person who (as a youth himself) is already standing up for the things on the right side of the fence.

The world has evil and the world has good. Now, I'm not saying that Tony Douglass is Clark Kent and that he is going to save all of us here in Metropolis by himself. But, I am saying that since I know ***this*** young person, that anyone reading this certainly knows ***someone else*** like him who will also stand up for the right things (like helping kids) when the times comes for them to do so. In this way, society will be prepared to continue the strong fight until the Master decides to draw down the Big Purple Curtain at the end of the Final Act. And, I (for one) am not going to waste time worrying about it. Good job, Mr. D. The future awaits...

* * * * * * *

## "Hope"

Many years ago in late August a very small kid with blonde hair stood hesitantly with his tray in the lunchroom of Parkview Elementary School. He was a first grader and for them, being at school all day long is an entirely new proposition. The friend who told me this story, Margaret Johnson (wife of Don Johnson, not the former Miami Vice Star, but the guy who runs the library here in Valpo), said that she saw a look of uncertainty on his face. All the other kids had taken their trays to the tables and had begun munching away. Margaret, a former instructional assistant at our school, approached the little guy and asked him if something was wrong. He looked at her and said, "When are we going to say the Blessing?" Now, that momentous little inquiry raises a whole slew of questions about public education in America, which I don't have time to address here. Margaret, to her credit, handled the situation brilliantly. She just put her arm around his shoulder and said, "Honey, we won't be doing that together here at school like you do at home. But, you can certainly say one yourself before you eat."

A few years later that same kid was playing after school in the Intramural Basketball program. The girls play on Tuesdays and the guys play on Thursdays. Before we start with games the kids run, do a few calisthenics, and then we shoot some free throws. To make it interesting, the coaches (Bryan Benke, the other fourth grade teacher, and myself) shoot ten free throws. Then, anybody who beats us wins a drink from the machine. On this particular day the coach (remember that I was eight years younger) was in good form. I sank 9 out of the ten charity tosses. I said, "Okay fellas. Today, anybody who beats me gets a drink, a candy bar from the teachers' lounge, *and* a dollar." In normal years with normal 4th and 5th grade kids, this would have been like betting on the Yankees in 1927 to win the

Series. The blonde kid (who really hadn't grown all that much since 1st grade) took the ball and calmly sank ten free throws in a row. There was no chest thumping. No 'woo - wooing'. At the end of Intramurals when I gave him the rewards he said humbly, "Thank you, Mr. Karas."

Now, eight years after that the world is a mess in many ways. Bombs blow up daily. Groups misunderstand and hate with a growing fervor and intensity, and I haven't heard of anymore kids in the lunchroom asking about when we're going to say the Blessing. But, there is still Hope.

Hope because the blonde kid is not quite gone yet. He is a Senior at Valparaiso High. His name is Brent Kimmel and he is the best thing to happen to Valparaiso Basketball since Bryce Drew and Tim Bishop worked in the backcourt together.

Junior High Coach Matt Thomas described to Benke (who is the now the 8th grade B team coach) how hard Brent works in the offseason. Four or five hours every day. The hotter the better. Thousands of shots. Hours of ball handling drills. Weight lifting. Passing drills. Running. Free throws. He still is under six feet tall. He only weighs 140 pounds. And that doesn't matter one bit because his heart was made with the same pattern God used when he carved out Bobby Plump, Oscar Robertson, Larry Bird, Steve Alford, and Damon Bailey. Those guys loved basketball the same way Brent Kimmel does. That love led them to great things in life and he is heading down the same path.

Coach Bob Punter has a really good squad this year. Besides Brent, there is McMillan, Moon Dog, Thomas, Nupps, and great kids off the bench like Ozzie, Heckard, Reinhertz, Pease, and the Lieske twins. These kids have been enjoyable to watch all season. They play as a team, they shoot out the lights, and they make it look fun. Remember fun? It was why games were invented in the first place. This fan, for one, would like to thank the team and Coach Punter for their hard work and exciting brand of play.

And especially, this fan wants to thank Brent for turning out to be the kind of young man that all his teachers (Kindergarten through College) will be able to recall with pride in the years to come. Your parents, Steve and Cindy, and your sister Heather (now Treece, who teaches at Hayes Leonard School) share this pride in your work ethic, values, and the positive approach you bring to the game and to life. No matter what happens in March, you are already a Champion in this fourth grade teacher's book! Thanks for the Hope.

Brent Kimmel
(Currently teaching at Valparaiso High School)

* * * * * * *

## "Wayne, Garth, and Lois"

Something really cool happened at our school last week. It seems that many years ago a woman named Lois Anderson used to teach in our building. Lois is 92, and of course has been retired for several years. She wanted to make a visit to her old place of employment. Our principal, an energetic, caring, and intelligent young woman named Stacey Schmidt, had a few ideas on how we might welcome Lois back.

She asked the staff to brainstorm ideas as well. One teacher, Mrs. Moran, planned to have her class make a big welcome banner. Someone else (I think it might have been Kindergarten Teacher, Donna Battista) thought we could do a "Clap Out" for Miss Anderson. A "Clap Out" is something we give the graduating 5th graders each year. Everybody else in the building lines the hallways, and the 5th grade students, as they are preparing to move on to middle school, march through the hallways, and everybody claps. That doesn't sound like much, but you should see the looks on the faces of the 5th graders as they walk by and see people cheering and clapping for them. It is pretty sweet. Our class decided to prepare a poem for Miss Anderson. Here's that poem:

"Once a Teacher, Always..."

The school that we're all learning in,
Was built quite long ago,
And as the years fly by us,
Well, there's some things you should know.

There used to be sixth graders here,
Though that's hard to believe.
Perhaps they liked the place so much,
They didn't want to leave.

And other teachers used to roam
These halls we know so well.
And kids that used to go here
Now are Grandparents; Do tell!

And once there was a teacher here,
And Lois was her name.
And verbs were verbs, and nouns were nouns,
And books were just the same.

This Lois…called Miss Anderson,
She really loved to read.
She knew if kids would love it too,
Well then, they could succeed.

She worked right here,
In Miss Knauff's room.
It then belonged to her.
And she was quite a teacher then,
The History books concur.

So all these years have passed us by,
And Lois has retired,
But think about those children
She has long ago inspired.

They all grew up, and they read books,
Had children of their own.
She stretched their minds, and filled them up,
And that's how they have grown.

So thank you, kind Miss Anderson,
Your life has made a mark.
You brought light into places,
That would otherwise be dark.

For once you are a teacher,
You're a teacher evermore.
And the difference that you made right here,
We see today for sure.

*Thanks to Lois Anderson*
*From the Appreciative Students and Staff*
*Of Parkview Elementary*

<>

So, we got all this stuff ready for Miss Anderson's visit and then her brother called and said that Lois would not be able to come after all. She had been feeling ill and this illness was going to force her to cancel her trip over to Parkview. But, her brother said that he would like to stop by instead. Stacey reported to us that he was a very nice older gentleman and they sat and talked for a while in her office about how Lois loved teaching, and really loved reading and the teaching of Reading class. Then, she said he started looking through his wallet. He couldn't seem to find the thing he was looking for. Stacey figured that he was going to hand her a twenty dollar bill, or some similar token of appreciation.

She was correct about the gesture, but wrong about the amount. It seems Lois wanted to give Parkview $5,000.00 to help enhance the instruction of Reading for our elementary pupils. So, he pulled a check out, handed it across to Mrs. Schmidt, and there you have it. Oh yes, there's one more part to this story. Mr. Anderson didn't stop there. He asked Stacey for directions over to Northview School (which is also here in Valparaiso). It seems that Lois had spent part of her career there as well. Mrs. Schmidt gave him the directions, he walked out to his car, drove across town, and then repeated the whole procedure. Isn't that nice? Ten thousand bucks given away in about a half hour. Wow!

So, you might (right about now) be glancing back at the title of this piece and wondering where in the world it came from. If you were lucky enough to see the hilarious film, "Wayne's World", you will remember the scene where Wayne Campbell and Garth Algar received $5,000.00 each from the sleazy TV executive "Benjamin" (I love it when they call him "Bun-jamin") and go dancing through the street singing, "We got five thousand dollars. We got five thousand dollars..." Maybe the next time we see Mrs. Schmidt and Mr. Hershberger (the principal over at Northview) together, they will be doing that same little song and dance! Wouldn't that be something? All because of Lois...

* * * * * * *

## "The 'Smart Kid' Banquet"

Sometimes, I think back to a day in 1976 when my boss at Wickes Furniture asked me if I would be interested in joining the Manager's training program. I told him that I had gone to school to become a teacher and that I wanted to see that idea through. He told me that I was going to make "Peanuts" as a teacher and that it would be a decision which I'd regret for the rest of my life. I was management material (he said) and the rewards from a career in supervising individuals selling furniture would far outweigh whatever I would encounter in a classroom.

Now, there was the guy who owned the Titanic. I think he said, "God Himself could not sink this ship." Then, there was the person in the front office of the Chicago Cubs who decided to trade Lou Brock for Ernie Broglio. And finally, there was Pat, the Wickes Manager who told me that the rewards in helping to sell Crestline plaid sofas would far outshine what I might encounter in a life spent teaching young people. Now, I happen to know a guy (the smooth Mr. Dale Bagnall) who runs a furniture store and I don't mean to denigrate what he does for a living. He helps a lot of people furnish their homes and he does make more dough than I could ever hope to shake a stick at.

But, the idea that people (namely Pat) can miss the target by such a wide margin is one that often intrigues me. I know that I've done it lots of times myself. Now, I don't have a shipping expert to talk about doomed ocean liners, or a baseball general manager to talk about bogus trades. But, I'm here to tell you that Pat was as wrong as wrong can get when he gazed into what he thought was the crystal ball of my life.

Here's why: I recently was invited to the Valparaiso High School "Smart Kid Banquet" at the Strongbow Inn. Here is how it works. Each year, the top 10% of the 500+ member Senior class at Valpo High is invited to a banquet which celebrates the four years of hard work it took to place them at a class ranking higher than the other 450 some odd kids in the class. These kids in turn invite a teacher who has had the "greatest influence" on them to attend. I suppose calling it the "Smart Kid" banquet (and that is of course, ***my*** name for it) might be a mistake. It might also be called "The Hard Working Kid" banquet. Personally, as a teacher I prefer the hard working kid to the smart kid. More often than not at this particular event, you get the same thing all wrapped up in one package. That is pretty sweet.

At each year's banquet they ask a speaker to come and talk about life and success. One day (right here at a Kiwanis meeting) I was talking to Judy Rooney-Davis and she mentioned that they had asked Joe Crowley to come and speak at this year's event. This made my eyes light up. Joe was in my first class at Parkview. To say he was one of my favorite students of all time would be an understatement. I've written a previous piece about Joe entitled "Fireball Joe Crowley".

Joe is currently a hotshot publicist on the NASCAR circuit. He works for Tony Stewart, and hangs out with people like Troy Aikman and Joe Gibbs. Even though he gets to walk about in that rarified air, Joe almost always gives me a call when he gets back into Valpo. Often, we'll go out for dinner. It would have been a real treat to hear Joe speak. When I emailed him about it, he joked that he had been in the bottom part of the class at Valpo High and he wondered what he might come up with to say to the really smart people at the top. Believe me, he could have come up with a LOT to tell them. He is a guy who will never forget his roots.

Unfortunately, Joe could not make it to the event. NASCAR obligations prevented him from speaking to the graduating kids at his alma mater. I certainly hope the committee keeps after him. I have a feeling he would give a tremendous speech.

So, who ***did*** the Science Department (the high school folks running the banquet) find to speak instead? Well, they found Bill Hanna. Bill is the Executive Director of the Northwest Indiana Regional Development Authority. Talk about somebody who has had a stellar career. After graduating from college Bill joined the military and became a guard and trainer at the Tomb of the Unknown Soldier at Arlington National Cemetery. Locally, he has had a meteoric rise which has led to his current position. Now, I also knew Bill when he was a 4th grader. He was not in my class back when I taught at Morgan Township, because there were two sections of fourth grade, but I coached and worked with Bill and remember him as a kind, funny, smart, hard working, and respectful kid.

I do remember Bill's ***class*** quite fondly indeed. One day in the 1990's my phone rang. A girl named Dena Ailes asked me if I remembered her from 8 years before. My reply was that of course I did, because Dena was one of the most unforgettable kids I'd ever known. Dena said, "Well, we have a favor to ask you. Would you mind being the Commencement speaker at our graduation this year?"

Now, that would be like asking a minor league ball player if he'd like to come and play at the All Star game out in Left Field while Roberto Clemente is prowling Right and the "Say Hey Kid" is in Center. So, I got to buy (under my wife's watchful eye) a brand new suit and talk to a gym full of people about what they should expect to give to and get from the world. It was without a doubt one of the pinnacle experiences of my 54 years on the planet.

At the "Smart Kid Banquet" this year, Mr. Hanna gave a very fine speech about what the kids can and should do as they step out into the world with the considerable gifts God has granted all of them. As I watched Bill speak I thought back to the kind of kid he was and marveled at the great things he has accomplished as an adult. I remembered his parents and his sisters and I reflected that when everybody does what they are supposed to do (kids, parents, and hopefully teachers too) this "education thing" works out quite nicely.

Now, the girl who invited me to the "Smart Kid" banquet is not only smart and hard working. She is talented athletically, artistically, and also with words. She is a track star and she has won big distance walk race events all throughout this country. When I sat down with Melissa and her parents at a table in the Strongbow's dining room she handed me a poem. Usually, (and there are probably whole sectors of the population by now who are pretty fed up with it) I am the one handing people a poem. So, it was absolutely delightful when Melissa gave me those two pages. Here are my favorite lines from that creation of hers:

***"His heart was open, his eyes were bright,***
***He became wild characters on Friday Night."***

This is a reference to our school's annual **"Friday Night Live"** reading event, which Melissa had attended when she was a 4th and 5th grader. For her to remember that event and me in that wonderfully generous fashion, instantly brought tears to my eyes.

I have actually taught three girls from the Moeller family. Jackie, Jamie, and Melissa. Their dad, Martin, runs a local funeral establishment here in town and Martin and I share a birthday (except, he is ***much*** younger). Here is one thing I've found out about all of them. They live life to the fullest. One summer, Martin joined a team of people who dipped their bike tires into the Atlantic Ocean, hopped on, took a little ride, and then dipped their tires into the Pacific Ocean. He came to school to show slides of that trip to my class. You see, I think because the Moeller's work with people who have come to the end of their time cards on a daily basis, they know (probably much more than you or I could know) that this deal down here has no guarantees. Jesus can ring the bell in 20 years from now, or 20 minutes from now. And nobody knows the hour.

Anyway, I had a wonderful time talking with Melissa and her mom and dad at the banquet. While listening to them it occurred to me that the supreme thing I have found about teaching is that you ***learn so much yourself.***

I'm sure that every teacher who has ever had the sublime joy of being asked to attend that dinner, could explain all these feelings to you much better than I'm doing in this slipshod endeavor.

So, the evening was going along swimmingly and then the VHS Science Department got up to hand out mementoes for the night. I saw a bright young science teacher walk over to help present the award boxes to the Seniors. Her name is Jackie Collins. That is her name in 2009. When I knew her a lifetime ago, she was a little kid named Jackie Howard. I actually got to teach Jackie when she was both a $4^{th}$ and $5^{th}$ grader. Every year, Jackie would show up at the Morgan Township Elementary Science Fair and absolutely kick butt up and down the block. I remember her professional looking displays, the hard work she put into her projects each year, and the excitement on her face when she would bring her stuff in with her mom. It was "Blue Ribbon City" all the way.

Besides being a "Young Einstein" at the Science Fair each year, Jackie was the kind of kid who just put a smile on your face when she walked through the door each day. So bright. So hard working. The tiniest bit shy. Funny. Modest. Kind. You know, the whole deal. To see that she has grown up, become a successful teacher herself, and is now inspiring a new generation of learners pretty much capped off the night for me in a most delightful fashion.

So let's see, the first speaker selected was a former student of mine who now hangs out with Troy Aikman, and travels to NASCAR events throughout the land. His replacement is the head of the Regional Development Authority and used to serve as a guard and instructor at the Tomb of the Unknown Soldier. The kid who invited me to the banquet thrilled me by handing me a beautiful poem written because she said that I had inspired her to do so. And the person who helped hand out the awards was one of my favorite students from way back at Morgan Township in the 1980's. You know the part of the 23rd Psalm which says, "My cup runneth over"? That's kind of how I felt as I sat there that night watching everything unfold. Somehow, the fact that my life had intersected with the lives of all these wonderful people was a little unbelievable, and more beautiful than if I would have been able to script it myself.

I thought that that night had been about as perfect a night as a teacher could have. After I thanked Melissa again for inviting me, I looked up and saw another Parkview student from 8 years before standing across the room with his family. I walked over to congratulate him on the wonderful achievements of being smart and working hard. After shaking hands and exchanging a few words with the young man, I stayed and chatted with his parents a few more minutes while he drifted to another part of the Strongbow's dining room to talk with more of his friends. A lot of the crowd had dispersed by now. The dad said, "Hey, you know our son picked ***you*** as his most influential teacher too. But, apparently he procrastinated turning in your name, so Melissa beat him to it. We just thought you'd like to know that." As I went out to the parking lot at Strongbow's, my feet didn't really hit the ground; I just sort of floated above the asphalt with my keys in my hand.

We tell students in creative writing class that their pieces ought to have interesting and meaningful conclusions. In the case of this story that is proving difficult to do. Part of me feels like this has been a several page exercise in self aggrandizement. Part of me feels like I ought to hit my knees right away and thank God for sending me so many blessings, so many times. I could talk about how wonderful it feels to work with little 9 year olds, see them step into a Time Machine, let the red and blue lights flash, and watch as successful, self assured, and stellar adults appear at the other end. In some ways, a beautiful cloud of mystery seems to hover above the whole thing.

In any event, thanks for the heartfelt advice, Pat. It was the best talk I've ever ignored.

* * * * * * *

## "A Horse, a Hornet, and a Moment of Horror"

My dad (who passed away in 2002 at the age of 82) told us a hundred stories when we were growing up. Lots of them were about his WW II experiences on the U.S.S. Bennington. Sometimes they were about exciting adventures he had had (shining John Dillinger's shoes one day in front of the family business or riding his bike as a 13 year old from East Chicago to Chicago for the 1933 World's Fair).

But, one of the best stories he ever told us involved a mean kid on a farm, his baby sister Joan, and a huge horse. In the summertime the family would leave East Chicago and head south to spend some time on a friend's farm. There were five children in my dad's family: Dennis, Anthony (my dad), George, Bertha (fans of "My Big, Fat, Greek Wedding" will be delighted to learn that Bertha is also known as "Tula" - I kid you not), and the youngest, Joan sometimes also called Joanne). George, Bertha, and Aunt Joan are still among us. Dennis and Pops have left the building.

The chance to spend time out in the country was a very special experience for these city bred kids. Apparently though, there lived on this farm a boy who made it his business to make everybody who came to visit feel miserable. Maybe he made fun of their more formal East Chicago clothing. Perhaps he didn't like the fact that they were children of recent immigrants. It could be that he was just a jerk. I don't recall the specific details.

I just know my dad suffered a number of indignities at the hands of this boy and as the visit one summer was nearing its end, he saw an opportunity for vengeance.

They were playing a game of baseball in a field

which was adjacent to a large, fenced in pasture. The pasture held a horse of enormous proportions (to hear my dad tell the story this equine wonder could have been the prototype for the Trojan Horse). I mean, this monstrous horse would make a Budweiser Clydesdale look like a Golden Retriever puppy. Mean Kid (let's call him Rex) was pitching. The field was arranged in such a way that a massive oak tree was spreading its branches over the players. One branch was directly above the head of the pitcher. My dad's eagle eyes had noted that a large hornets' nest happened to be suspended almost directly above Rex's head. Now, if at this moment you're wondering (as I always did when hearing this story) if that constitutes a *magnificent* coincidence, you are correct. However, I must tell you that I *caught* my dad lying only once in my entire life. He probably caught me 1000 times.

Rex hurled the ball. My dad sized up the situation, stepped into the pitch, and cracked a screaming line drive. Yes, your assumption is correct. That line drive made a bee line (or more appropriately, a hornet line) directly toward the nest. The papery container filled with potential mayhem was struck and fell like a buzz bomb squarely on top of Rex's noggin. 257 angry hornets immediately exited the nest and 256 of them stung Rex on the face, neck, legs, and arms. In short, nearly every square inch of his body was assaulted.

I neglected to tell you that Aunt Joan (who was a mere baby at the time) was lying peacefully in her perambulator, at a safe distance from any stray pop ups or other errant batted balls. Yia Yia (my dad's mom) and Rex's mother were chatting peacefully near the fence as well.

The 257th hornet flew straight at the horse and stung him on the rear end. He reared up on his hind legs and let out a piercing whinny that could be heard as far away as

Northern Michigan. Then he started to gallop *straight toward Baby Joan.* There was the fence, Joan's buggy, and a hand operated water pump all in a direct line. As Rex ran toward the pond screaming in dismay and pain, all eyes turned in the other direction toward the rampaging stallion. If the horse crashed into the fence the snapping boards would certainly smash into the baby. He had enough momentum to trample both the fence and the buggy. If he crashed into the metal pump handle, the consequences could only be imagined. My dad's moment of triumph had instantly turned into his worst nightmare. His batted ball was going to lead to the death of his own baby sister.

The moment was frozen in time (such were my dad's skills as a storyteller, that even though this happened in the early 1930's I can vividly see the farm, the horse, the buggy, the tree, the hornets, and the horror filled faces of the characters as clearly as I can see the keyboard at my fingertips). Think of all the times in your life when destiny has turned upon a particular instant....

The speeding car spins and careens out of control on the ice, but stops just short of a disaster. You ask the love of your life to marry you and the reply is either yes or no. You look at the person offering you that one particular job and the decision is...

Had the horse slammed through the fence and crushed the Baby Joan all would have changed. My Grandmother would have faced *two* crushing blows in one decade. The loss of her husband *and* her youngest child. My dad's life could have been ruined as well. He might have become a guilt ridden recluse who chose to never marry and then... (you wouldn't be stuck reading this right now). But, the horse leapt high into the Hoosier sky. Somehow, I imagine that he followed the same arc as beautiful rainbows I have seen spread across the horizon from time to time in our fair state. He cleared the fence, the buggy, and almost the water pump. If my dad is to be believed, sparks flew off his rear hoofs as they scraped the metal handle of the pump. He then trotted peacefully down into a nearby gully and rolled around on his back to scratch the hornet's stinger.

Everyone there (especially my dad) breathed a huge sigh of relief. The two women shifted their attention from one crisis to another. They ran towards Rex who was covered with hornet welts and sobbing uncontrollably. My Yia Yia had a thousand home remedies and she knew exactly what to do with those hornet stings. She grabbed big handfuls of fresh horse manure and smeared them onto every welt she could find. My dad watched with a huge grin on his face.

Post Script - Aunt Joan is an (incredibly young looking) retired school teacher who now resides in Coronado, California. When our very own Orville Redenbacher moved out to Coronado, Aunt Joan would often see him doing his marketing at the local grocery store. She tells me that he was just as pleasant as we all remember him. It has been more than 70 years since she survived that brush with fate.

* * * * * * *

Left to Right Bertha (aka Tula), Dennis and Baby Joan, George, and my Dad, Anthony T. Karas (Photo - 1932)

* * * * * * *

## "On Board the Bennington"

My Dad had Alzheimer's Disease during the last few years of his life. Once, when he was hospitalized for a heart condition, I showed him a picture of his seven beautiful grandchildren. I asked him if he could remember any of their names. He stared at the picture for a few moments, waved his hand vaguely and said, "No. I don't know who those people are." When you first see someone do something like that (especially someone you love, especially your father) you think at first that the person must be joking. How could anyone in the world forget their own grandchildren? I'm sure everyone reading this has had similar experiences with a family member or friend who has been afflicted with this horrible disease. It is bewildering and depressing, and of course we all fervently hope and pray that it won't happen to anyone else we love (or ourselves).

Interestingly enough there were only pockets of my Dad's memory which had been destroyed. He was able to recall some astounding bits of information. One of the most amazing things I ever saw was when the Old Man was staying at our house for a weekend. This was after I had asked him the question about the grandkids. We were sitting up in the Bonus Room which is equipped with a computer. I had found a website dedicated to the aircraft carrier he had served aboard during World War II, the USS Bennington. This is a remarkable website with photos, crew listings, anecdotes, and a timeline detailing everything the ship and crew had ever experienced. Aboard the carrier the Old Man's job was to prepare a plane for flight. This entailed fueling, making sure the ammunition was properly loaded, checking the instruments to be certain they were correctly functioning, and doing anything else which the pilot felt was necessary. He was always proud of the fact that ***his*** plane was the Captain's plane.

As we looked at various items on the website the Old Man was riveted. He sat next to me on a rocking chair and stared at the screen. It was as though we had stepped through a time tunnel back to 1944 and 1945. The amazing thing was the accuracy with which he could recall events. When we were looking through the ship's timeline he said, "Find December 21st, 1944. That's the day we went through the Panama Canal." Now remember, this was a man who could not recognize his grandchildren's faces just a couple of months earlier. I scrolled down to December 21st. Sure enough it said, "Transit of Panama Canal" and went on to list the time it took to cross through from one ocean to the other. I just looked at him with amazement. He did that again and again with other events which had been seared into his memory. I sat next to him, totally dumbfounded.

Once, their ship plowed into a supremely unlucky whale while steaming ahead at full speed across the Pacific. My brother Tom, sister Toni, and I had heard that tale from him on dozens of occasions. Someone had recorded the event photographically and posted it on the website. He sat there staring at the screen and the poor impaled mammal. He stared and stared at that picture for the longest time. I leaned over and nudged him, "Papou? Papou?" He was thousands of miles and half a century away, back in the South Pacific. "Look at that poor whale," the Old Man said. Even though this had happened in 1944 he still felt awful about the death of the unfortunate creature. Divers had to actually go into the water and dislodge the whale's carcass using explosives. Here is the very picture the Old Man stared at.

Another time the ship had run right through the middle of a Pacific Ocean typhoon. He used to tell the story about the unbelievable fury of that storm and say that the front of the carrier's deck got bent over, "***just like a Hound Dog's ears***". As I searched through the website with him, we found the following picture. I couldn't help thinking that ***he*** might have been one of the young men standing up on the deck surveying the tremendous damage and contemplating the fury of the storm they had just survived.

He told us a story about a Kamikaze plane streaking right toward the ship. To hear the Old Man recall it, he was standing on the deck watching the plane roar right toward his head. His colleagues were firing bullets at the man in that enemy plane who ***knew*** he was going to lose his life in the next few seconds. The only question was whether or not he would take American Sailors with him on that final journey. He could see the pilot's face, his teeth gritted and his hands clenching the controls. The Japanese Zero (apparently riddled with bullets), burst into flames, overshot the deck and crashed violently into the blue Pacific. The men aboard the Bennington cheered and once again counted their blessings. Here is yet again, another photo from the Bennington website showing the Kamikaze exploding. This photo was reportedly taken from the deck of the USS Wasp. It is amazing to me that photos exist from nearly all of the Old Man's best stories.

He told yet another story about the time rounds from a gun accidentally were shot on the flight deck. He could hear the bullets whizzing above his head. Every time he related one of these “near death” experiences it struck me how things might have turned out differently. What if the Kamikaze pilot had actually hit his target? How would things be changed if those stray bullets had been aimed at a slightly different angle? What if the Bennington had capsized in the typhoon? Of course, none of those disasters happened. But, reflecting upon all those long ago moments it occurs to me that in each case the future of our entire family was always hanging in the balance…

The Old Man ***was*** able to return stateside after the War in the Pacific had been successfully concluded. He came back to Indiana, got married, and helped raise his three children. He was born in 1920 and died in 2002. He's been gone seven years now. This month, on the 11th of November we are supposed to take time to remember the Veterans of this country who risked (and in many cases, gave) their lives so that we can continue to enjoy the incredible freedom and under appreciated abundance our land has to offer. I know which Veteran I'll be remembering. How about you?

**"On Board the Bennington"**

**Half a century ago in 1944,**
**All the world was shadowed**
**By the tattered clouds of war.**

**One ship sailed through the seas,**
**Stocked with bomb and plane.**
**One ship traveled toward Japan,**
**Through the waves and rain.**

**CV - 20 Bennington, Pride of all the Fleet,**
**Did her part with all the rest,**
**To make the job complete.**

**Once a typhoon bent the deck,**
**Just like a "Hound Dog's Ears".**
**A Kamikaze buzzed us once,**
**His widow now cries tears.**

**Unlucky whale met the bow,**
**And an untimely end.**
**Lightning struck while battles raged,**
**Our country they'd defend.**

**The Hummingbird Defenders**

One man, one of thousands,
Signed the rolls and made the trip.
One man did his part,
To ready planes there on that ship.

Saw his duty to his country,
Helped preserve the "Freedom Land".
Risked his life to win those Battles,
Followed leaders who'd command.

The plane he readied was the first,
When we bombed Tokyo.
The weapons and the gasoline were ready,
You should know.

Tony Karas served this great land,
On that rolling deep blue sea.
Did his part to keep our Country,
Free for you and free for me.

A thousand, thousand sailors,
Need to hear our words of thanks.
Say it now before the brave ones
Are called Home and leave our ranks.

For people died and families cried,
And that's the way war goes.
What matters is, when all was done,
The Flag with Stars still shows.

So thank you Seaman Karas,
For your service without fear.
Cause your honor and your courage,
Are some reasons why we're here!

The Bennington has been scrapped. The ship's bell is kept in a place of honor in Bennington, Vermont. Individuals interested in the history of the carrier should visit the award winning website:

**www.uss-bennington.org**

* * * * * * *

## "Hot Roast Beef Sandwich, Mashed Potatoes, and Gravy"

The last time I saw my dad was in the nursing home. I knew that since he was in California and I was heading back to the airport that it was probably going to be the last time I'd see him in a vertical position on this earth. He was sitting in the dining hall having a roast beef sandwich with mashed potatoes and gravy. When I walked in he had said, "Well, here's my brother, Chris." The funny thing is, he never had a brother named Chris. Alzheimer's Disease had pretty much robbed him of his mind. Sometimes I wondered if decades of breathing in dry cleaning fumes might have exacerbated his problems. In any event, I'd been there for a few days visiting him because the prevailing medical opinion was that he was starting the long slide which eventually leads us all to the final stop on the train line.

We visited for a short time (my mom and my sister were there too). My dad continued to eat his lunch and we engaged in the weird type of conversation which takes place when three people know what is going on and one of them has little or no idea. I remember looking at my dad and watching him eat.

I closed my eyes for a moment, and suddenly it was 1960. I was a 6 year old kid walking down the sidewalk in East Chicago, Indiana. The Old Man, 42 years younger, was by my side. We wheeled into the Olympia Restaurant and sat right at the counter. My dad was wearing a short sleeved white shirt, blue slacks and his dark hair was parted on the side. He told Gus (or Louie, or Stavros - I can't really remember) that we'd both have the Roast Beef sandwich with gravy. He got a cup of coffee and ordered me a Chocolate Malt. I looked around the restaurant at the dozens of people who were having lunch. Ashtrays and sugar jars peppered the counters and mini juke boxes were affixed to each booth table. Smoke, laughter, arguments, and hand gestures filled the air. Ike was still in the White House. My Old Man talked easily with almost everybody in the room. That guy could talk to anybody. Years of waiting on customers had perfected his delivery. The image he projected was one of friendliness combined with a knowledge of how the "world worked" which caused a 6 year old to stare at him in awe...

The food came. A chocolate malt never tasted better. Steam rose off the fragrant gravy and mashed potatoes. I wolfed down my lunch like only a chubby, hungry, little 6 year old Greek boy can. The Old Man paid Stavros, left a tip, and we both headed out the door back toward the dry cleaning shop.

I shook my head and there we were back in the dining hall of the nursing home. I glanced at my watch and noticed that it was time to catch the shuttle to the airport. I leaned over and gave the Old Man a goodbye kiss on the top of his balding head. "Okay, Papou. I gotta go now. I love you."

"Okay. I love you too." He smiled as I left and I'd like to think that he knew that it wasn't his brother "Chris" who had just kissed him goodbye for the final time.

* * * * * * *

## "Soldier (In the Army of the Lord)"

Last year in December something happened which I believe was a miracle. You can read this story and judge for yourself. Skeptical people will say it was just a coincidence. Other kinds of people (my kinds) will probably agree that it *was* a miracle. I promise you that everything I write in this story happened exactly the way I say it did.

On December 15th, 2006 I turned 52 years old. The day was a Friday. One of my students, Julia Manion, and her mom, Lora (who also works at the school as an Instructional Aide) gave me a present. The Manions are the kind of family who've kept me going in this profession for over three decades. Father Patrick is a creative and loving dad who has crafted wonderful things to make our school a better place. He once built a rolling jail cell for us that we locked the Principal up in to help raise money for Riley Children's Hospital. For our annual Friday Night Live reading program, Mr. Manion has designed and built elaborate and unbelievable sets, which have delighted the 4th and 5th grade students. He's the kind of guy who dresses up on Halloween with his kids because he wants to have fun. He's smart, nice, and funny and he's survived a harrowing health condition with optimism and courage. Mom Lora is an artistic wonder. She also has designed and put together breathtakingly creative displays for Friday Night Live and she has painted murals throughout our building to make it a warmer and friendlier place. Additionally, she plays wild and wacky characters at our annual reading event in a way that can simultaneously embarrass and delight her daughters (this is quite a trick). The Manions are peaceful, friendly, sharp, engaging, and fun people. Oh, and they really love music. The importance of that will be revealed momentarily.

Their two daughters, Dorian and Julia, did not fall far from the tree. Both girls are "A" students, polite, kind, considerate, and the type of individuals who will add much more to society than they will ever take away. As I said, these are the kind of people who make teaching such an enjoyable and rewarding profession. They are the kind of family who give teachers birthday gifts on December 15$^{th}$ and *another* present a few days later for Christmas.

I looked at the wrapped present and it was obvious that it was a CD. That was great because I love music too. One day I'd mentioned to Mrs. Manion that I really enjoy the music of "The Blind Boys of Alabama".

They've recorded a Christmas CD called "Go Tell it on the Mountain" which is absolutely delightful. I unwrapped the present and saw that it was another album by the Blind Boys entitled, "Spirit of the Century". I thanked the Manions for their kindness. Lora told me that I was really going to enjoy the songs on that disc. She had seen the group perform in concert. As I prepared to leave school for the weekend I looked around my classroom for the things I needed to take away. I found my keys, grabbed my black briefcase, slipped on my winter coat and hat, and headed out to my 1999 Honda CRV. And, I took that Blind Boys CD with me as well. I hadn't looked at the titles of any of the songs. I had never heard this particular music before in my entire life.

That afternoon I was not going straight home. I had one stop to make first. I got into the car, started it up, opened the CD case and popped the gift into the player. Now, there are twelve songs on the disc. They have titles like 'Jesus Gonna Be Here", "Good Religion", "Amazing Grace" and so on. I immediately started bobbing my head and slapping the dashboard in time to this heartfelt and soulful music. I was driving in a northerly direction toward Route 6. I remember that it was pretty cold out and since it was Friday, and my Birthday, and getting close to Christmas Vacation, I was in a positively ethereal mood. I kept on driving as the music blasted out of the speakers and turned west onto U.S. Highway 6. I always like the fact that this particular roadway stretches all the way from New York to California. I sometimes think about the idea I could be (and probably am) sharing the road with a west coast surfer dude, a grizzled rancher, an Iowa pig farmer wearing a John Deere cap, and a stunning long haired model on her way into New York City.

It gets dark early in December and as my journey unfolded I was treated to some beautiful light displays in the yards of houses along the way. Six songs had played. While they weren't strictly "Christmas songs" like the other Blind Boys CD, they talked about God and were definitely putting the listener into the right frame of mind. All the songs were between 3 and 5 minutes long. The seventh song started up. Before the Blind Boys began singing on this particular number there was a long and intriguing intro featuring an acoustic and an electric guitar which "talked" to each other for several bars before they were joined by a driving rhythm section. While this was playing I was waiting to turn left off of Route 6 because I had almost reached my destination. I turned south onto Capital Road. The car rolled on several hundred feet until I reached the parking lot of the building where I was headed. Another left turn was required to get into the parking area behind my destination. The introduction continued (I checked later on the computer and found out that the intro was exactly 50 seconds long).

Now, ***here comes the miracle part***. As soon as the wheels of my car came into contact with the parking lot I was pulling into, the voices of the Blind Boys of Alabama began singing. As someone with the middle named Milhous once said (and I assure you I am being more honest than that person was wont to be), "Let me be perfectly clear."

This didn't happen a few seconds ***after*** I pulled into the lot. It didn't take place a couple of seconds ***before***. It happened ***instantly*** as the wheels touched the lot. Powerful, deep, and rich voices of old, blind, black men rang out:

***I'm a Soldier, in the Army of the Lord,***
***Soldier in the Army.***
***I'm a mighty good Soldier***
***In the Army of the Lord…***
***Well now, when I get to Heaven, I'm gonna sing and shout,***
***Ain't nobody there who can turn me out…***
***I'm a Warrior in the Army of the Lord…***

Now, you may have guessed already where I was headed. I was pulling into the parking lot of the Salvation Army Church to pick up kettles for our Student Council's volunteer bell ringing the next day. For about 20 years kids from our school have been spending a day in December (in hour long shifts) ringing the Salvation Army Bell. I had to sit there for several seconds before I got out of the car. The fact that the Salvation Army is organized in military fashion, with Captains, Majors and the like struck me in the face like an enchanted and painless sledgehammer. I looked up through the cold windshield at the old building. I stared down at the car speakers still pulsating with the vibrant song. I gazed up at the darkening, star strewn Heavens. I shook my head in wonder at what the Lord can do.

Many beautiful things have happened over the last two decades as a result of our association with the Army. I remember once I read in the paper that the United Way had decided to drop the Salvation Army from their list of agencies because of something called "duplication of services". I remember the total amount was in the hundreds of thousands of dollars. I walked into the church during the week I read about that and expected to see the people in charge deflated and depressed. Major Mary Postma was working away as busily as ever as I entered to pick up some bells, aprons, and kettles for our shifts the next day. I told her that I was sorry that United Way had decided to cut them from the list. She looked at me with a big smile and said, "You shouldn't worry about it. I'm certainly not going to. You know, the Lord ***will*** provide. Ever since the story ran in the paper that phone has been ringing off the hook. We'll make up that money in no time. I'm not worried about a thing." I stood there with a stupid look on my face and hoped for the day that I would have 1/10th, nay 1/100th of the faith that this little grey haired lady had.

I could go on and give lots more examples about things which have happened to some of the kids when we've rung those Salvation Army bells. One day (after I retire) I promise to write another article about the Salvation Army. I'm just not allowed to do it yet.

So, in any event, that's my miracle. I know that it isn't like seeing Jesus walk out to a boat in the middle of a storm, but I'm figuring that God gives out miracles according to the stature of the folks involved. I got a small one, cause I'm just an aging 4th grade teacher driving his old Honda around Northwest Indiana. But you know what? I wouldn't trade in my miracle for all the tea they once dumped into Boston Harbor. It's my miracle and I'm grateful to God that He saw fit to give it to me. I'm guessing that many people reading this have had similar experiences of their own. Maybe not in the specific circumstances, but in the feeling of wonder which comes over a person when That Hand reaches down right into our lives. That Loving and Incomprehensible Hand.

Merry Christmas, Happy Hanukkah, Blessed Kwanzaa, Joyful Festivus, and Wonderful Whatever it is You Celebrate to everyone. May God richly bless you all the days of this Holiday Season and throughout the coming New Year.

* * * * * * *

## "Kyle Price - A Christmas Toast"

This Christmas, when you sit down for that wonderful dinner (either on Christmas Eve or Christmas Day) I'd like you to fill your glass and join me in drinking to someone's health. Most toasts can be summed up in a line or two, but for this one to have more meaning it will take a bit of background.

Less than twenty years ago a baby boy was born. He was healthy and kind. He grew up tall, and straight, and honest. His parents took him to Church, and made sure he brushed his teeth and did his homework. He went to Elementary School at Memorial. He went to Middle School at Ben Franklin. He was also (with the support of his parents) involved in Scouting. The Scouting was such a big part of his life that he worked all the way up to the Rank of Eagle Scout. He graduated from Valpo High. In high school he played bassoon in the band. He notes that he enjoyed VHS band because he got to play wonderful music with lots of great people, *and* band is the place where he met his girlfriend. He has a younger brother and hard working parents who love him, and he could have easily stuck around town and worked or gone away to school. But, he didn't do either of those things. Instead, he did something for you and me. He did the thing which earned him that Christmas Toast.

He signed up to be a United States Marine. He traveled to Camp Pendleton out in California. Imagine living the life of the typical American teenager one week and suddenly being thrown into the firestorm of military training the next. Imagine getting up well before the sun and having a Drill Sergeant in your face as soon as your feet hit the concrete. Imagine running mile after mile in the hot sun, in combat boots and full uniform, while carrying a rifle and loads of gear on your back. Pushups, sit-ups, obstacle course, rifle training, no phone, no TV, nothing at all easy, day after day, week after week. Sweat, pain, homesickness, fatigue. Then, imagine that you come down with pneumonia. It sets you back two weeks and there isn't a thing you can do about it except wait until you recover. The young man went through all of that and then (ah!!) Boot Camp was over.

When I asked him about what it meant to him to be serving his country, this young man had a very interesting reply. He said, "To serve one's Country is not only a job for those in the Service. Taking the time to help a neighbor in need is just as meaningful as our forces going out to fight in the war." I wanted to say, "Maybe just as meaningful, but certainly not as dangerous." If I go out to help Mrs. Young next door when her car gets stuck in the snow, I'm not very likely to encounter land mines waiting for me on Wedgwood Drive. Never once have there been snipers on the rooftops of our subdivision waiting to cut me down as I participated in neighborhood "landscaping day". When I helped the old gentleman put his groceries in the back of his car at Wise Way there was no one blasting rocket propelled grenades at me from across the street in the K-Mart parking lot. I might give my *time* to help others. You, young man, have purposely put *yourself* in harm's way so that our society can keep rolling along. The difference in the quality of sacrifice is incomparable .

The thing which impressed this young Marine the most about his training was the fact that a group of people from all over the United States with tremendously dissimilar backgrounds could be brought together and formed into (his words) "A Band of Brothers" through rigorous physical and mental training. His Eagle Scout experience helped him during Boot Camp because it allowed him to attain the rank of "Private First Class". Additionally, he tied for Top Ranked Shooter in his platoon with a rating of "Expert Marksman". These achievements serve to make his parents (Dale and

Diane) proud, and they should garner a share of appreciation from everyone who hears his story. This kid did it the right way as he was growing up, and he continues to do it the right way now that he is one of "The Few, The Proud, and The Brave."

Next, I asked this young Marine where he was headed from here. He said that after a short leave he would be flying back to Camp Pendleton for Infantry Training. That would entail 6 to 7 more weeks of intensive work. From there he would receive his assignment to a "duty station." This, he noted, might be "anywhere". Then, the young Marine had another very interesting comment. He said, "The future for myself is the same as it is for every other person. ***Unknown***. I have a plan for a while, but *nothing* ever goes totally according to plan." Those words were carefully considered and full of wisdom.

Every individual can be located at a certain point along the political spectrum. Some people think that the current war is the correct and necessary way to begin the eradication of terrorism from our planet. Others think that we're making a costly error (in both human and financial terms) by pursuing the present course of action. Some folks, just aren't sure what to think about it at all. Here's the deal. Whatever *we* think, sitting around our coffee tables, and lecture halls, and computer chat rooms, pales in comparison to what this Marine (and his parents, and his brother, and his girlfriend) think(s). Because, you see it is the Marine who takes the step into the Dangerous Unknown. He follows orders so that we can go to Church Services this Christmas Eve in peace. He packs up his gear and heads where he is told because he loves America and everything that word stands for. He does it really because he loves all of *us*. He might have private opinions about government policy, but he puts them on the back burner because doing his *duty* is more important. He just picks up that rifle, shuts his mouth, and heads to the most dangerous parts of the globe, for you and for me.

So, how about it? This Christmas Eve or Christmas, can you pause right about the time when that warm Holiday glow is surrounding you and everyone else at the table? Can you stop for just one moment and think about a guy (and thousands others like him), who gave up the warmth and comfort of Christmas by the fireplace for *you*? Can you spare a moment to raise your glass to the health of Private First Class Kyle Edward Price, United States Marine Corps? It won't take but a moment. Wherever he is in the world, it'll be worth it! Semper Fi Yule!

(Kyle Price did end up serving in Iraq.)

* * * * * * *

## "Merry Christmas, Martin Homan"

Here's what happens to boys in around the 7th grade. They go crazy. I can remember the specific moment that I lost my mind. It was actually in the waning days of 6th grade. I was sitting across from Jenny Treder in Mr. Bonner's class at Elliott School. She was wearing a plaid skirt (the colors were green, blue, red, and white - I totally remember) and she crossed her legs. Now, I had probably seen Jenny Treder cross her legs about a hundred times since second grade. But, all those times happened before I had lost my mind.

The social and biological reasons why junior high boys lose their minds are probably too well known and elementary to go into here. Suffice it to say, my mind was gone. When JT crossed her legs it was the slightest nudge that was needed to topple my psyche down into full blown lunacy.

So, for the next few years I embarked upon a pattern of behavior which would cause great turmoil (both in my mind and in our family). It could almost be called my own private "Idi-Odyssey". Jenny Treder's legs alone probably were not the sole cause of my precipitous slide. I'm sure other factors entered into the equation. The event I'm about to describe was just one of many episodes which were laced with adolescent insanity. Most of them were just stupid and fairly harmless. This one teetered right along the darkest edge of darkness.

Previously, I had always been a good student, earning all A's and B's in school. However, when madness descended upon me my grades began to plummet. C's in our house were bad. D's and F's were not even discussed because my older brother and sister (National Honor Society material) had never earned them.

So, it was with great consternation that I received my 7th grade report card which had a line that read, "Social Studies - D". There was also a line which was provided for comments. Mr. Alex Bochnowski, my 7th grade Geography teacher, chose not to write one. I decided to fill in the blank for him. I clumsily wrote "High D", as though I had only been a few points away from a "C-". I think I had been drinking a lot of the soft drink called "High C" at the time. The strategy backfired.

Mr. Bochnowski busted me. He summoned me up to his desk and said that my mom had called and was wondering just how "High" of a D it actually was. When he informed her that it was not high at all (it was actually, in all likelihood, closer to an "F") her "Mom Radar" went into overdrive. She scheduled a meeting with Mr. B. after school where they intended to get to the bottom of the phony report card note. Mr. Bochnowski told me that if I wanted to play football (which I passionately did) that shenanigans like that would not be tolerated at Wilbur Wright Junior High.

I spent the rest of the day dreading that evening. Remember, I was suffering from 7th grade insanity. I pictured my Mom and Mr. Bochnowski talking at his desk. I thought about all the teachers who had compared me to both my brother and sister (always unfavorably). Tom would eventually become a "Sunkist All American" high school football player. Toni was a National Honor Society member in the first ever graduating class of Munster High who had thought up the nickname, "Munster Mustangs". I was the fat little pimple faced slob, who goofed off in class and got D's in Social Studies because I was day dreaming about girls like Jenny Treder. It was a highly miserable realization.

As I walked home, my gloom deepened. The weather was dreary in a way that was peculiar to Northwest Indiana. Not only was it cloudy and overcast, the "pollution smell" was drifting in from Hammond and East Chicago. It was damp. It was cold. I am ashamed to admit it, but I began thinking about the knives in our kitchen drawer. Would it hurt? Would I have the guts to do it? If I did it, how sad would everybody in the family be? I was worthless, so what was the point of going back to school every day and finding out how stupid and unlike my stellar siblings I was. Filled with self-pity and self-loathing I continued the trek down Elliott Drive which would ultimately lead me to my home. I again thought about the knives.

Suddenly, a voice behind me said, "Hello, Greg." It was a deep and resonant voice. A very "unkid" like voice. It was the voice of Martin Homan. Martin was (by far) the largest kid at Wilbur Wright Junior High School. People (myself included) had made fun of Marty ever since he had moved into Munster. His stentorian tones and gargantuan frame set him up as the perfect target for the taunts and jeers which came so easily to junior high school lips.

Marty was different because he didn't really seem to care about all the silly kids who teased him incessantly. Indeed, looking back I realize now that he was tremendously wise beyond his years. For one thing, Marty was not afraid to talk about his faith in God. I had never really heard a kid in junior high dare to do this. Of course, many of our parents made us attend Sunday School and church. But, to actually talk about God and how having faith in Him was the path in life to take? It just didn't happen. It was the kind of thing we scoffed at. Most of us were busy seeing if we could "out-cuss" the other kids on the block. I can remember hearing Marty speak in school about his goal of becoming a preacher one day. As he caught up to me as we journeyed down the sidewalk, I think he could sense from my body language that I might have been in trouble that afternoon. "How are you today?" That was the simple question he asked.

Immediately, I spilled my guts. I told him the whole story about changing the report card, being caught by my teacher and mom, and the meeting between them (which was probably taking place at this very moment). Then (surprisingly) I told him about the kitchen drawer. I think I had seen a western where one of the characters opined that his life "was not worth a plugged nickel.".

Martin stopped walking and put his hand on my left shoulder. "Greg. Never think of that. This is one small problem in your life. The sun is going to come up tomorrow and God is going to give you another chance to do things the right way. He will always forgive you for the mistakes you make in life. You simply have to ask Him. The life he has given you is a great gift. You should ***never*** think of throwing it away."

For a moment, I felt like we were in a movie. I can still the see the look in Marty's deep and expressive eyes as he said those words to me. Years later I realized that we were in something much more important than a movie. We were in real life and Martin Homan had (in all probability) just saved mine.

Forty years have flown by since that pivotal moment. When I married my wife Liz, I thought about Martin Homan. When my son Nick and daughter Natalie were born, I thought about Martin Homan. When we bought our dog Tracker and subsequently watched him swimming through the cool water of Flint Lake, I thought about Martin Homan. When I have an extraordinarily memorable meal, or I'm having a wonderful experience on a trip somewhere, I might stop and think about Martin Homan. When a thousand and one different delights have given me beautiful days and memories on this planet, I think about Martin Homan. I don't believe I ever thanked him for saving my life on that cold and dreary day.

When I sat down to write this story I started by firing up the Internet and typing the words "Pastor Martin Homan". I had not seen him in all those years, but my mind told me that he had to have followed his dream of becoming a Minister of God's word. He had. I saw various references to the work Pastor Homan has done in different churches he has served throughout the midwest. And though it is about four decades overdue, finally I want to say. Thank you, Martin Homan. Merry Christmas.

* * * * * * *

## “Angels and Asparagus"

On December 24th, 2005 my wife and I were in the Wise Way grocery store on Route 49 in Chesterton, Indiana. I happened to glance at my watch when the event which I am about to relate took place. It was exactly 3:47 in the afternoon. Though it was Christmas Eve, I had not been drinking any Egg Nog, eating Rum Balls, or in any other way imbibing in holiday related festivities at the time of this unique occurrence. My mind was clear, because Liz and I had just been out for a jaunt through the scenic nature trail at Coffee Creek. We were picking up a few last minute dinner items before heading home to get ready for a Christmas Eve church service.

Every December for about the last twenty-five years I re-read A Christmas Carol by Charles Dickens. I especially love the way Dickens describes Scrooge's outer room as it appears when he is being paid a visit by the Ghost of Christmas Present. It is a beautiful passage which never fails to bring about many of the warm feelings associated with Christmas. Here it is so that you can see just what I mean:

***"It was his own room. There was no doubt about that. But it had undergone a surprising transformation. The walls and ceiling were so hung with living green, that it looked a perfect grove; from every part of which, bright gleaming berries glistened. The crisp leaves of holly, mistletoe, and ivy reflected back the light, as if so many little mirrors had been scattered there; and such a mighty blaze went roaring up the chimney, as that dull petrification of a hearth had never known in Scrooge's time, or Marley's, or for many and many a winter season gone. Heaped up on the floor, to form a kind of throne, were turkeys, geese, game, poultry, brawn, great joints of meat, sucking-pigs, long wreaths of sausages, mince-pies, plum-puddings, barrels of oysters, red-hot chestnuts, cherry-cheeked apples, juicy oranges, luscious pears, immense twelfth-cakes, and seething bowls of***

***punch, that made the chamber dim with their delicious steam. In easy state upon this couch, there sat a jolly Giant, glorious to see: who bore a glowing torch, in shape not unlike Plenty's horn, and held it up, high up, to shed its light on Scrooge, as he came peeping round the door." ****

Therefore, as my wife did the actual important work of shopping I stood in a happy reverie daydreaming about the bounty of Christmas time as it appeared to Charles Dickens and as it was being displayed for the hundreds of shoppers in the store at that particular moment. From where I stood I could see much of the same fruit Dickens described, vegetables, chocolate cakes (Wise Way offers this incredible 30 dollar cake with the appropriate title, "Death by Chocolate"), candy, nuts, wine, and a thousand and one other delights. I closed my eyes and inhaled deeply. The rapturous joy of Christmas filled the store and my soul simultaneously.

Suddenly, I heard a voice. It was pinched, raspy, exasperated, and discordant. It instantly and completely shattered the beautiful mood I had drifted into just a few moments ago. The voice said, "What do you mean, you don't have any asparagus? This is Christmas Eve. I have 14 people coming. I ***need*** asparagus. You're going to ruin my Christmas dinner!" I looked over at the speaker. She was probably in her 60's. Her attire was not festive. Her eyebrows were set at a perpetually self pitying angle resembling high mountains in Asia. I could see a pack of cigarettes peeking out from the top of her purse. There were some plastic bottles of cheap diet soda, boxes of nasty looking crackers, a cheeseball wrapped up in shrink wrap, and a package of Twinkies already inside her shopping cart. But, the asparagus was missing and she was consequently far from being amused.

The white shirted produce clerk who was fielding her complaint had the countenance of Saint Francis. He stood patiently listening to her. He apologized. He told her how much asparagus they had ordered, but that people seemed to be snatching it up in something resembling epic proportions. He offered to call the other Wise Way stores to see if they had any asparagus left. He told her he could go in the back and check again to see if any asparagus had been somehow overlooked. I think if he had had the time, he would have offered to grow her some asparagus out in back of the store.

Nothing sufficed. The woman's face grew red. She pointed her index finger at the young man's chest. "You idiots know how many people are going to be buying asparagus for Christmas! Don't you even have enough brains to know how to order a simple vegetable?" I thought of Charlie Brown's friends ranting at him, "Don't you even know a good tree from a poor tree, Charlie Brown?"

Suddenly, the music on the overhead intercom stopped. The lights in the aisles faded down and turned from their normal fluorescent brightness to a rich and majestic shade of calmest blue. The entire atmosphere of the store was instantaneously transformed in the winking of an eye. A vaguely familiar and very appealing voice spoke vibrantly through the store speakers, "Attention Wise Way Shoppers, this is Clarence Oddbody A-1C, calling from Heaven. I'm here to address all the shoppers, but especially Vivien Skinkle, who is currently in the produce aisle complaining loudly about the lack of asparagus. Those of you who know me, also know what we are capable of up here in Heaven. Remember when we had to take away George Bailey's life for awhile to show him just how precious it actually was? Well, we have other methods available to us up here also." I glanced around the store. Everyone was frozen, staring at the ceiling with stunned looks upon their faces.

Clarence continued, "Vivien, in a moment I can make this entire store vanish and you will find yourself standing in an overpopulated city in India where this very night people will fight for garbage scraps to survive. Some of them will not. Or, I might transport you to a village in Africa where over half the population is infected with HIV. How would you like to be in a Women's Prison in New York, where the Christmas Eve menu is going to be a cold cheese sandwich featuring stale bread with watered down tomato soup? Why, even the rich will share in the misery. This very moment in a wealthy suburb of Minneapolis, a Cadillac Escalade has flipped over into a snowy ditch, and it is not certain whether the occupants of that vehicle will ever taste asparagus, or anything else again!"

"Vivien, you are right. There is no asparagus in the store this night! But, look at what there ***is***! That is what we are calling upon you to do. Look at the wonderful bounty God has provided for you. Can you imagine what a young child from that impoverished city in India would say if he were to stand in the aisles where you now complain? He would be overwhelmed, Vivien. The choices would nearly crush his uncomprehending mind. And, if he were to see you, with that awful, sour, disgusted look upon your face, he wouldn't be able to tell where it came from or why in the Universe it was there. You have become spoiled, Vivien. You stand in the midst of plenty and you are blind! You need to change nearly everything about your attitude, and you need to change ***now***, this very night, this very instant! You need to become filled eternally with what we call in Heaven, 'The Philosophy of Gratitude'!"

Suddenly, the doors to the meat department flew open and an army of butchers came dancing out in unison, carrying meat cleavers and carving knives in their hands. They juggled the sharp implements and danced throughout the store while singing, "We Three Kings". Then, women from the floral department dressed in long flowing garments of red and green, who were carrying large Santa Claus sacks over their shoulders, came bouncing out of their section of the store on pogo sticks which were festooned with twinkling Christmas lights. They deftly pogoed with one hand up and down the aisles, all the while tossing roses, pine cones, and beautiful red poinsettias into the baskets of shoppers. I looked over at my wife, who was standing there dumbfounded with a bottle of sparkling peach juice in her hands. She seemed as young and beautiful as the day we were married, twenty five years ago. Young baggers appeared on ice skates (how these worked on the store linoleum, I do not know, but they did), carrying bags of the richest Swiss chocolate, which was molded into coins and wrapped in delicate golden foil. They flipped these coins through the air where they landed in the hands of grateful shoppers, both young and old. Angels flew down from the rafters and dropped enchanted Minty Candy Canes into the carts of everyone inside that Northwestern Indiana grocery store.

Vivien fell to her knees, quaking with terror, regret, and shame. Her face changed upon the instant. She cried out, "Oh, I'm so sorry. I see what a selfish and thoughtless fool I have been. I am surrounded by blessings and all I do is curse. Please, please Mr. Produce Clerk, can you see it in your heart to somehow forgive me?" The clerk, who had joined the chorus line of dancing butchers, said that he certainly would. Vivien took the cigarettes out of her purse and tossed them into the nearest trash bin shouting, "I won't be needing these any more!"

The entire store broke into a rousing rendition of Handel's "Hallelujah Chorus". My wife and I joined the conga line which led to the express aisle, and attempted to pay for our items (we were told that everything today was going to be "On the House"), so we loaded up our treats, hopped into our CRV, and headed home to get ready for Church. As we drove away we could see the entire store bathed in the light of a Christmas Eve Aurora Borealis. I glanced into the rear view mirror and noticed protruding from the top of the paper bag, a batch of the greenest, freshest asparagus my eyes had ever seen.

Happy New Year, everyone!

* From Charles Dickens **A Christmas Carol** 1843

* * * * * * *

## "Wild Thing"

The place was Royal Cleaners in Hessville, Indiana. This toxic den of commerce (which my Dad reminded us every day was "Our Bread and Butter") was located right on Kennedy Ave. next to the I - 94 Expressway. The year was 1966. The Old Man was gone. Maybe he was across the parking lot talking to Juicy Roth at the "Dunkenberger". Perhaps he was over at Dr. Parker's, the Dentist who shared space in the building. He could have been right next door talking to Shirley at the "Chez Joey" Beauty Parlor. I don't remember where he was that afternoon, but he was gone.

I was in charge of watching the counter. At the age of 11, I was lousy at making change, but I was good at finding the orders on the revolving clothes spinner machine. If you happen to get there before me and see my Old Man in Heaven, don't tell him, but I used to turn it on, pull myself up on the metal bars and let it carry me around the store. Being a portly little dude, it was a surprise that I never broke it, but it sure was fun.

Lots of days my brother Tom and my sister Toni would be in there serving time with me, but today for some reason both of them were absent too.

The radio to the left of the cash register (a plastic, yellowish, chipped window up to Heaven) was tuned to WLS (which I found out later meant "World's Largest Store"). Songs would come and go, the DJ would yak, and commercials would play. When customers came in we were instructed to turn down the sound, and say "Good afternoon, may I help you?"

Some of the songs coming out of the radio were forgettable. But, every once in a while a song would come on which spoke directly to my soul. Some of the songs which helped to ignite my imagination back in '66 were "Kicks" (by Paul Revere and the Raiders), "Devil with a Blue Dress" (by Mitch Ryder and the Detroit Wheels), and "Sunshine Superman" (by Donovan). But the song that really flipped my switch into the "Go" position was "Wild Thing" by The Troggs (definitely with two g's). Do you remember it? If you've qualified for your AARP card, you almost certainly will.

"Wild Thing, you make my heart sing.
You make everything groovy.
Wild thing, I think I love you,
But, I want to know for sure.
So, come on and hold me tight...
I love you.

Those three little dots (I think they are called "ellipses") in that lyric excerpt are by far the most important part of the whole thing. The singer, after rumbling out the phrase, "But I want to know for sure, Come on and hold me tight," pauses for exactly the right amount of time.

It is just enough so that you can imagine the young man actually giving his girlfriend a heartfelt embrace. Then he continues, "I love you." The emotion in his voice leaves no doubt that the hug has done the trick. He truly loves her.

I think I remember something in the film "Amadeus" about the spaces ***in between*** notes sometimes being more important than the notes themselves. Even though I'm a long way from being a trained musician this song taught me that that particular assertion can be true.

So that day in the cleaners, with the Old Man gone, and

with plenty of time to kill I was listening to that wonderful song (which believe it or not, had been written by the brother of actor Jon Voight, a fellow named Chip Taylor). There were no customers, so I was vigorously singing along at the top of my lungs.

I had my “Microphone” (the silver stapler from the counter) firmly grasped in my right hand. My eyes were closed and the pivotal moment in the song was approaching…

“But, I wanna know for sure,
So, come on and hold me tight…
(Long Pause)
I love you.”

Right after that there is a prolonged and slashing guitar part combined with a flute solo. The Troggs musical style has been described as “Caveman Rock”; indeed Troggs is a derivative of “Troglodyte” - which is a type of primitive cave dweller. I tossed the stapler onto the “Pre-spotting Table” spun around and (still with my eyes shut) launched into an “Air Guitar” solo. I did this with an extra flourish since the lyrics had already whipped me up into a pre-adolescent frenzy. At that moment Jeff Beck, Eric Clapton, and Jimmy Page had nothing on me. Noises from my mouth echoed the guitar notes. Satisfied with my work I opened my eyes and prepared to bow to the sold out arena…

☺

How long they had been standing there I had no way of knowing. You will recall that for much of the number my eyes had been shut. There stood a Mom and her two daughters. One of them was about 6. The other looked to be my age or perhaps a bit older. Worse yet, she was adorable; with long blonde hair, sparkling blue eyes, a white t-shirt and stylish Levi blue jeans. Just the kind of girl I had been singing about a few seconds ago.

The 6 year old stared at me and then turned to her Mom. "Mommy, what's wrong with him?" The Mom and the older daughter struggled with suppressed laughter. "Nothing honey. He's... he's just listening to the radio."

I wanted to crawl under the nearest caveman rock, but of course, none were available. I lunged for the radio to turn down the volume. I clumsily banged into it so that it slid off the table. I barely caught it by the cord before it hit the floor. I stammered, "Good after***goon.*** C-can you help me? I, I mean, can I help me. I, I mean, can I help you?"

The lady handed me her dry cleaning ticket. She said, "I want to pick up these dresses, please." How red a person's face can become before it actually catches on fire is a matter for the dermatologists to discuss, but I'm sure that my face had (and for that matter has) never been redder in my entire life. I touched my ears and nearly got 2$^{nd}$ degree burns on my hands.

I found Mrs. Cartwright's order, told her the cost, took her money, messed up her change, thanked her for her business, watched them walk back to their car laughing hysterically, saw them drive away, and spent the next 42 years contemplating just how humiliated a human being can become.

So, the test of a truly great song is this... Even though that moment was one of my very worst ones on the planet, I still love the song. Given the choice between having that song not exist and being able to escape that moment of crippling embarrassment, I'd keep the song.

Wild Thing, I think you move me,
But I want to know for sure.
So, come on and hold me tight...
(During the long pause I always see the faces of Mrs.

Cartwright and her two daughters)
You move me.
Come on, come on, Wild Thing.
Shake it, shake it, Wild Thing.

* * * * * * *

## "Dermo's Halloween"

When I was a child "Trick or Treating" was an art form. First of all, parents were not invited. Nowadays, because of safety concerns parents often accompany their young charges as they make their annual October rounds. Back in our day, that would have been unthinkable. I believe I was about 4 when I first ventured out with just my older siblings around to keep an eye on me. Secondly, we *ran.* I mean after all, ***candy*** was at stake. To the young child candy outshines almost any other attraction in the known universe. I honestly believe that if Bill Gates were to walk into my 4th grade classroom toting large golden bricks from Fort Knox in one box and Reese's Peanut Butter Cups in another, that most kids would make a bee line for the peanut butter and chocolate.

The choice of a costume back in the 60's was not an overly complicated affair. Ghost, Pirate, or Bum pretty much summed up the male possibilities. Ghost proved to be pretty bad because the sheet made it hard to see and run. So, Pirate or Bum would usually win out. In either case, it was always great to use something like charcoal to draw a beard on. Scars were always cool, too. There was a place in Hammond called "Wayne's Trick Shop" where we would go to pick up cool things like "Stick on Scars" (they also had a wonderful assortment of fake vomit, phony doggy doo, "Ew, My Finger's Chopped Off" boxes, and cheesy decks of magic cards).

I remember one year my parents let me get a giant novelty cigar (a real one) from Wayne's to complete my bum outfit.

So, when darkness fell upon the hazy Northwest Indiana sky, we ventured out into the streets of East Chicago (and later Munster) to become fast moving, weird looking, miniaturized candy magnets. It was, as we used to say back then, "A Blast".

Today however, I'd like to pay tribute to the "Master" of Halloween. His name was Jim Dermody and he was in my brother's class (which meant they were a couple of years older than my pals and me). One Halloween night in Munster I saw him put on a performance which boggled my mind then, and still to this day fills me with admiration. Jim's costume (when I first saw him) consisted of an ugly troll's mask, a pair of jeans, a loose fitting sweatshirt, and a pair of fast tennis shoes (as we called them back then). Instead of a paper bag to hold his candy, Jim utilized a pillow case. He explained that if it rained, paper bags could get soggy and break. Additionally, pillow cases were larger and easier to hold as one sped through the "candy collection zone."

But, here was the true genius behind "Dermo's" methodology. Inside the pillow case, carefully concealed beneath the first few layers of candy, Jim carried 4 or 5 "alternate" masks. We watched him at work with a sense of overarching awe. He ran (as we all did) from house to house and rang the doorbells with anticipatory glee. When the door would open he projected a very distinctive deep voice which bellowed the familiar, "Trick or Treat". After the adult would toss candy into the bag, Dermo would graciously acknowledge the gift with a "Thank You", in the same dulcet tones. He made a mental note of what type of candy had been dropped into the bag. Full sized Kit-Kat's, large Three Musketeers bars, big bags of M&M's, and several others were considered "Winners". Apples, bubble gum, and a few other non-descript items were labeled "Losers". At a loser house, Jim uttered the obligatory "Thank You", and then high tailed it to the next abode.

However, at the house of a "Winner", we were privileged to see a performance which Sir Laurence Olivier would have envied. Jim would sprint around the side of the home, quickly remove the troll mask, replace it with a devil (or an old hag, or a lizard's head) and then instantly attach himself to another batch of doorbell ringers. When the door would open a second time, Jim (who was a tall and lanky boy) transformed his entire persona. He literally became several inches shorter (how he did this, I do not know to this day).

He drifted to the back of the crowd and appeared to be the most reticent of Trick or Treaters. His voice, which previously had been "basso profundo", suddenly transformed into a squeaky, utterly convincing "wimp voice". He also sized up the age and visual acuity of the candy donors. Old fogies and trifocal wearers were capable of being bilked up to four times. With each successive ring, Jim's appearance and voice would change. I don't believe he was ever suspected, let alone caught. Dermo was an artist. We youngsters followed him from house to house to watch his con game in progress for a short while. But, he was too speedy for us to stay with him for long. Ahh, how I admired that scam! So it is, that whenever I see a batch of Trick or Treaters going from home to home, my mind drifts back to that cool and magical night long ago. I can still see Dermo, dashing from door to door, with a sense of joy, excitement, and mischief, that even now brings a smile to the face and a warmth to the heart.

I happen to know which profession Jim chose, and today it will serve as the basis for a little quiz:
After reading this story, do you think Jim Dermody is currently:

A. An Attorney in South Bend
B. A Middle School Principal in Laporte

C. Proprietor of an Off Track Betting Establishment in New York City
D. A Minor League Baseball Coach

(Correct Answer is B. Jim Dermody is currently Principal of Boston Middle School in Laporte, Indiana)

* * * * * * *

## "Just a Normal Day"

G.K. Chesterton once wrote that lying in bed would be an altogether ideal pursuit, if only one had a colored pencil long enough to reach the ceiling. I thought about that for awhile and decided that the pencil wouldn't have to be so long, provided that the legs on the bed were tall enough to get us closer to the ceiling. Or, we could have the carpenters make our bedrooms with very low ceilings so that we could easily reach them with our magical sticks of color. Failing all those options, we could just fill assorted squirt guns with food coloring and blast away without worrying about pencil length, bed height, or ceiling proximity. Of course, then we would have rainbow decorations all over the comforter and our spouse's face as well as our own.

Come to think of it, that might be a very nice byproduct of the endeavor. Imagine that my wife walks into the hospital and begins attending to her patients. One of the cardiologists, Dr. Serious for instance, strolls into the room and notices splatters of orange, blue, and green sprinkled merrily across her face and hands. Mistaking her decorations for a rare tropical disease he turns tail and runs down the hallway to check the medical literature in the hospital library. The patient in question drowsily opens her eyes and notices my wife closing in with her stethoscope. Coincidentally, at that very moment this patient falls into cardiac arrest. The Code team springs into action and the zapping machine is quickly rolled into place. Heaven protect us, but at that very instant a huge power failure sweeps across the entire northern third of our fair Hoosier State. The automatic backup generator kicks on, but at *that* very moment a large sewer rat (don't worry, this is a made up story and I can almost totally assure you that there *are no sewer* rats wandering the basement of Porter Hospital) darts into the generator and 50,000 watts go coursing through it's body, rendering both him and the generator lifeless. The hospital grid is down and a true state of crisis looms on the horizon.

Back up in room 117 the patient's eyes come into focus and she clearly sees the gleaming riot of hues dancing across her nurse's (my darling wife's) face. This, in and of itself, provides the necessary shock to restore the patient's heart to a normal sinus rhythm. Had she not been "colorized" the previous evening, the consequences could have been extreme. Dr. Serious reenters the room and explains to my wife that she is afflicted with a rare disease known as "Rainbowpigmentosis", which unfortunately in most cases proves to be fatal.

My wife calmly walks over to the sink, washes her pretty face (thereby removing my art work from the previous night). At that very instant the crack NIPSCO power restoration team has discovered that a farmer in Hebron has stuck a fork into his toaster (again), causing the massive outage. They remove the fork and electricity is restored. Dr. Serious, for once, is humbled. The rat is dead. The patient is alive. My wife has removed my Picasso like decorations and stands ready to complete her shift. At that very moment our good Reverend Jim (who is in the hospital attending to the spiritual needs of some parishioners) walks by the room, pops in his head and inquires if all is going well.

My lovely wife responds, "You bet. Just a normal day."

* * * * * * *

## "If you see a Mouse who Boogies*"

Have you ever noticed that it is fun to be outside? I mean, think about it; usually if you are outside something good is probably happening. You might be taking a walk, or rolling along on a nice bike ride, or sitting in a park having a picnic with someone you love, or catching a fish, or watching a football or a baseball game (I can't stand domed baseball stadiums). I told this theory to a rather pessimistic acquaintance once (the idea that being outside is usually fun). She replied that both wars and burials took place (mostly) outside and those things *weren't* much fun. I had to grudgingly concede her point, but overall I will stick with the original assertion. I think the unpredictable-ness of going out into the big world might have something to do with it.

I hope some of you have read what G.K. Chesterton has written about being outside in weather which certain people might consider to be "bad". If you have read his ideas, you will know why storms (rain, sleet, snow, wind, thunder, or otherwise – and you'll notice I'm kind of stopping short at tornadoes, hurricanes, and typhoons) are really things we ought to cherish rather than dread. If you don't understand how this might be possible, you can probably stop reading right about now...

One of the things I've enjoyed doing outside since I was 23 years old is running. The sad fact that I've slowed down to the extent that you would hardly even *call it* running anymore, doesn't diminish the fact that it is a fun activity. I am still outside, and my feet still move (a little bit).

Lots of cool things have happened while I've been on different runs. Brilliant sunsets have revealed themselves, blizzard force winds have held me up (or pushed me along) with an intensity it is difficult to describe, rain has pelted, heat has wilted, darkness has baffled, and each time out has brought a different type of adventure. I've met some strange and unusual people, I've fallen down a few times, and I've had many chances to "pray to Him who made us all" while I've been out there. Fun, fun, fun, and nobody has taken the T-Bird away (not just yet, anyway).

One of the most enjoyable aspects of being out on a run is the potential for animal encounters. Coming across a friendly dog is usually a happy moment. At places like Coffee Creek and the Indiana Dunes you can often see deer. A rare treat is to see a buck. That has probably happened only four or five times lo these many years. Last week when trudging along up at the dunes I saw a beautiful brown and white hawk swoop down onto the snowy ground between the trees and then rise again majestically into the grey sky. I was kind of hoping to see him carrying a little "happy meal" aloft, but alas, his talons were empty. I think whatever he was going after made an underground escape just in the nick of time.

Anyway, since I am talking about adventures I want to tell you about a wintertime episode which happened a few years back at Rogers - Lakewood Park (which is about a mile and a half away from where we live). I was running on a very bright and sunny day on those trails which wind around close to the Soap Box Derby hill. The ground was covered with a few inches of snow and I was coming to a loop near the eastern boundary of the park. Suddenly, a small brown mouse dashed out onto the trail directly in front of me...

*At this point in the story we'd like to pause for a brief moment and pay tribute to mice of note. People who've read "The Chronicles of Narnia" by C.S. Lewis will be familiar with that most heroic mouse, Reepicheep. If I were to compile a list of "Greatest Mice of All Time", Reep would certainly top the list. But how about Gus and Jaq, the two little mice from the animated Disney classic, "Cinderella"? I love those guys and Jaq has a place every year right on our Christmas Tree. Consider Mighty Mouse, Mickey & Minnie Mouse, Itchy from 'The Itchy and Scratchy Show", Pixie & Dixie, Jerry from "Tom and Jerry", the Metal Munching Moon Mice from "Rocky and Bullwinkle" and all the other little cartoon, movie, or literary mice people have been delighted by throughout the years. I'm sure to have forgotten some of your favorites.*

*Contrast all those happy fictional mouse memories with what **actually** happens when people (I'm thinking about my lovely wife and a few other folks I've known) encounter these furry little dudes in the real world... The reaction doesn't really compute, does it? In the book or on the screen they are adorably cute. In your kitchen pantry at 6:30A.M., it is an altogether different scenario. Well, I'm sure some psychologist somewhere has devoted his or her entire professional life to the study of mouse attraction/revulsion, but we have to get back to the tale...*

Or perhaps it is the ***tail***... When the mouse skittered out in front of me on the snowy trail, he immediately realized he was not alone. He put on the "Flintstone" brakes but I don't think he realized how treacherous the footing was. He spun in a wild circle, slid, and then kind of did a back flip in the snow. Now seeing this was really funny. Of course, I stopped dead to avoid crunching him with my ploddy size 12 / 4E New Balance Clod-Hoppers. I think he and I were equally surprised to meet one another.

Here comes the portion of the story where you are really going to have to trust me. As the mouse attempted to right the ship he found himself standing up on his back legs. I had never seen such a thing before. I think his tail was helping him to balance. OK, are you ready? For a few seconds the amazing little creature ***seemed to dance***. His miniscule front paws kind of moved in two clockwise circles. His feet flew across the snow in an intricate, scampering pattern which is difficult for a non-dancing layman to describe. I would say the entire episode lasted somewhere between 4 seconds and 100 years (depending upon your "wonder co-efficient").

Now, I've been pondering this for awhile and I've been trying to figure out the type of music a mouse might be dancing to. I actually consulted a dance professional about the whole business and was told that mice ***might*** like to impersonate John Travolta from "Saturday Night Fever", so he could have been dancing to a

Bee Gees song. Maybe the mouse was tap dancing, so perhaps he'd been watching some old film clips of Bill "Bojangles" Robinson dancing with Shirley Temple. It was winter, so could the mouse have been attempting some ballet moves lifted from the "Nutcracker Suite"? There are mice in that, right? Remember "Singin' in the Rain", starring Gene Kelly? Maybe the little guy was attempting a remake entitled, "Scamperin' in the Snow".

Deep down though, I'd like to think that the mouse was listening to a little rodent I-Pod (too small for me to see) and he had the Sonny Terry and Brownie McGhee number "White Boy lost in the Blues" playing (here are some lyrics):

"You bought you a six string Gibson
You bought you a great big house
You try to sing like Muddy Waters
And play like Lightnin' sounds

But since I blowed my harp
You feelin' mean and confused.
It got you chained to your earphones,
You just a white boy, lost in the blues..."

You see, maybe the mouse wasn't startled by my presence at all. Maybe he went slip sliding onto that part of the trail and danced every day. Or maybe he thought, "Well, here's a gigantic audience member. Let's show him what we've got. It's time that relations between our two species got onto a better footing."

I don't really know what was going on that day, but I do know this. If God can make the icy rings around Saturn, and huge blue whales in the incomprehensibly vast ocean, and towering Redwood forests which have stood before the time of His Son's life on this world, He can most certainly come up with a little mouse who dances for a few moments inside a snowy park. As to whether or not this story is to be found on the fiction or non-fiction shelves, I guess you'll have to decide that for yourself. Ramandu's daughter said it best in The Voyage of the Dawn Treader, "You can't ***know***. You can either ***believe***, or not."

Happy New Year to All, and may the adventures you have each day (both inside your home and out) serve to light up your mind, your heart, and your soul. And may they help you to believe as well...

* With apologies to If you give a Mouse a Cookie author, Laura Joffe Numeroff

* * * * * * *

## "John's Musky"

Our recent trip to Northwestern Wisconsin was the best kind of vacation; both relaxing and exciting. We've been going up there for more than 25 years and fishing is the main activity. John and Bob (brothers of Mrs. K.) are the real expert fishermen. The types of fish we usually catch are Bass, Walleye, and Northern Pike (with an odd Crappie, Bluegill, or stray Perch thrown in from time to time for good measure).

Everybody up there dreams and talks about the legendary fish called "The Musky" (Muskellunge), but in the 50 some odd years ***Liz's family*** has been going up there, NOBODY had ever caught one (they might have hooked a couple, but they are so huge and powerful that they just snapped the lines). When you go into the town of Hayward, they have one of the World Record Muskies hanging up on the wall inside one of the bars. These monstrously ugly and wonderful fish are the stuff of legends.

Each year when we are there my lovely wife prepares a huge spaghetti dinner for all the members of her far flung family who make the trip up to the Northwoods. I help a little, like maybe I get to make the meatballs, cut up the red peppers for the salad, or whip up the Brownie mix. Anyway, on the night of July 25th we ate this beautiful dinner and then Bob and I went out fishing in one boat and Liz and her brother John went out in another. The Upper Eau Claire Lake is one of the most peaceful places I have ever experienced in this world. I hope you have been there (or somewhere like it) or can get up there sometime.

Well, we were out on the water as the sun was going down and everybody was just sitting in our respective boats talking, and suddenly my brother-in-law John hooked a Musky. You should have seen his fishing rod bend! He played that fish for about 15 minutes while everyone else watched in amazement. At one point in the proceedings that fish leaped out of the water. I don't have the proper skill with the English language to explain what that looked like. I wish I did.

Our two boats were about 20 yards apart. John and Liz didn't have a big enough net in their boat to handle this prehistoric beast. Bob rowed our boat closer to theirs and it suddenly became my job to use our larger net to land the fish. Now, a 4-5 pound fish is a nice catch. A nine to ten pounder gets talked about for years. A handful of times in the last two decades someone has broken the ten pound barrier. But, this is extremely rare…

The Musky John caught that night weighed over 20 pounds! Now, we didn't actually get to weigh it, but I have picked up lots of 40 pound bags of salt for our water softener and I have hoisted up a fair number of pretty good sized fish. Trust me, it was well over 20. Bob and I lifted the beast into the boat, then both boats raced back to shore to show Grandpa, and John's wife and kids. I had to use all of my power to keep the Musky from thrashing around the boat as we headed into shore. The word "strength" won't suffice for what was lurking inside that creature's muscles. I read later that experienced Musky fishermen often ***wear gloves!***

Judy (John's wife) took pictures of this incredible monster. We released him back into the Upper Eau Claire Lake and he swam around with his head above the water looking at us for a few minutes before he disappeared. It was a very surreal experience. The whole thing was like nothing I've ever experienced in all the years we've been going up there.

This little poem tells the story of that night in verse. If you don't know who Louie Spray is, here's the short version. He caught three of the five largest Muskies on record at one time. Of course, controversy surrounds these fish. Some people think that old Louie exaggerated the size of his catches… Maybe he did and maybe he didn't. One of the stories I read said that ***all*** Musky fishermen are liars! I know that that can't be true, because Liz's two brothers are probably the most honest guys I've ever met.

In any event, here's the poem…

## "John's Musky"

The Sun began to set, we heard the crying of a Loon,
The clouds were pink and peaceful, on an evening late in June.
A Yellow Lab lay on the bow of one boat quite nearby,
And talking in another boat there sat a girl and guy.

The Texan, lean and angular, with wisdom on his brow,
Had nodded to his sister and said, "Well, let's go in now."
They'd only brought a few worms plus one Chubb, and so you see,
They hadn't really meant to fish, just sit, and talk, and ***be***.

They started winding the rigs in, He said, "My bobber's down.
Perhaps a bass has hit it, or a Northern swimmin' round."
But then he felt and saw some things,
Some things which were quite rare,
'Twas hard to find the adjectives, the past did not compare.

Earlier, they'd looked at pictures of Old Louie Spray,
But little did they know, his spirit rode with them that day.
For this fish was a Musky, rippled muscle, razor teeth,
A creature huge, from frigid depths, the water far beneath.

Then John played him skillfully, as he swam round the boat,
The others watched in disbelief,
"Let's move those poles and coat."
And then he jumped, Dear Lord, he jumped,
I wish you could have seen!
The power and the majesty, the background so serene.

The other boat pulled closer, skillful Bobby closed the gap,
The Monster used his tail to give the waves a fearful slap.
The net was lowered down and then the Musky swam right in,
They lifted him into the boat, and then, a fearful din.

He crashed against the metal and he thrashed from side to side,
Then both boats fired the engines up,

And kicked them to full stride.
For they were racing 'gainst the clock,
They knew that time was short,
They knew if all did not go well, their mission would abort.

And Liz ran up the hill to gather Grandpa, Claire, and Dan,
And Judy grabbed her camera, and then everybody ran.
She snapped the photos, then the fish was put back in his world,
All went inside and talked about the things which had unfurled.

The 25$^{th}$ of June, Upper Eau Claire, Two thousand eight,
We ate spaghetti, drank some wine, had brownies on a plate.
Then John asked Liz if she would like to fish until it's dusky,
And don't you know,
That that's the night God sent their boat a Musky!

* * * * * * *

## "Fail-Safe"

When my sister Toni was in the 10th grade, one of her teachers at Munster High School gave the class an assignment. It was to go to a local theater and watch the movie, "Fail-Safe". My parents took my brother Tom and me along.

Of course, I had been scared by movies before. My dad used to lie on the couch and pretend to be the Boris Karloff character from the classic horror film, "Frankenstein". He'd have us flicker the lights in the living room on and off (to simulate the electricity going into the monster's body) and then he would wiggle one little finger. Then, he'd move his whole hand. At this point, all three of us would be screaming in terror. Finally, he would rise up from the sofa in a thoroughly frightening fashion and stagger through the house after us with his hands extended and we could almost see those little metal things popping out of the side of his neck. That was one kind of fear. But, when I sat outside later on in the sunny backyard and analyzed the whole thing, I knew that it was just a scary *story.* No ugly green dudes with zig-zagging scars would actually be coming to chase us around 1535 Melbrook Drive.

However, sitting inside the darkened theater that night watching Sidney Lumet's classic masterpiece regarding accidental nuclear war, I remember thinking that everything which took place in ***that*** film ***could*** actually happen.

Henry Fonda gives an excellent performance as the President of the United States. In the black and white classic with no background music, both the Soviet Union and the United States utilize complex technological systems to make the other side's systems go haywire. The result is that a team of United States bombers, equipped with two twenty megaton hydrogen bombs is streaking through Russian air space toward Moscow. The pilot has been given instructions to not listen to radio communications after a designated point in the attack route. Even when the President and the pilot's wife get on the radio and tell him that the whole thing is just a mistake, the pilot (Grady) refuses to listen. You can see in his eyes that he ***knows*** it is his wife and the President, but he is too good a military man to ignore orders.

When it becomes clear that the plane will get through and destroy the entire city of Moscow, the President makes an unbelievable decision. Rather than allowing a total nuclear holocaust to take place, he proposes a trade to the Soviet Premiere. Even though he knows his wife is there visiting, he tells the Russian leader that rather than unleashing the vast nuclear arsenals of both nations, America will destroy New York City as well as Moscow. Through this course of action both sides can agree to call the whole thing even without further loss of life. Watching this incredible sequence numbed my young mind.

I don't know if parents in those days discussed what the effects of certain things were on their kids. But, I can remember lying in bed and wondering what was happening at the Strategic Air Command for several nights in a row. I remember thinking about how deep the Presidential Bomb shelter really was and what they might have to eat or drink down there. There was a Nike Missile site a few miles from our home in Munster. I rode my bike over there and stared through the fence, thinking about what was going on under the ground in those missile silos. What if one of the technicians at that site was mentally unbalanced? I wasn't sure whether or not those weapons were tipped with nuclear warheads at the time (they weren't), but I did know that they were missiles, and that they were just a few miles from my front yard.

One of the most poignant parts of the film takes

place when an American officer is on the phone with a Russian officer near the end of the story. As they confront the mutually assured destruction of their two greatest cities, the men talk about the experiences they shared during World War II and how they both loved the city of London. The Russian tells the American officer that "the great cities are the ones in which you can walk." The American sees the family photograph in the dossier of the Russian and realizes that the Russian officer's wife and children may be destroyed in the impending conflagration. Their conversation ends with a staggeringly sad, "Goodbye, my friend," uttered by each soldier.

For years, this movie has haunted me. So, the other night I rented it. I wondered if my fear had mainly stemmed from the fact that I was 9 years old when I saw it. I wondered if the story would hold up and be as utterly believable as it was in 1964. I thought I remembered pretty clearly the final scene which shows different slices of life taking place throughout New York City. Teenagers dancing, kids jumping rope, motorists arguing, birds taking off in a flock, all accompanied with a countdown to impact. Then, everything stops.

The movie was even better than I had remembered. Here is what it taught me. We live each day (whether we're aware of it or not) on the precarious edge of a razor. On one side are sunsets, wrestling with Golden Retrievers in the backyard, our wonderful wives, daughters, and sons, old films of Willie Mays catching Vic Wertz's World Series shot, mountains, bike rides, starry nights, steaks on the barbecue, walks through the woods, ethereal music, and a thousand and one other things which make life beautiful and worth living each day. On the other side is Pearl Harbor, the Holocaust, nuclear explosions, astronauts blown up in billion dollar machines, pollution, abuse, car wrecks, crime, disease, people with evil hearts boarding planes on sunny September mornings, and a thousand and one other things which have the capacity to fill us with dread. The terror of the bad things is partially what causes the good to be so sweet. The splendor of the good things is what makes the bad so awful. Each side gives power to the other. In "Fail-Safe", mankind slips off the edge and tumbles into the shadow. Watching this film after a gap of 42 years caused me to once again reflect on the nature of this life. Conclusion? There must be a Satan. There must be a God. And we must stand with God.

* * * * * * *

## "Jane"

When G.K. Chesterton was in the process of becoming the monumental genius who would go on to pen scores of books, hundreds of essays, and brilliant poetry like "Lepanto" (among other things) one of his teachers met with his mother. The teacher described the young man to Mrs. Chesterton as "Six foot of genius." When his mother innocently asked, "What shall we do with him?" The teacher's reply (which we hope all parents might take note of) was splendid. "Cherish him, Mrs. Chesterton. Cherish him."

This school year (2007 – 2008) I find myself in a similar position to that teacher in England many years ago. For one day in December I picked up a paper in my classroom and read:

*All the woodland animals gathered around the big fir tree. They were about to decorate it with big glass balls of deep and rich crimson and gold, purple and silver, patterns of cascading lines, or an intricate pattern of swirly shapes. This was a holiday tradition. The tree was never cut down, but held up all year round, and specially decorated in December. Rabbit was there, along with Mr. and Mrs. Cardinal, and Rudolph with his special friend, Clarice. Everyone came when the sun went down. It was a joyous time for all. Tinsel and garland with delicate ornaments decorated the tree until it twinkled. Mr. and Mrs. Cardinal put on the star. Just as everyone gathered around the tree to admire the glowing decorations, a snow began falling. It was fluffy and pure white. It surprised and delighted the dear animals. They ran and leaped about. In the end, they again formed a half circle around the tree, sharing memories of Christmas long ago.*

Every time my class writes something this year, I read words like that from the pencil of Jane Tullis. Now usually when a 4th grader's story has phrases like "intricate patterns" and "cascading lines" you can pretty much rest assured that it was a homework assignment and an overzealous mom (or dad) has been pumping the thesaurus for all it is worth. Jane wrote those words sitting a few feet away from my desk with no prodding or adult interference of any kind.

Now, I have been doing this job for 31 years and I have met many wonderful children, Some of them have been tremendous athletes. Others have been blessed with talent in the realm of acting. A select few have been able to sing with power and beauty. Others have had extraordinary ability with a musical instrument of one sort or another. Some are splendid artists. As I watch and work with these children (and I must say honestly that the truly "gifted" child in all of these areas is indeed a rarity), I am filled with a type of awe. Has the talent simply been "bestowed"? Have parents worked to develop it? Is the child herself aware of how hard it is for others to do what she can do with (apparent) ease? These are questions I ask this year each time Jane hands in another "assignment".

One day I asked the class to randomly write down questions which popped into their minds. Here are some of Jane's:

* *Why does pride have to come before doing the right thing?*

* *Why can't the USA and our fellow countries decide not to have wars, but to be peacemakers?*

* *What was Methuselah's health condition during his long lifetime?* (Methuselah was the oldest person mentioned in the Bible at 969 years of age).

* *How long was there utter blackness before God created Earth?*

* *How did people get* <u>*last*</u> *names?*

* *Why does the devil have to exist?*

* *What was going on in the Roman soldier's heads while nailing Jesus to the Cross?*

* *How did God become God?*

While many of the other kids were writing questions about how many touchdowns Devin Hester scored, or whether or not Mr. Karas will let us have a longer recess today, Jane was mulling over issues of war and peace, the nature of God's existence, and the physical condition of a man who almost lived to be 1,000 years old. She also had inquiries about criminals, abortion, terrorists, what type of job she might ultimately have, and the pollution of our planet (among other things).

You may have noticed that themes of faith enter into Jane's ruminations. Her Dad, Garner, is the Pastor of Bethel Valparaiso Church. Her Mom, Mary is one of the most committed parent volunteers I've seen throughout my three decades in this profession. There are four Tullis girls. I have already taught Molly and Marilee (who are both now in middle school). The youngest daughter, Rachael is a first grader. It is quite a family. When Marilee was in my class Hurricane Katrina took place. She went down (as a fourth grader!) to help with the relief effort. Molly has penned a full length fantasy story and is an accomplished actor. The family's faith, positive outlook, and zest for life always leads them into areas which produce interesting results.

One day Jane wrote about visiting the Broadmoor Hotel in Colorado with her family when she was of

Kindergarten age.

*...My favorite part was the pool. At my age it looked terrifying. There I stood clutching onto my Dad. I saw a high pavilion with two slides coming down from it. One was straight, and I mean straight! It looked like a monster to a five year old. I saw a more curly, less dangerous slide. It curved into the rock that held up the pavilion. I didn't dare go on those slides, straight or not...*

Jane explained how being unable to summon up the courage to climb those slide ladders haunted her. I can only surmise what it is like for a child this young to have such a vivid imagination and the ability to articulate it at such a high level. Time passed, but she did not forget the strange attraction coupled with the powerful fear.

*The feeling of not going on those slides gnawed at me...*

Years later (she does not specify in the piece exactly how many) the family returned to the Broadmoor.

*Again, the hotel looked magnificent, but I wanted to go to the pool, the slides! The moment arrived. I was at the top of the straight slide... It was my turn... I remembered the gnawing feeling. Suddenly, I just raced down. The rush was exhilarating! I went on again and again. The Broadmoor Hotel is just amazing.*

Now, Jane is human. She spelled exhilarating with an "e" in the middle and she started gnawed with a "k" instead of a "g". Chesterton himself had similar misspellings as a child, but the important thing is the quality of her thought. I am continually dumbfounded by the way ideas seem to flow from her mind onto the paper. Two of Jane's former teachers,

Mrs. Wolf and Mrs. Moran, experienced similar astonishment when reading things she had written in their classes.

When I try to remember back to the kinds of things I could write in the 4th grade and the kinds of things I see her turning out every week, I simply sit and shake my head.

We read a book in class entitled, Black Cowboy, Wild Horses. As a concluding activity we wrote a letter to Bob Lemmons, the fictitious cowboy who is the protagonist of the story. Here is an excerpt from Jane's letter.

*I truly think that riding a horse all day and living with a herd of mustangs must deliver some kind of impact on your life, a respect for nature. So many people nowadays would rather have memories of video games instead of memories of horses, the sun on your back, tall grass brushing against your feet. It sounds like you and Warrior were a great team!*

In December Jane decided to surprise her younger sister Rachael with a letter from Santa Claus at the North Pole! Here are a few of "Santa's" words to Rachael...

*Rudolph's nose is shining brighter than ever before. Dasher and Dancer might need to work on their landing a little, so if you hear a small crash, don't worry. It's just them.... Oh, the Reindeer would like to thank you for the carrots and water. It's such a long journey, so having a little snack helps them... I want to tell you a big secret, I only pick 10 kids to write a letter to and every year you are at the top of my list. Oh my, the elves need me. They said the cocoa machine is having problems.*

*Ho Ho Ho,*
*Santa Claus*

It seems in little snippets like this one that Jane has already discovered one of the splendid secrets pertaining to great writing. It has the capacity to delight others. How a 10 year old child has already figured this out is beyond me. I think it is marvelous that Jane decided to use her skills on a project which was designed to ignite the wonder of her younger sibling.

So many kids think of writing as a chore and consequently they approach it with dread. To Jane, the world of writing is like a vast playground where she is allowed to utilize her considerable skills and explore the landscape of her unusually vivid imagination.

Obviously, the other side of the coin when discussing outstanding writing is quality reading. Jane is an avid reader. When taking the Accelerated Reader placement test which determines the grade level of particular students, Jane maxed out the system at 12.9+ (this means her reading ability is roughly that of an incoming college freshman). Jane reads all the time. She had devoured the "Chronicles of Narnia" by C.S. Lewis before she'd completed third grade. She's read many of the Little House books by Laura Ingalls Wilder. In the age of instant messaging, cell phone toting, two minute attention span elementary students, I can't tell you how truly refreshing that is.

About "The Chronicles of Narnia", Jane has written,

*The purpose is to delight children and adults and invite them into a magical world... nothing could have the depth and passion these books supply.*

Before I sat down to write this I wondered about the effect it might have on Jane. For instance, would seeing these things in print give her a "big head"? Since I know

Jane and many of you reading this don't, I can tell you that that is probably the last thing in the world which will happen. Not only is Jane humble about her abilities and accomplishments, she is the kind of kid who spends so much time being a good friend and thinking about other people that it is inconceivable that she'd entertain any thoughts which were laced with conceit. And, she's a kid. She loves dogs, people, hot cocoa, and laughing (among many other things). If I thought saying any of this stuff about her might have had a negative effect, I would have left the laptop closed.

Earlier in the year (at parent teacher conferences) I related the story about Chesterton's instructor to Garner and Mary. Of course, I didn't have to tell them to cherish Jane. They'd had that emotion toward all of their daughters since the moments they had entered the earth.

So, what about me and other teachers who will be blessed to work with Jane as the years unfold? What are we supposed to do? I suppose a number of suggestions might be made. I am certainly not an expert regarding the development of individuals with such prodigious talent. I've taught precious few kids in Jane's league in regard to writing skills, and she is standing atop the pyramid. Double promotions, enrollment in special university programs, writing workshops, and the like will leap into the minds of some observers. I have one humble suggestion… Give her a pencil and get out of the way.

* * * * * * *

## "Courage"

Each year the local Boys and Girls Club in the town where I live hosts an unique and entertaining event called "The Steak and Burger Dinner". At this function kids from B&G Clubs in the area are VIP guests. The children eat steak while adults from businesses and civic organizations who help sponsor the night, eat burgers. (Now, some of us savvy veterans have figured out how to trade our way up to steak by using monetary bribes or well placed compliments - but that is a story for another article). Our Kiwanis club always buys a table full of tickets. I look forward to the event every year.

During the evening, young people win new bikes in a raffle, sign autographs in deluxe programs, wear colorful "kid designed" t-shirts, and get a chance to listen to exciting motivational speakers. A couple of years ago the speaker was Dan Hampton, the Hall of Fame defensive lineman from the Chicago Bears. At the end of the evening I got in line to shake his hand. Now, I am a regular sized person (sort of), but when I glanced down at Hampton's huge hand as it engulfed mine, mine seemed to disappear. He had given a good talk about the old days with the Bears and the crowd of adults and kids had loved his Super Bowl tales.

The next year's speaker was completely different. Kerri Strug, the Olympic Gold Medalist from the 1996 Atlanta Games came to Valparaiso to discuss her quest for athletic excellence and her life after that experience. After having taught elementary school for 30 years and being around dozens of 9 year old girls who would some day ***like*** to win Olympic Gold, it was fascinating to hear her talk about the sacrifices which were necessary for that event to ***really take place***. As Ms. Strug talked about the spartan conditions and rigorous regimen at Bela Karolyi's Texas training camp, it became patently obvious that those young ladies earned each and every moment in the spotlight. Her description of the training and necessary sacrifices champions have to make was absolutely riveting.

It seems like failure and heartbreak are lurking around each and every corner for competitors like Kerri Strug and her teammates. The more difficult the skill being attempted, the greater the likelihood that the performer will experience a horrible crash landing. Even if the humiliating disaster does not take place, one tiny slip in a routine can mean the difference between a medal and the feeling that the last four years of work have not brought about the result one intended. The pressure, the stress, the incredible weight of the world which must descend on the shoulders of these young athletes all seems to me to be incalculable.

In the weeks leading up to the event I had thought a little bit about the night Kerri Strug turned in her incredible performance. Thinking about that inspiring show of courage planted the seed for a poem. Here it is:

**"Courage"**

**There are 40,000 people watching in this crowded room,**
**And the camera lenses (there are many) all are set on zoom.**
**Plus millions (probably billions) more are viewing in their homes,**
**Then don't you know (ten years from now) some people will write poems.**

**Because the first time that she landed after soaring through the air,**
**Her feet felt for the mat below, but it just wasn't there.**
**She landed with a wrenching twist that filled her being with pain,**
**And some folks thought, to go again, well that would be insane!**

**Then this girl looked around the Dome and thought about the task,**
**The ligaments were torn, perhaps that's just too much to ask.**
**But then, she saw the faces of her Coach and of her Team,**
**And thought about the years that they had all worked for this Dream.**

**So she limped back to the runway, and she filled her heart with steel,**
**And she told her mind the pain was something she chose not to feel.**
**Then she sprinted down the pathway, and prepared to spring the vault,**
**And she never thought of failing and she never said, "My fault".**

**Well, she soared into the Georgia sky and spun and flipped and twirled,**
**And people held their breath in every country of the world.**
**Landing with but one good foot and triumph on her face,**
**The crowd erupted, it was like explosions in that place!**

**And that's what "Courage" means my friends, to battle when you're down,**
**And that's how Gold is gathered, how a Team can earn renown.**
**And that's what Kerri showed us on that warm day in July,**
**How even with a damaged wing, determined birds can fly!**

I wanted Ms. Strug to have a copy of that poem, but of course felt awkward about just walking up to her and handing it over. The fear of feeling foolish can be a pretty overwhelming one at times. Therefore, I enlisted the help of one of the young kids at my table. I asked her to take it up to one of the people in charge of the event. I figured that way, if it was meant to get into her hands, it would.

As we sat there eating dinner and talking at the Kiwanis table with our kid guests, I found myself enjoying the evening immensely. At this function you get to talk to the kids from the different Boys and Girls Clubs in Porter County and find out a little about them, their families, and their schools. When we ask the kids to sign the program booklet underneath their names, we tell them stuff like we'll keep it until they are famous. If you get the kids to open up a bit and talk about themselves, it is really a wonderful thing. One year, the kid who had designed the T-Shirts was sitting right nearby, and we all made it our business to make a big deal of praising her for her cool design. You could tell that this girl enjoyed the recognition and was really proud of her shirt.

Anyway, we were sitting there eating (I'm pretty sure it was Ron, George, Mary Ann, Judy, the kids, and myself) when Dr. George Vrabel, the Assistant Superintendent for Elementary Instruction (and that night's MC) walked over to our table.

He said, "Hey Karas, come with me. There's somebody who wants to talk to you." Of course, I'm thinking that he's going to take me over to the head of Security and have me arrested for stalking the evening's speaker. This is doubly bad, because not only will I be arrested, I will be arrested right in front of one of my bosses.

Actually, that's not what happened. In reality, Kerri Strug liked the poem and had asked George if she could meet me in order to thank me. Talk about making an Old Man's day! Do you know what she told me when I got the chance to talk to her for a moment? She told me that her ***Mom*** was going to love the poem. Then, I remembered that this young lady was still in her ***twenties***. George's wife Kathy snapped a picture of me next to Kerri (it is up on the bulletin board of my classroom). The gymnasts in this year's class (there are 3 or 4) really loved seeing that picture - not, I'm sure because of the presence of my round belly or gray hair!

I once met Muhammad Ali at O'Hare airport. He did magic tricks for a crowd of people as we all waited for a plane to arrive (remember when you could go right to the gate and wait for your loved one to de-board? That's where we were). I mentioned meeting Dan Hampton the year before at this same event. But for my money, Kerri Strug is the greatest athletic performer I've met (or probably ever will meet). Here's why:

A. Her potential window for success was miniscule.
B. The white hot focus of the Olympic gymnastics competition seems more full of pressure and potential disaster than any sport I can imagine.
C. She took a horrendous spill in the biggest competition of her life, which injured her severely and which would have sent most teenage girls hobbling toward the ambulance.
D. Then, she "sucked it up" to a degree most people would have found unimaginable and proceeded (with her last vault) to light up that entire arena and television sets around the globe with billions of people watching. If you are old enough to remember Willis Reed limping out onto the floor of Madison Square Garden, watching the severely injured Kirk Gibson smash that World Series Home run for the Dodgers, or if you can recall the game when Michael Jordan was doubled over with the flu and still incredibly led his team to victory, you know exactly which emotions were activated by Kerri's monumental display of courage.
D. And, she told me her ***Mom*** was gonna love the poem.

* * * * * * *

## "Kofi"

Recently my wife and I attended a Derek Trucks Band concert. Lots of people in this club might not know who that is, and I don't have adequate space or expertise to explain about the styles of music his band plays. Suffice it to say, in my humble opinion, he is the greatest living guitar player on the planet and if reincarnation was real (which I don't think it is), then the spirit of the greatest living guitar player in the *history* of the planet (Duane Allman) would be walking among us once again. In any case, I do think a little of that spirit was thrown his way.

However, the thing I want to relate is an episode that happened before the concert. We arrived kind of early (the show took place at the Park West, which is right by Lincoln Park), so that we could sit where we wanted. We chose seats up in the balcony right next to where the technicians were to work during the show. We met a very friendly lady who was working the venue as a security guard. She told us all about the shows she had worked (Eric Clapton, the Marley Family, Phil Collins). She was a very nice person and she obviously loved her job.

At one point I went down to the bar to grab something to drink. When I climbed the stairs back up to the balcony I noticed that our friend the security guard was talking to another person. He was a friendly looking kid in his late twenties or early thirties. Since I had already struck up a conversation with the security guard, I kind of nodded at both of them as I went to resume my seat.

The young man shook my hand and said, "Did you come out to see Derek tonight?" There was another band (from Chicago) playing beforehand, so there was a possibility that we had come in to see them. I told him that we indeed had and that we were really looking forward to the show.

He looked truly happy (and almost a bit surprised) that the band we had come to watch was his.

He then told me who he was, "I'm Kofi Burbridge. I play keyboards and flute in the band." I had seen pictures of him on the band's CD's. In those photos he sported a fairly large Afro. He was wearing a knit cap with African colors. He removed it with a smirk and said, "I kind of cut off all of my hair." He told us how long he had been in the band (six years). I told him that I also admired his brother, Oteil Burbridge, the bass player for the Allman Brothers. We stood there pleasantly chatting for a couple of minutes and then he said the words that were to stick with me for the rest of the night (and I think for perhaps quite a bit longer).

Kofi Burbridge said to me, "I really want to thank you, man. The reason this is all happening for us is because of people like you."

The implication was that the fans, by purchasing tickets to the show and buying the band's CD's were responsible for the group's livelihood. That sentence shocked me so much, I didn't know what to say. I must have mumbled something like, "Our pleasure." But then, I thought about it. If no one had purchased tickets, or nobody ever bought their CD's, they might be back in their hometowns, unloading trucks. He was truly grateful.

I then ruminated about the entertainers in our society (other musicians, athletes, & actors) who could really take a lesson from the attitude of young Mr. Burbridge. Really, how many times have you sensed that some of these folks are indifferent, and indeed sometimes outright contemptuous in regard to their fans. It just made me so happy that somewhere along the way, this young person had picked up the idea that other people in the world were worthy of gratitude.

I just wanted to tell him how much that sentence meant to an old guy like myself. I thought that somebody raised that kid the right way.

I went to the show in Chicago expecting to listen to some jazz and blues on the slide guitar. I came away with an unexpected lesson in gratitude and humility. Bonus time again!

***(I sent this story into the Derek Trucks Band and got a nice letter back explaining that Kofi Burbridge was actually in his forties. That was hard to believe.)***

* * * * * * *

## "Sara Stone"

A very long time ago my wife and I worked at a Horse Camp in Mazomanie, Wisconsin. It was called "Hoofbeat Ridge" and it is one of the most beautiful places I've seen on the planet. I didn't know much about horses, but I knew a little bit about kids, so they let me be the "Program Director". Children (from about age 9 up to 15) would come for two week sessions and ride horses, canoe down the Wisconsin River, swim in Devil's Lake, take hikes, sing at campfires, and generally do all the fun stuff that kids do at camps. We stayed there the whole summer and met many wonderful humans, dogs, and horses. I worked there for three summers and my wife Liz was there for the last two of those. She served as Camp Nurse.

Since I had never done any camping type things as a child, it was great to do them as an adult. My job was to help plan and supervise activities for the sessions which ran from June all the way to August. The camp is still there, run by a wonderful man named Ted Marthe (whom I have not seen in over 25 years). Ted is the head of a large and accomplished family and a person who is full of what I'd call "natural wisdom". He ran a fun and very cool place.

The reason I never did anything like camping as a kid is because my family never had that magical thing called "Disposable Income". We had instead, "Drycleaner's Income". It was enough, but it certainly was not ***more*** than enough. Instead of camp, my parents took us to the Dairy Queen. Obviously, some of the kids who came to this camp were in a completely different financial league. We would find out that a certain camper's Dad had worked in the Nixon Administration, or somebody else's Grandpa was on the Board of Carson Pirie Scott (or some such big time thing). Some of those kids were brushed with a sense of entitlement because of their family wealth. They usually weren't that much fun to be around. The operative word was "Snooty".

One day however, we were in the camp office and saw a letter stating that a girl named Sara Stone was coming to visit Hoofbeat Ridge. The note went on to explain that Sara was the Granddaughter of W. Clement Stone, one of the richest men in the world. Now, the note didn't actually say the part about W.C.S. being one of the world's richest men, but everybody in the room knew who he was as soon as we read the name.

I remember looking at Amy (the secretary) and Margaret (one of the staff members), and saying something like, "Oooh. Hoidy Toidy! W. Clement Stone! I wonder if she is going to bring her own maid and butler along? Do you think she'll request a private cabin and have a special King Size Bed flown in? I wonder if she'll bring along the family chef, or her own private jet?"

Looking back at all the stuff I said about Sara and her wealth makes me totally ashamed of myself even to this day. Here's why:

When Sara arrived (in a remarkably plain looking vehicle with her Mom and Dad) she was wearing a light blue T-Shirt and a regular pair of blue jeans. She was about 12, fairly tall, blonde, athletic, and quite intelligent looking. When she was introduced to you she smiled, looked you straight in the eye and said, "Nice to meet you," while she gave you a warm handshake. She carried her own duffel bag up to the regular girls' cabin. One thing I remember about Sara was when she came into the Camp Kitchen and Dining Hall one day early in the session when I had table setting duty. She started helping me and another staff member do the job. "Is it okay if I help?" she asked as she grabbed napkins, plastic glasses, and silverware. Lots of the other kids were outside, playing frisbee, petting the dogs (Riboflavin, Barney, or Misha), or just goofing around. Sara chose to come in and work. "Uh, yeah," I said. "That would be great. Thanks." Then I wondered, "What's this rich kid's game?"

On another day Sara got up early and walked to the barn where all the horses were stabled. She asked the British girl in charge of the stables (whose name escapes me) if she could help feed, water, and brush the horses. Most of the other kids were still sleeping or blearily preparing for breakfast. Sara did this work with a smile. She truly loved horses. She went up to help like that every morning.

Unfailingly, she was the most polite, the most involved, the most considerate, and the kindest person at the whole camp. There was nothing phony about this. It was not an act. It was truly her personality. She was funny. She was smart. She was "in tune" with whatever was going on around her. It drove me nearly out of my mind. Here was a child I was prepared to resent. Here was a child ***I knew*** was going to be the worst "Spoiled Rich Kid" on the North American Continent. The only problem was, she ***wasn't*** obnoxious and she wasn't spoiled. She was the exact opposite of everything I had expected. She made friends easily and I don't think the other kids knew (or if they knew, didn't give a rip) who her rich Grandpa was.

She quickly became my favorite kid and (after eating a big bucket of crow) I finally just learned to enjoy her personality. One day a few of us were just sitting around talking and I admitted my prejudices. I told her about the conversations we had had prior to her arrival. I told her that I had been prepared to dislike her because her Grandpa was rich beyond my wildest dreams. Then, I just went ahead and asked her, "Sara, why are you so nice? How come you're not a spoiled brat?"

She said, "My Mom told me a long time ago that because of who our family was, I had to make a choice. She said that people were going to be prepared to hate me because of the money our family had. But, she told me that if I was a certain kind of person, that I could show them that that was wrong. She said that anybody can be nice and if you're truly, genuinely nice, people will forget about the money. She told me that it was a lesson that ***she*** had to learn. If she wanted to really have friends she'd have to show them that she was worthy of their friendship and the money didn't have anything to do with it." That story boggled my mind. It still does. What a perceptive Mom! What a smart kid to accept her advice!

So, that's the story. I've been wrong about lots of things in the last five decades, to be sure (just ask my wife). But, I'm not sure if I've ever been so magnificently, wildly, or unfairly wrong as I was about Sara Stone. I remember when Dr. King said that he had a dream about his little children being judged not by the color of their skin, but by the content of their character. Well, here's a little addendum to that great thought, "I have a dream that all of God's children will not be judged by the weight of their purses, but by the purity of their spirits." Sara's spirit went shooting up past mine on the very first day I met her, and I'm still gazing up into the clouds to see exactly where it went.
I wonder where she is now?

* * * * * * *

563 Wedgwood Dr.
Valparaiso, Indiana 46385
May 25, 1997

Dear Mr. Schulz,

Since I was 7 years old I have been reading your comic strip. In the Chicago Tribune and in paperback editions that have come out from time to time, I have enjoyed the Peanuts characters and the situations you have created for them. Each morning for over 35 years you have given me the gift of a smile. You don't even know my name, but your funny children and animals have helped to create a wonderful little landscape in one very important corner of my mind. I know that since this has happened for me, it has happened for millions of other fortunate readers as well.

My friend from high school (Terry Lavery) and I used to read your work and marvel at your sense of humor. Do you remember the "Touched the Dog" strip? It is the one where Sally tells Charlie Brown to wash his hands again because he "touched the dog"? When Snoopy goes into the Bubonic Plague and the handful of germs routine, I just fall apart. Nearly every time I pet my dog, Tracker (a 12 year old Golden Retriever), I think , "touched the dog".

I read your biography recently and I noted that everyone who writes to you always wants something. I want something too. I want you to know that you are one of the great artistic geniuses of this century. I want you to know that I (for one) appreciate the work you have done for me every day. I want you to know that as a teacher I often invoke the example of people like Michael Jordan (who was cut from his high school basketball team) and Charles Schulz (who earned terrible grades in high school). I tell my class that if they want to be a success at something they will need to have the same kind of drive and character that people like Jordan and Schulz have shown during their lives (even if they meet with failure early on). I want you to know that I believe your work will be studied hundreds of years from now as an example of one of the truly great cartoonists to ever work in the genre. I want you to know that there is something so special about the world which you have created, that when you finally quit working it will seem like a member of my own family is missing. To have read the other cartoonists comments about you confirms my thought that you are an individual of great dignity and class.

So please, don't bother to write back. I don't want an autographed picture of Snoopy, or Charlie Brown, or Linus. I just wanted to say, "God Bless you. Thank you for the gift you have given me each morning for the last 35 years."

Believe me, your effort has been worth every drop of ink and every mental exertion that you have spent.

Most Sincerely,
Gregory J. Karas

(I wrote this letter to Charles Schulz in 1997. A few weeks later I received a very nice letter from his personal secretary and a book signed by Mr. Schulz himself. Later, his wife (Jeannie) wrote to me to ask permission for them to display my letter in the new Charles Schulz Museum in Santa Rosa, California. I guess the point of the story is, if you admire someone for the work they have done, let them know it before it is too late.)

* * * * * * *

## "Father's Day"

This Father's Day (2006) is one I'm going to remember for a long time. Not because of something which happened between my dad and me. Nor, because of something which happened between my own kids and myself. My dad passed away a few years ago and of course I always still think about him on Father's Day. I got great gifts from own family (a new bike, an I-Pod, and this really cool photo display with each letter of my name illustrated - the two G's in Greg stood for "Goofy" and "Gimpy").

However, this Father's Day will be memorable because of something which happened between my friend and his daughter (who also happens to be my God Child). Her name is Libbie Gilliland and she just finished up her Freshman year at Valparaiso High School.

Typing the words "God Child" just now gave me a chill, because I am certain God has been present in this event from the first moment (as He has been in *every moment* since He decided to make this staggering universe). We got a call a couple of weeks back telling us that Libbie had been rushed to Porter Hospital in Valparaiso. Worse still, an MRI had discovered that there was a large (golf ball size, was the way it was first described) mass inside her skull which was pressing down on her optic nerve. She had been having terrible headaches for the last couple of weeks. By the time we got to the hospital, they were waiting for the helicopter to airlift her to the University of Illinois Medical Center. Immediate brain surgery was indicated.

The control center called and said that the wind was making it too risky to attempt a landing on the roof of Porter Hospital. Remembering back to when a helicopter crash landed on the roof of that facility, everyone in the room thought that the slightly slower ambulance ride would still get Libbie to the new hospital on time. It did.

Doctors at the U. of I. Med Center performed more tests and then told the Gilliland family the straight truth. The tumor was life threatening. Libbie could get sleepy, slip into a coma, and die within a matter of hours. The surgery itself was precariously risky. There was an 80% percent chance that Libbie would lose her vision, even if the tumor were to be successfully removed. Her entire skull would have to be opened, her brain "flopped out", and the tumor would have to be extricated (while angels stood over the shoulders of the doctors and nurses in the O.R.). The surgery would start early in the morning and possibly continue to 6:00 or 7:00 p.m. that night.

When the surgeon walked into the room Libbie looked at him and said, "Well, Dr. Hahn, did you have a good night's sleep last night?" The venerable physician, Dr. Yoon S. Hahn took a step back in amazement. He happens to be one of the top Neurosurgeons in the nation. "Why, yes. Why do you ask that?"

Libbie answered, "Well, if you're going to be poking around inside my brain all day, I just wanted to make sure your hands are going to be steady." He laughed, wiggled his fingers with a mock tremor, and replied, "Well, my hands are a little shaky today." Then, they wheeled her in.

The doctors, nurses, and angels all did their jobs correctly that day. The surgery worked wonderfully. Libbie did not lose her vision. She did not slip into a coma. She did not die. They had to insert a drain inside her skull. There was talk of radiation treatments in the future. People prayed. Friends visited. Libbie's mom (Denise) adorned the walls of her room with get well cards, photos, and a huge poster sent over by Jeff Samardjiza (the Notre Dame football star and recently signed pitcher of the Chicago Cubs who happens to be a friend of the family). Someone could write an entire book about the strength the family displayed during this crisis. They spent many nights at the Ronald McDonald House (and are simply full of praise for what ***that*** organization can mean to people in unimaginable situations like the one into which they were hurled).

As the days of Libbie's recovery started to turn into weeks, she looked at her dad Keith (shortly before Father's Day) and said, "So what time are you leaving for the Senior Olympics?" Keith looked at her in dismay. He was amazed that she even remembered. For the last several months Keith had been practicing the discus because he had planned on competing as a fun summer diversion in the Indiana Senior Olympics. Now, with the tremendous family crisis at hand (and by no means had anyone yet walked out of the woods), driving all the way to Carmel, Indiana to throw an overweight frisbee through the air was *the very last thing* on Keith's mind.

"Well, I'm not going. Are you kidding me? Libbie, there's no way that I'm going all the way down there and leaving you here. Besides, I'm exhausted. This was hard on you, because you're the one sitting there with the big scar running through your head. But, your mom and I've been through a few moments of our own. This is no time to go traipsing all the way down there while you're still here in the hospital getting better."

She gave him the same look she'd given Dr. Hahn on the morning of surgery. "So, I guess you lied." Keith's eyes narrowed. "Lied about what?"

"I guess you lied when you said that we were gonna make it through this thing because our family never gives up. I guess you lied when you said that we could whip anything because we weren't quitters."

Keith got on the phone and contacted Dr. John Kostidis (a local Chiropractor, who had also been practicing to compete in the Senior Olympics - his event was the 100 meter dash). They rode down to Carmel discussing the events which had turned the Gilliland family upside down during the last two weeks. They competed in the Indiana Senior Olympics. Athletes at the state competitions who earn a Gold, Silver, or Bronze medal automatically qualify for next year's National Senior Olympics in Louisville, Kentucky. Keith didn't even think about that. He hadn't lifted a weight or touched the discus in over two weeks. He was just there to show his daughter that he *wasn't* a quitter. John ran his race. Keith took his throws. Then, they got into the car and drove back north.

Meanwhile, Libbie, her mom, and her brother Bo remained at the hospital. More cards arrived, more people visited, more friends prayed. In the film "The Shawshank Redemption", Morgan Freeman points out that "Prison time is slow time." But, at least the Prison had an exercise area ***outside***, and you went ***somewhere else*** each day to eat your meals. When you're in the hospital, you're ***in*** the hospital. As Libbie's condition improved (and the word "miraculous" was tossed around a few times in regard to how she was making it through this minefield) the walls of the room started sliding in a little closer to her bed. She talked about what it would feel like to walk through the front door of her house, to hug her family's three dogs, to lie down again *in her own bedroom*. She was getting ready to get out of there and start taking advantage of the miracles which had parachuted down to her from Heaven in the last two weeks.

Keith walked into the room. He gave Libbie a hug. He put something down on the bed next to her pillow. It was attached to a long ribbon. It was Silver. He'd had the longest throw of the competition, but he'd fouled when he did it. Otherwise the medal would've been Gold.

He'll be heading to Louisville, Kentucky next summer to compete at the Nationals. Bet you I can guess who's gonna be right there cheering him on.

That's gonna be one Happy Father's Day.

* * * * * * *

## "Kobayashi Maru and Barabara Pedersen"

I am not a big fan of the Star Trek television show or the movies of the same name. However, there were three scenarios in that series which I have never totally been able to shake from my memory:

1. The episode where two half black and half white men are mortal enemies. These fellows were vertically divided right down the center of their bodies. They spent much of the program attempting to kill one another. The absurdity of their hatred was revealed when one of the men explained that the important thing is *which side* of one's body is black or white.

2. The film where Spock went into the Enterprise's damaged reactor in order to save everyone else on board the ship. As he emerged with the leak stopped and his body riddled with radiation, he explained to Captain Kirk, moments before his death, that "the needs of the many, outweigh the needs of the few, or the one." (Kirk actually finished the last part of this quotation for him).

3. The final episode is the one in which James T. Kirk was forced to play a computerized battle simulation entitled the "Kobayashi Maru". This took place when he was at the Federation Academy learning how to become the captain of a starship. The simulation presented a no win scenario which was intended to reveal how future commanders would handle defeat. Kirk, realizing that the game was impossible to win, went into the computer (without his superior officers' knowledge) and changed the program so that he ***was*** able to win. He ultimately received a commendation for his innovative approach to the situation.

Today, I write in an effort to exercise my own private "Kobayashi Maru". In other words, I am going to cheat because cheating is the only way to succeed in this particular endeavor. For years I have been fascinated with the grants awarded by the John D. and Catherine T. MacArthur Foundation which are informally known as the "Genius Grants". Each year when the MacArthur Fellows are announced I read through the list of names and attempt to learn a little about the recipients. Typically, they are incredibly gifted and innovative individuals who sincerely deserve the recognition and reward ($500,000.00 of no strings attached grant money) associated with this program.

Inevitably, as I read about the grantees and the things they have accomplished, it comes into my head that the task of choosing these individuals must be an extremely fun and rewarding thing to do. Imagine what it must be like to learn about an outstanding person, research his or her accomplishments, interview people about that person and the work that he or she does, and then contact the individual with the following information:

"You have done unique and important work and people who are in a position to reward it have done so. We are going to give you a $500,000.00 grant spread out over the next 5 years so that you may be able to continue and enhance this work." I'd just love to see the individual's face when they are given news like that. Do you remember the look on George Bailey's face when all the people in Bedford Falls put money in a basket to save him from his legal difficulties? They did it because he was a worthy and deserving fellow. They gave him that money (and $20,000.00 more if necessary from Sam Wainwright) because the kind of life he had lived had made him worthy of receiving it. Yes, the people who choose the MacArthur Fellows have a truly wonderful mission in life.

Here's where the Kobayashi Maru comes into play. The Foundation stipulates that only nominators selected by the organization can put forth the name of an individual to be considered for a "Genius Grant". This is of course, understandable. If the general public had the ability to send in names in regard to this program, the response would likely be overwhelming. People would send their Uncle Harry's name in because he had invented a new type of mustache trimmer out in the garage. Second grade teachers who put on nice puppet shows would have parents from the PTA nominate them. Makeup artists who think up a new way to apply mascara would be touted as worthy geniuses. It would, on the whole, be an untenable situation.

However, the current system places ALL the trust into the hands of a few select individuals. Nominators chosen by the Foundation are charged with finding people from a variety of fields and bringing their accomplishments into the light of day. It would be safe to say that no matter how adept they are at this task, in a country with over 300,000,000 people, nominators are bound to miss talent. Of course, I don't mean to insinuate that the nominators are doing an inadequate job. On the contrary, when I read through the list each year I am always extremely impressed by the accomplishments of the people who have been selected. I just think that once in a while, just to shake the cobwebs out they ought to look in places that they may have never considered before. They ought to hear from people whom they've never met. In short, they should listen to me, because I have a person in mind who should have been awarded one of these Fellowships years ago.

Think back again to Captain Kirk and all the potential Starship Pilots who had failed that Kobayashi Maru. Obviously, the word had gotten around the Academy that no matter what you did, you were not going to pass this test. All Kirk did was think about the problem with a *different light* shining on it.

For a moment, he must have considered that cheating would "get him into trouble" because he was not following "the rules". Then, it must have occurred to him that the instructors had already seen multiple candidates fail this test. Then, he probably said something like, "Well, I'll open up the back of the computer, rig the game, and let the cards fall where they may. If nothing else, I should be credited with thinking originally."

That's what I'm going to do right now. Can I "get into trouble" by not following "the rules"? Maybe. But, here is what I'm guessing. I'm guessing that once the nominators really find out something about the person I'm proposing, they will forget about their rules and procedures and say, "Well, that fellow came up with an interesting way to bring this candidate to our attention. And it turns out that her work ***is*** outstanding. So, instead of being angry with this person, we're actually going to take his suggestion to heart."

The candidate I'm proposing for a MacArthur Fellow Grant is named Barbara Pedersen. Barbara is the Director of an Educational Organization in Lebanon, Indiana known as C.L.A.S.S. (Connected Learning Assures Successful Students). If I were to state that Barbara and her staff plan and execute educational training sessions which enhance instruction in our schools, the reader's eyes would immediately start to glaze over. Lots of people do that. I've been teaching for over 30 years and I have been to any number of educational workshops. Most of them are forgotten by the end of the week, if not by the time you are pulling out of the parking lot.

Barbara has done something else; something which is unique and unforgettable. What she's done is taken research on the brain and crafted it into a seamless model of how our schools should look and run. The three separate strains of "Climate", "Community", and "Curriculum" have been *thoroughly* thought out in her system. Schools which choose to follow her lead have become infinitely more compassionate, creative, and successful places to work and learn. Additionally, Barbara is the type of communicator who can touch your soul. People who spend time with her become better people. Teachers who learn from her become better teachers. If you are ever lucky enough to spend time with her, you'll find out exactly what I mean.

Space limitations prevent me from even beginning to delineate all the terrific things she has created or inspired. I would simply state the following. She changes schools. She changes hearts. She changes lives. All for the better. All within the context of solid research pertaining to the human brain. Any MacArthur Fellow nominator worth his or her salt will do a Sherlock Holmes on Barbara Pedersen.

Start at www.indianaclass.com. Then, go find some of the schools and teachers she has touched. If my hunch is correct, by the time the next group of Fellows is announced, her name will be right at the top of the list. And then, just like with Captain Kirk, they'll call me up and give me a commendation. Even though I've cheated.

* * * * * * *

## The Hummingbird Defenders

## TEA (Tessa, Emily, and Alyssa)

Parkview School
1405 Wood St.
Valparaiso, Indiana 46383

Dear Admissions Director:

Generally speaking, high school students tend to shy away from asking their former elementary teachers to write letters of recommendation on their behalf. Probably, the experiences of high school itself are so fresh in their minds, and their days in that earlier institution so remote that such a request would seem unnecessary if not faintly ridiculous.

Indeed, the subjects of this letter have not requested that I write such a document for them. However, something they have done over the last 3 years has compelled me to take the time to inform you about it.

When Tessa Meyer, Alyssa Walter, and Emily Longhi were in middle school they belonged to the Kiwanis organization known as Builders Club. While attending a convention for that group they had occasion to hear someone speak who belonged to a K-Kids Club (once again, a club sponsored by Kiwanis which draws membership from elementary schools). The three girls (only 8$^{th}$ graders at the time) returned to Valparaiso determined that they would form a similar club. They approached Cheryl Highlan and myself and asked if we would be willing to serve as teacher sponsors.

They secured permission from the Principal. They jumped through the necessary Kiwanis administrative hoops. They held recruitment meetings in our building. They figured out how to collect dues, get T-Shirts made, procure membership materials, and generally showed the type of organizational savvy and leadership which many individuals twice their age cannot figure out.

For three years we watched them provide meaningful experiences for the 4th and 5th grade students in the K-Kids group. Members worked with Special Olympians, helped Senior Citizens, held a car wash for a family which had lost their Kindergarten daughter, visited with Miss America, raised funds for Relay for Life, helped Riley Hospital in Indianapolis, babysat at Kiwanis Pancake Day, and generally learned what it is to be a citizen in society who takes the time to "give back" in meaningful ways. Besides all of that, the girls made belonging to Kiwanis fun!

The students who worked with Tessa, Emily, and Alyssa looked up to, emulated, and learned from these young ladies. Can a person put a price tag on an experience like that? I really don't think so. I watched kids without strong families benefit from the time they spent with our Kiwanis leaders. Our K-Kids sponsors could have their pictures in the dictionary next to the term "role model".

Now, these three girls are Seniors in high school and ready to take the next step in their lives. Are they all good students? Certainly. You can see that from glancing through their application materials. But, if you take the time to look a little deeper you will see that they are already good citizens. That is something which some people take many years to figure out.

I simply wanted to take the time to let you know that if one of these girls is applying to your institution, you would be making a tremendous decision if you decide to admit her.

I have been teaching the 4th grade for 31 years and I have encountered lots of remarkable young people. Many scholars, musicians, athletes, and other gifted individuals have blessed my time in the classroom. However, these three young ladies have done so much ***for other people*** that they stand out from the crowd. I am available to speak to you or one of your representatives if you would like to hear more wonderful things about any of these three remarkable young people.

Thanks for your time and best wishes as you do the important work of selecting scholar / citizens for your fine institution.

Respectfully,
Greg Karas
Parkview Elementary

* * * * * * *

## "Bo"

Many years ago during a Kansas City Chiefs football game my phone rang. I answered it anxiously and listened. An elated voice told me, "He did it! He won! Make sure you watch the tape at halftime." I assured the caller that our whole family would be watching. *He* was Bo Gilliland, a nine year old third grader from Valparaiso, Indiana. The thing that he had won was the National Punt, Pass, and Kick Competition. I had been with Bo and his father and mother, Keith and Denise for some of the practice sessions leading up to that competition. They always made it fun, but they also made sure that Bo knew it was *work.*

Years before that I had been around as Bo was growing up. I am an elementary school teacher and I have had a chance to see (and evaluate) the mental and physical progress of hundreds of young children. As I watched Bo catch, throw, and kick different balls around the yard as a two and three year old, I told his mom and dad that his levels of strength and coordination were extraordinary for a child of that age. And they were. The kid did stuff that made the adults stop and say, "Whoa! Did you see that?"

During the years that Bo played Pop Warner Football I was lucky enough to serve as the Public Address Announcer for the team. Once again, he did things (catching, running, kicking, punting, throwing, blocking, and tackling) that seemed to suggest that he was either an older child (he wasn't), or that he had come from another galaxy (he may have). Once again, his parents were an integral part of his success as a gridiron prodigy. Keith served as Head Coach for Bo's teams during every year of his play. Mom and Dad also were the Directors of the League (the patriotically named "Valpo Americans") throughout Bo's tenure. They did such a good job running that league that one year Denise was chosen as the Pop Warner "Volunteer of the Year" for the entire United States of America and Canada.

Hopefully, the picture is starting to emerge that this is a family which loves football, loves their children (Bo has a sister in Middle School named Libbie who is talented in both volleyball and basketball), and are willing to do what it takes to succeed and to help their kids succeed. Bo continued to star in the Middle School program. Sometimes he played quarterback. Sometimes he played running back. He always played defense.

I can remember being at a game during Bo's Freshman year. They had him up on the varsity covering kick-offs. I was standing with Keith on the sidelines as Bo raced down and "cleaned the clock" of an upper-classman who was returning one of those kicks. Dad's eyes filled with unmistakable pride, he pumped his fist and shouted, "Yeah, that's my **boy**!"

Bo has been playing full time since his sophomore year. And when I say full time, I mean ***full time***. He kicks off. He punts (his average during his junior year was 38.7 yards per punt). He returns kicks. He kicks field goals (in practices he has nailed many well over 50 yards). He ran the ball as a halfback extensively as a junior (rushing a 109 times for 613 yards, which is a 5.62 yard per carry average in the very tough Duneland Athletic Conference of Northwest Indiana). He was the middle linebacker and signal caller for the defense. As a junior he had 153 tackles (47 of those solo tackles). He's intercepted the ball at key moments, jarred loose fumbles, pounced on fumbles, made tremendously exciting long runs, and generally thrilled football fans of all ages in this town for about a decade now.

If I was forced to pick out one thing that I have seen Bo do the *best* on a football field, it would be a very difficult task. But, I would have to say "sticking people" would be it. I was standing close to the playing field during a game against LaPorte High School. The quarterback rolled out to pass near the sidelines. The play was going to be made just a few yards from where I was standing. Bo delivered a hit which would have been worthy of the old NFL highlight film entitled, "Crunch Course". Everyone in the crowd gasped. The quarterback was taken away in the ambulance for precautionary reasons (fortunately his injury was not serious or lasting). The funny thing is, I've seen Bo make hits like that since he was in elementary school. The phrase, "What God had in mind there was a football player," appears in my brain whenever I see Bo Gilliland, either on or off the field.

While some players make it their business to excel against mediocre opponents, Bo has made it his priority to do just the opposite. State (and indeed National) Powerhouse Penn High School visited Viking Field during Bo's Sophomore year. The meetings between Valparaiso and Penn during the last decade have become legendary throughout the state of Indiana. Late in the game Valparaiso held a precarious lead and Penn was marching toward the goal line. At the pivotal point in Penn's drive, Bo knifed in front of a receiver to snare a game saving interception. During the meeting between the two squads this year (a heart wrenching overtime victory for Penn) Bo made an astounding 24 tackles (12 of which were solos). Time after time I've seen Bo come up big when it counted for his teammates.

Then, in Valparaiso's sixth game of Bo's Senior year, he tore his ACL. Nobody touched him. He was returning a kickoff early in the first quarter against Crown Point. He planted to cut and just went down. When I saw him lying on the ground, I knew something bad had happened. Bo *never* just lies there on the ground. The trainer, Kathy Levandoski (who is one of the best trainers I have ever seen operate at any level) brought him over to the sideline, looked him over, and hooked him up with a large bag of ice. He looked like a lion who had spent his entire life on the Serengeti Plain suddenly being brought to a cage in an old fashioned urban zoo.

The next day, MRI results confirmed the bad news. Bo's high school career was over. He wouldn't pass Garrett Gray on the Valparaiso all time tackle list (he had been on track to do just that). He wouldn't get a chance to lead Valparaiso to a Duneland Conference Title. He wouldn't get to play in his final round of state tournament games.

Sometimes things in life don't seem fair. Bo's family has had their share of challenges. Besides this knee injury they had to live through a serious car accident which Keith was lucky to survive. Sister Libbie had a brain tumor which required emergency surgery. She too was fortunate to come away with her life. I don't know why some families are given more challenges than others. But, I know one thing. This family is tough enough to take everything that's dished out. I'm glad I know 'em. I'm glad I saw Bo play. He stuck people like nobody's business. I wish you would have seen it.

* * * * * * *

## "Minh's Dad, Freedom, and Life"

One of the great things about teaching is the people you meet. Some of them are little people, some of them are middle sized people and some (like me) are great big jumbo sized people. We (teachers) spend most of our time with kids. We read stories, learn how to do long division, play spelling games, find out about the Emancipation Proclamation, write book reports, explore computers, make dioramas, throw the football at recess time, and generally have enough fun to recall the Steve Martin phrase, "And the most amazing thing to me is, I get paid for doing this."

In addition to working with kids, we also get to meet periodically with their parents. I have met many impressive parents during my 32 years in the classroom. Some are impressive because of the educational opportunities they provide for their kids (ask me sometime about the Dulla family and the wonderful things they have done for their two daughters, Kathryn and Whitney). But today, I want to tell you about Minh's dad.

Minh was a boy in my class whose family had emigrated from Vietnam. Minh was a very good student, but his dad insisted on having a signed note come home from school *every day* spelling out *exactly* what Minh was required to do for homework. He told me on the first day of school that "Minh must work very hard in school & all work must be right."

His parents run the manicure shop which is located inside of Wal*Mart. The night of the conference, Minh's dad was the last person on the schedule. He came at 8:20 and was scheduled for a 20 minute session. For the first 15 minutes we discussed Minh and his strengths (there were many) and his weaknesses (there were very few) as a student. I found myself wondering why Minh's dad insisted on such a high level of accountability from his son. I asked how long the family had been in America. There is a map of the world (the old fashioned roll down kind) in the front of my classroom. He walked over to the map and we pulled it down and he showed me where they had been in Vietnam.

Then, he told me about being held in a Prisoner of War Camp by the North Vietnamese. Then, he told me about his parents being murdered in that camp. He told me about how he and his wife escaped from the camp. He told me about how they were recaptured. He told me about how they escaped again and journeyed on a raft to the Phillipine Islands. From there, they made their way to America and were sponsored by a Catholic family until they were able to strike out on their own.

The conference had stretched on for over an hour. I was spellbound listening to Minh's dad. This was someone for whom the idea of freedom in America meant so much because he had experienced a place and a time with no freedom at all. Indeed, this was a man who had lived through the unimaginable. After talking to him it was a little easier for me to understand why he wanted his son to make so much of his opportunities here in our land. It made me think about my 4 grandparents, who had come over to this country in the early 1900's. It made me look at Minh, his dad, and our country in a new light. Indeed, it made me open my eyes and really ***see*** this country for the first time. I wish you all could have been there that night. I wish you could have seen the look in the eyes of Minh's dad as he talked about what it meant to be here, in the United States of America.

* * * * * * *

## "Incongruity"

Today I went to visit my Aunt Bertha at the hospital. She is 83 years old. She fell in her kitchen and broke some bones (her pelvis and her shoulder). I think it hurts her quite a bit. I have 7 broken bones and all of those hurt. I broke mine when I was young and stupid. She broke hers when she was older and at a time of life when it is harder to bounce back.

I walked in at about the same time the physical therapist came to take Auntie Bea to her group therapy session. I offered to go along and push her wheelchair. The therapist was happy because she was already rolling a different chair with an older gentleman (who had recently lost both of his legs from the knees down). Muzak played in the elevator as we headed up to the fourth floor.

All four of us got off the elevator and rolled into a large room where over a dozen wheelchairs (loaded with people) were all set up in a circle. In the middle of the circle there was another physical therapist sitting on a round leather stool with wheels (this allowed her to spin around and face all of the patients any time she wished). I pulled up a chair in the circle too. It was really interesting to see the different people and how they approached the session.

As the therapist led them through exercises you could see that on the whole, most of them would have rather been in Philadelphia (all you youngsters run over to the internet and look up "W.C. Fields" to find the significance of that statement). One fellow however, was the life of the party. He was a tall, African American gentleman, who happened to be wearing a helmet. I wondered if he had had a brain injury. He, I am sure, was on the road to recovery. He laughed, engaged others, participated in the exercises whole-heartedly, and knew the answers to many of the Trivia Questions the therapy team asked (in order to keep the patients alert). He would have been a fun guy to have over to your house one night for dinner. Other people in the group looked as though invisible demons with drills were crouched below their chairs searching for the most painful spot (and having great success finding it). You had to feel for these people.

As the session continued I glanced around the room. There were about 5 people on the PT staff who were standing by to help out if needed. The therapist did a wonderful job of putting the patients through their paces with stretches, ball bouncing, and a variety of other activities designed to get them moving again in the wake of their injuries.

I noticed that there was also music playing through the speakers (which were mounted in the ceiling). Now, I would have assumed that for the age group involved in the therapy session (most of these folks were in their 70's or 80's) we might have been listening to Lawrence Welk, Rosemary Clooney, Old Blue Eyes, or Muzak similar to what had been playing in the elevator. I was wrong.

The first song I became aware of was the Talking Heads number, "And She Was". Here are a few of the lyrics:

"And she was drifting through the backyard
And she was taking off her dress
And she was moving very slowly
Rising up above the earth
Moving into the universe
Drifting this way and that
Not touching ground at all
Up above the yard..."

I glanced around the room to see if some of the elderly patients were registering anything in regard to the music, or especially in regard to the *lyrics* of the music. None of them were.

A younger worker however (perhaps an "Orderly" - if that is still a term used in the hospital) was bobbing his head in time to the tunes and you could see that ***he*** saw the wonderful incongruity of the moment. He nudged his partner and nodded up toward the speakers. They both giggled.

The next song was even better. It was "Smells like Teen Spirit" by Nirvana:

"Here we are now - Entertain us
I feel stupid and contagious
Here we are now - Entertain us
A mulatto, An albino
A mosquito, My libido
Yea, Yea, Yea, Yea, Yea".

The slashing guitar and drums and angst ridden voice of the late grunge rocker, Kurt Cobain juxtaposed with my sweet little Aunt Bertha from East Chicago (sitting there in a wheelchair with a sling protecting her right arm) is something which I couldn't have made up if I had had a thousand years in which to do it. And yet, somehow the whole thing was okay. Nobody looked up with a pained expression and said, "Oh for goodness sake, turn that trash off!" I think most of them had enough to deal with just trying to keep up with the exercises. At one point, I actually think I saw an old guy on the other side of the room kind of nodding in time with the tune.

Then, it hit me. Kurt Cobain was already dead (of an apparent suicide at the age of 27). But those folks in the therapy room who were old, battered, some with legs removed and parts of their brains no longer functioning, were still giving life their best whack. I thought about Aunt Bertha (who had lost her husband way back in WWII) and the courage with which I have seen her face her difficult existence. I looked around the room at the other people (with missing legs and damaged eyes from strokes, and who knows what else) and I wondered what would happen to me if I am blessed enough to make it up to that advanced age. Would I have the same type of courage these folks were displaying after eight decades of everything life could throw at them? We'll see. Somehow, I got the idea that Faith was playing a big part in what was going on in that room for lots of the people. Especially, the irrepressible guy in the helmet and my Auntie Bea.

And the tune just kept pouring right out of the speakers:

"Here we are now, Entertain us..."

* * * * * * *

## "Inciting Wonder"

When I was three or four I had a green and blue toy bug with multiple suction cups for feet. If I smushed the cups onto the wall of the front porch in our East Chicago home and pulled the string in the bug's tail, it would miraculously climb right up that wall. At the time, I did not understand many of the "principles of science". So, in my mind what was taking place was magic. My dad also showed me how to rub a balloon briskly through my hair and make it stick to the wall as well. Now, the bug was better than the balloon because it moved. But, the balloon was pretty cool because it would stick to the wall (you see, nothing else I knew of without glue or tape would do anything besides fall down if I placed it against the wall).

I'm pretty sure these were my first experiences with wonder. I hope everyone has read the autobiography of C.S. Lewis (**Surprised by Joy**). There is a memorable episode early in the story where his brother Warren creates a miniature garden in the lid of a biscuit tin. Lewis vividly details the emotions he felt while gazing at that "Toy Garden". He describes the feeling he got while looking at his brother's handiwork as "Joy", and much of his subsequent life was spent searching for that same emotion. When I saw that bug climbing up the wall of our Grand Boulevard home, I had a similar experience. It was (and still is) an excellent sensation. I'm pretty confident you can recall the same type of thing from your own childhood.

As the next fifty years have rushed by, I've discovered that the feelings of Joy and Wonder are best and most pure when they take us by surprise. I have also noted that there are certain people, places, items, or moments in time which tend to incite those feelings of wonder. For instance, the first time I set foot inside of Comiskey Park in the 1960's as a small boy, the floodgates were flung wide open. That was no ordinary space. Recently, some friends and I visited a place right here in Valparaiso which opened up the doorway to those same emotions.

Our school puts on an overnight reading event every May called "Friday Night Live". Parkview Elementary has been doing this for 24 years. There are a few thousand people alive who have been to one of these things. *Those* people know what the night is like. I've never really tried very hard to explain it to other people. Basically, an army of parents spend several months planning a night designed to make a 4th or 5th grader say, "Whoa, dude. ***That*** was the coolest night of my life." Each year a theme is chosen and this army works to transform the school into a setting which fits that theme. T-Shirts are designed, backpacks are purchased, sets are built, decorations are painted, toys and treats are procured, skits happen, copious amounts of food are purchased and prepared.

Wild Things take place. But, as I said, unless you've been to a Friday Night Live, it remains largely unexplainable. This year was really cool because as we were working one night on the decorations, one of the Moms told us that she had *been* at the first Friday Night Live, as a 5th grade student! Now, she's 34. Her daughter Brittney is a 4th grader.

This year's theme happened to be "**Night at the Museum**". As we were planning the activities for the evening, one Mom mentioned to me that she had seen a wonderful "Haunted House Evening" down at the Porter County Museum (formerly known as The Old Jail Museum). Now I had not visited that building since the early 1980's, and my recollection was that I wasn't missing much. However, this Mom insisted that the place was "so cool", and the guy running the place (his name was Kevin Pazour) was such a "neat guy" (her phrase), that I simply "had to go meet him".

I contacted Kevin and the two Moms in charge of the program and I drove over to the Museum one day after school. I was dreading talking to him because as I mentioned, the population at large doesn't really have a clue what we try to accomplish with this event. You see, *nuttiness* is a big part of the experience, and "nuttiness" and "Museum" are not usually words that end up in the same sentence. One year we had a 30 person Pirate Battle and a fireworks show on the shore at Lakewood Park. Last year we had a surprise, private outdoor rock concert by the band, "State Park". There have been live tigers at Friday Night Live. People have driven Harley Davidson Motorcycles down the hallway into the gym!

I was hoping that I wouldn't have to try and explain (for hours) what we were trying to achieve by visiting the museum on the night of FNL. I dreaded the prospect of meeting a stereo-typical Fuddy Duddy Museum dude. I feared that Kevin would have clipboards with genealogical charts that he'd want the students to fill in for the previous seven generations. I expected a bow-tie. I was prepared for a highly nasal voice. Thankfully, I was wrong in every conceivable way.

Kevin stood outside the museum waiting for us to arrive. Tall, with bright eyes and an air of easy confidence, Mr. Pazour greeted the three of us (Mrs. George, Mrs. Tullis, and myself) warmly. He took us inside and showed us both floors of the museum. Everything from Civil War weaponry, to vintage art work, to dinosaur bones discovered in Porter County farm fields was on display. You could tell right away that it was Kevin's passion to get lots of human beings in there to see it all, be inspired by it, and learn from it. I was stunned by the amount of really interesting Porter County artifacts on hand inside that beautiful old building.

As we spoke about a possible side trip to the museum it took about two minutes to discern that he "got it". "I see," he said excitedly. "What about if we do a haunted scavenger hunt?" "We could have the whole museum be dark, except for these green lights (he demonstrated) and the kids would have to travel around and collect clues for the mystery you are trying to solve." I had to pinch myself because he was so unlike what I'd expected.

He was way ahead of me and I've been working on this

event for twenty years! When we asked about bringing in an army of Middle and High School kids his response was, "You can do that or we can bring our own people." When I asked about bringing in music to match the mood we were seeking, he was right on top of it too. "That sounds great. Whatever you need to do to make it work."

I can't tell you how refreshing it was to meet somebody who was so tuned in to what we were trying to accomplish and so accommodating about making it all happen. I left the museum (all three of us left the museum) filled with a combination of relief and great hope.

We showed up the night of May 9th with two busloads containing 104 kids and Kevin was better than his word. He greeted the excited kids warmly (on a cold night) and explained to them what they had to do. Every group entered the museum with a flashlight and a task. They had to search through the exhibits looking for their own particular clue. This was no mean feat because the building (which you really need to go visit) was shrouded in darkness, filled with music, and populated by dozens of creepy characters of every possible persuasion. Sounds of delighted screaming and laughter permeated the downtown Valparaiso air. The kids went through the museum diligently seeking their clues. Some were scared stiff, others laughed heartily, they all had a blast.

Outside on the museum lawn the kids collected their cards in order to find out the identity of our mystery criminals (the notorious Cheryl Highlan and her nefarious son, Zeke). After successfully assembling the clues, we crossed the street to the County Courthouse and the kids chased the dastardly thieves around the old building, recovered the missing ancient key (which was designed by the incomparable Pat Manion), and saved mankind as we have known it.

I've seen some pretty cool stuff in museums. For instance, I once touched a piece of the moon in the Smithsonian Air and Space Museum. When I look at the Tyrannosaurus Rex "Sue" at the Field Museum in Chicago, I can take pride in the fact that Sue Hendrickson (the person who discovered that massive and famous fossil) and I both attended the same elementary school in Munster, Indiana. Indeed, we both had Mr. Marciniak for our 6$^{th}$ grade teacher. But, now I would have to say that my favorite "Museum Moment" came on Friday, May 9$^{th}$, 2008, when Kevin Pazour turned the place over to a bunch of 4$^{th}$ and 5$^{th}$ graders he'd never met, just so that he could help to incite wonder. I wish you could have seen their faces as stepped in to that spooky and wonderful old building on that cold and exciting night. Thanks, Kevin. You went way beyond the call of duty!

* * * * * * *

## "A Tribute to Myron Knauff"

Lots of people have worked for the Valparaiso Community Schools. Several of those people have shown extraordinary dedication to the school system and to the community. I have lived in this town since 1972. I have not known an individual more dedicated to the children, parents, and teachers in Valparaiso than Mr. Myron Knauff. If you don't know Myron Knauff by name, chances are you've seen him. Perhaps it was at a High School basketball game; he doesn't miss many of those. Maybe you saw Mr. Knauff at a track meet, or at a Kiwanis meeting. Wherever you saw him, he was probably doing some good.

Back when Mr. Knauff was working for the school system, he was responsible for hiring many teachers and coaches. Mr. Knauff served as a principal and as an assistant superintendent. Several of the people he brought into the schools are still around today. If you ever have a moment, ask a teacher who has been with the Valparaiso Schools for a while what they think Myron Knauff meant to the school system. I don't play the Lottery and I have yet to set foot on a floating casino, but I would bet this week's paycheck that anyone with integrity you speak with will describe Myron Knauff as one of those rare individuals who *really* puts the needs of others before his own. I know that he is honest. I know that he is fair. I know that he cares about how things are done.

When he worked here he wanted to be sure that the children in town would learn, grow, represent the community with pride, and thrive as individuals because of the school system's policies and practices. Appearances mattered less to him than substance. He wanted to make sure that everything was done with the good of the child in mind. Another wise man I know, Coach Mick Cavanaugh, said that Myron Knauff taught him what the phrase "area of responsibility" really meant.

His sons, Mark, John, and Paul all work (or have worked) for the Valparaiso Schools. Paul is the principal at Thomas Jefferson Middle School. Mark and John both have been teachers and coaches at VHS (John recently retired). Perhaps the way to judge a man is to see how his children turn out. All three of these men spend several extra hours coaching, supervising activities, announcing at athletic events, and counseling students in order to make the schools the highly rated institutions which they are. These three gentlemen all went into the profession (I'm sure at least to a certain extent) because of the outstanding example their dad has set for them.

Myron Knauff has spent his life caring about others. He served his country with pride in the United States Navy. His long affiliation with the Valparaiso Kiwanis Club and organizations like Family House, the fact that he played Santa Claus for Valparaiso Elementary students at their Christmas parties, and his strong personal faith and character all serve to make him an outstanding community role model.

Usually, we wait until someone has passed away before we say all the kind things that can be said about them. I didn't feel like waiting. I know that in the grand scheme of things in a school system a fourth grade teacher has about as much pull as a flea on the rear end of an elephant. But, I wanted my idea to be heard. The idea is this: If they ever build a new elementary school (or any other educational facility in this town), it ought be named after Myron. Currently, naming a building after a member of the community is *against school system policy.* I guess my response to that would be that having women vote and helping slaves to escape were at one time against United States Government policy. When policies are outmoded or pointless, they need to be changed. If we can't honor a man in our midst who has made our children, our schools, and our town all better because it goes against a policy, then we'd better ask why the policy exists and what is the fastest way to alter it.

Thanks, Mr. Knauff, for everything you have done for our community, our schools, and us. Someone, and I'm sure I'm not the only one, has noticed and felt appreciation.

* * * * * * *

## "Amazing Grace"

Recently my wife's mom, Kathleen Foelber, passed away out in California after a long battle with Alzheimer's Disease. I could write several pages about what a wonderful woman Kathy was, the seven kids she raised, and how she and her husband Bob provided my wife and myself with a model of what a successful marriage looks like. I would be able to write a thousand and one other things about this remarkable couple and the splendid woman who is now reunited with her Savior.

I could also fill many pages describing her husband Bob's devotion to her well being throughout the course of their long and beautiful lives together. This devotion never wavered, even when Kathy was completely incapacitated by that horrible disease. Indeed, his devotion intensified in direct proportion to how ill his wife became. He has set the standard for everyone in the family at an unbelievably high level.

Bob was formerly a chaplain in the United States Navy and then a Lutheran minister in several churches throughout California. His specialty has always been moving into a church which had recently lost a pastor (for any number of reasons) and then shepherding the congregation through to the time when a permanent leader could be called. In these endeavors, Bob and Kathy always worked as a team.

Today, I'd like to relate one small event which happened at Kathy's memorial service. Now, this was a magnificent service which was complete with fine music, a more than memorable talk given by her eldest son Bobby, and the presence of hundreds of friends and family members whose lives had all been touched by Kathy in one way or another.

My wife and I were sitting with our son Nick, his fiancée Emily, and our daughter Natalie in about the third row of pews. Somewhere in the middle of the service four people I'd never met walked to the front of the church. A couple of them carried musical instruments. Two of them were men and two were women.

One fellow with a guitar stepped to the microphone and started addressing the people in attendance. He explained how several decades ago he was a person who didn't really attend church regularly. But for some reason, one Sunday he'd stopped by the church that Bob and Kathy were in the midst of helping. After the service Kathy was talking with people and she introduced herself to this fellow (his name was Mike Castlen) It came up that Mike played the guitar. Kathy asked him if he'd like to help out next week by playing the hymn "Amazing Grace" for the congregation.

This gentleman explained all the feelings that ran through his mind when he was given that request. C.S. Lewis wrote splendidly about the fear of being "pulled in" to something unfamiliar and unwanted. Lewis had this very real fear prior to accepting Christianity. This man had a similar fear. He had a little bit of nervousness as well. But, he also thought that he might have been asked to play that hymn for a reason. So, he decided to do the task. Remember, this request had been made by Kathleen more than 30 years ago.

Mike then related what happened ***after*** he had played that number. He told all of us sitting there in the pews that following that experience he eventually became the musical director for his church's congregation. He had been in that position for many years now, and if Kathy hadn't asked him to play on that Sunday morning long ago, he wasn't sure how things might have turned out for him. The way it did turn out, he was very grateful indeed. Kathy's request had brought him closer to his Maker, and the work he had done in the subsequent years had undoubtedly done that very thing for other people. That's how it is supposed to work.

At that point, Mike and his musical team (which included his wife) broke into the most beautiful rendition of "Amazing Grace" which I've ever heard this side of Judy Collins.

There was something extremely compelling about that

story and their performance, and on the way home in the airplane I sat reflecting about all the things it might teach a person.

When we got back to Valparaiso, I had a lot of catching up to do with my job. My class was in the middle of an Indiana History Unit which detailed the causes leading up to our nation's Civil War.

I had heard from another teacher about an excellent online video pertaining to slave ships. As the film unfolded it depicted the horrendous conditions which existed aboard these ships. The descriptions were vivid and if the intent was to make the students feel revolted at the living quarters aboard those despicable vessels, the director had done his job well. Then, the narration of the film spun off into a little side story. It was about the life of the British slave ship Captain, John Newton.

One day, the ship he piloted (the Greyhound) was caught in a tempestuous storm. The ship began to take on water and it appeared that it would go down and all aboard would be lost. In the middle of the night Newton cried out to God for help. Help was granted. The ship did not sink. The story goes on to tell how he retired from the slave shipping business, furthered his education, and eventually became one of the most popular clergymen in England. Then, the narrator related that John Newton had written one of the most beloved and poignant hymns in the history of the Church. Here it is:

Amazing grace! (how sweet the sound)
That saved a wretch like me!
I once was lost, but now am found,
Was blind, but now I see.
'Twas grace that taught my heart to fear,
And grace my fears relieved;
How precious did that grace appear,
The hour I first believed!

Thro' many dangers, toils and snares,
I have already come; 'Tis grace has brought me safe thus far,

And grace will lead me home.
The Lord has promised good to me,
His word my hope secures;
He will my shield and portion be,
As long as life endures.

Yes, when this flesh and heart shall fail,
And mortal life shall cease;
I shall possess, within the veil,
A life of joy and peace.
The earth shall soon dissolve like snow,
The sun forbear to shine;
But God, who called me here below,
Will be forever mine.

I don't know about you, but as I've grown older I find that I use the phrase, "Divine Intervention" a lot more than the word, "Coincidence". On one particular Sunday, we were all sitting in a church in California, listening to Mike tell his story about Kathy's request and how much it had meant to him. Then, we listened to a stunning rendition of that ethereal hymn. On Monday, I was sitting in a room full of 9 and 10 year olds in Indiana watching a film about how that hymn came to be written. When things like that happen, I'm convinced they happen for a reason.

There is something quite riveting about the line in that hymn which runs, "The earth shall soon dissolve like snow..." Kathy is Somewhere Else right now; for her the earth has already dissolved. But now, instead of just feeling occasional lightning bolts of grace (which are often interrupted by pain, disease, and all the despicable things which the Devil has concocted to distract us) she is in a place where grace surrounds one at all times. She is continually bathing in that celestial light, her mind fully restored, able to reach out and touch her Lord's hand at will. Amazing grace; how sweet that does indeed sound.

* * * * * * *

Kathleen Foelber and her Granddaughter Natalie Karas

* * * * * * *

## "Unsolicited Testimonial"

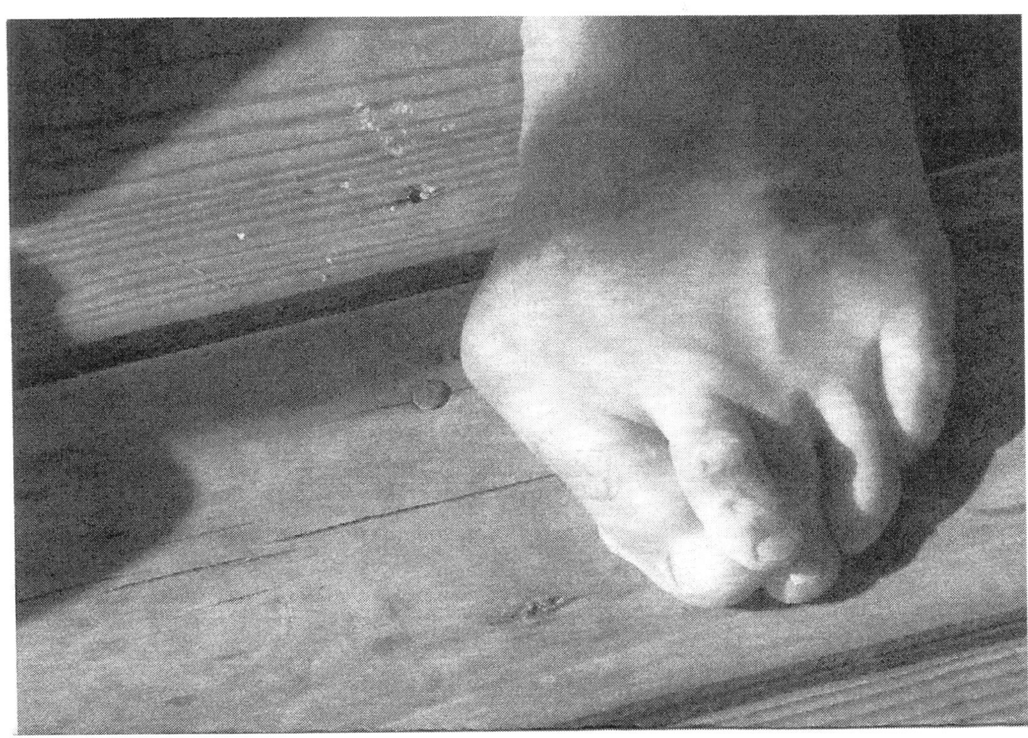

When I was a child I remember hearing a phrase again and again which puzzled me. That phrase was "Unsolicited Testimonial". When I was old enough to figure out what it meant, I was always on the lookout to make sure that those words contained truth. "Unsolicited" meant that no one asked you to endorse a product or a service. "Testimonial" meant that you were telling what it was about that product or service that you had personally found to be beneficial.

For many years I'd limp by my colleagues and students at Parkview Elementary. I'd had 7 different broken bones from car accidents, football games, sledding mishaps, and other assorted misadventures throughout my long and (apparently) clumsy life. As the years progressed I also developed some hammertoe and bunion issues which can only be explained with the title photograph (you know the old adage about "a picture being worth a thousand words"). People would often say, "What happened? Are you OK?"

One day at school I saw our Social Worker (Mrs. Kirkpatrick) wearing a surgical "slipper boot" on one of her feet. I asked her what had happened and she said that she'd had bunion surgery performed by Dr. Ron Izynski. After a brief discussion about her experience I slipped off my shoe and showed her my monstrosity. Her response was, "Oh, my." She then proceeded to give me an unsolicited testimonial about what a great surgeon and individual this Izynski fellow was. I was skeptical. I had spoken to other people before who had had elective surgical procedures done and weren't really wild about the results. What if I had the work done and my foot turned out to be worse than it was before?

I went home and discussed the whole issue with my wife. She's a nurse who has been helping people to get better for the last quarter century. She had seen how it had become harder and harder for me to stumble around during the last few years. She recommended that I go see the Doc.

I did. The immediate impression I received was that this guy was a ***Professional.*** Remember when we used to watch Michael Jordan play basketball? You just knew that *he knew* what to do with that ball in order for the team to succeed. It was the same with Dr. Izynski. As he showed me models of the human foot, displayed the x-rays of my foot, and talked about how the correction of my problems would be accomplished, he obliterated any reticence I had about getting the procedure done.

Additionally, the guy has the best bedside manner of

any physician I've ever encountered. Funny, confident, intelligent, genial, compassionate, insightful, and scientific are all adjectives one could employ to describe his character.

A few days after school let out in June the work took place. Anesthesia was administered, bones were broken and straightened, metal stuff was installed, the bunion was scraped off, and basically "The Frankenstein-ness" I'd been living with for the last several years was erased.

In subsequent visits to the Doc he has confirmed the only regret I had about the whole procedure. I'd just waited too long. As my foot grows stronger and I am able to resume physical activities which had long caused excruciating pain (have you ever read Tolkien's **The Silmarillion**? - "Suffering was graven in his face"), my admiration and appreciation for this surgeon's skill and professionalism grows.

So, this is ***my*** unsolicited testimonial. If you have problems with your feet go and find a telephone. Punch these numbers and ask for an appointment:
Valparaiso – 464 - 2205 / Chesterton – 926 - 3505. It was the best phone call I've made in the last 20 years.

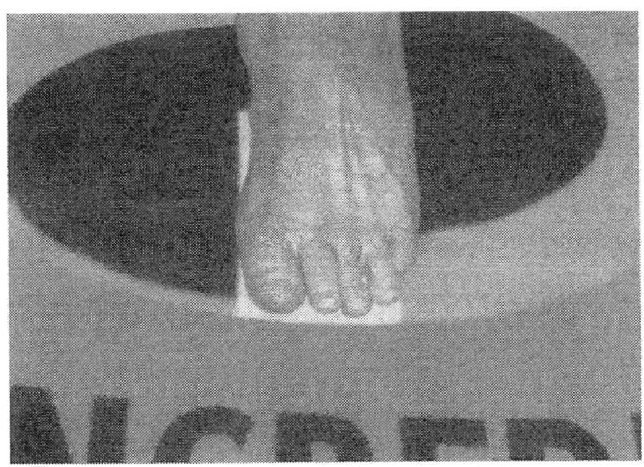

* * * * * * *

"Sue, Hal, and Joe… and One More Sue"

Here is today's homework assignment. The next time you check the Internet, type in the name of your high school (provided that you are old enough to have gone to high school) and the word "Wikipedia". I'm sure many of you have used Wikipedia, the online encyclopedia which is continually edited by users. I find as a teacher that I use it all the time. Things which used to involve long waits and trips to the library can pretty much be found out within a matter of minutes. (I know that you have to be careful because sometimes inaccurate info finds a way onto the site, but by and large it seems to be very well done).

Anyway, back to your assignment. Once you get to the Wikipedia page for your school, find the link which says "Notable Alumni" or "Notable People". You can find out really interesting information there. For instance, did you know that former NBA player and Valparaiso Basketball star (and current Associate Head Coach) Bryce Drew is married to the daughter of the child actor who played "Little Ricky" on the "I Love Lucy" show? That actor (and excellent drummer's) name is Keith Thibodeaux. Pretty cool, eh? I never would have known that had I not checked the Valparaiso High School entry.

Once you have clicked the link which says "Notable Alumni" you will see a list people who have left that institution to go on in life and perform feats which have been considered notable by the people who post the offerings. Depending on who is doing the work from school to school, the amount of people listed and the details regarding their achievements will (of course) vary. I have a friend from college named Paul Danatsko (aka Donuts). He attended Stuyvesant High in New York City. They have had ***4 Nobel Prize winners*** graduate from that school. Wow! That sounds like a pretty hefty achievement. Must be a great school. Unfortunately, Donuts was not one of the Nobel Laureates, or I ***really*** would have had a great story to tell. The very popular sports radio host Mike Greenberg (from Mike and **Mike** in the Morning) also graduated from Stuyvesant and the renowned author of Angela's Ashes, Frank McCourt was a teacher there. In fact, if you click on the list of notables from that school, you will be amazed.

Anyway, when I did the homework for ***my*** Alma Mater (Munster High, in Munster, Indiana), I found out about three pretty interesting people. Their names are Sue Hendrickson, Hal Morris, and Joe Mansueto.

The first thing I noticed about these three individuals was that they all had three letters in their names. That fact might be important, or it might be irrelevant, I'm really not sure. So, why are these individuals with just three little letters in each of their names accomplished enough to be listed as "Notable Alumni" from Munster High? Let's find out:

We'll start with Sue Hendrickson. First of all, I ought to note that technically, Sue Hendrickson is ***not*** officially an alum, because she actually did not graduate. Though a brilliant student (my sister, Toni remembers being in Student Council with her), Sue was stifled by formal schooling and she dropped out of MHS after her Junior year. She knew what she wanted to do with her life and she did not want to waste time with football games, proms, or study halls a moment longer. She started to explore the world (both in the ocean and on the land) to look for priceless treasures. By any conceivable measure she has been wildly successful.

One day in South Dakota (in the year 1990) she was exploring with her dog "Gypsy" and she discovered "Sue", the largest and most complete Tyrannosaurus Rex skeleton on record. Sue (the Dinosaur) currently resides at the Field Museum of Natural History in Chicago. She has also discovered cool stuff in shipwrecks, fossilized amber, and many other items in far flung destinations throughout our globe.

Our school got new reading books last year and one of the stories is about her. Since the theme of our school's special reading program this past year was "Night at the Museum" I sent an email to the Field Museum, hoping to get in touch with Sue. Surprisingly, she sent back a warm and funny message, talking about going to the wedding of the 6th grade teacher we both had (during different years), Mr. Marciniak. Apparently, her Mom made her wear a really dorky hat to that event. She remembered being in Student Council with my sister, and she remembered her bitter feelings toward school (at one point in the message, she jokingly referred to my students as my "prisoners"). I'd kind of hoped to call her for a taped interview for the Friday Night Live event, and she said that that would be okay. But, I also got the pretty distinct impression that she was a very private person, so I didn't want to push it. I decided to just leave her alone.

After the T-Rex was discovered there was a long and bitter legal battle to determine who actually owned the rights to the skeleton. A bunch of bad stuff happened to Sue Hendrickson during that ordeal and a lot of it left her a bit upset about a lot of things in this modern world. She went so far as to say that people should never discover anything really good, because there is always going to be a fight over it. But, she has nevertheless discovered (through digs and diving) tons of wonderful stuff. Never having met her, I still get the impression that she is a splendid individual. She is certainly someone who has followed her own drummer in life. And she certainly seems to have lived a very full life as well.

◇

The second person listed was Hal Morris. Sports fans, especially baseball fans will know that he was the longtime first baseman for the Cincinnati Reds. He actually started out with the Yankees in 1988 and put in short stints with the Royals and Tigers as well. Hal was a very good player. He holds the 5th highest rookie batting average in Major league history (.340). He had a lifetime average of .304. His fielding percentage as a first baseman was .994. If you know anything about baseball, you know that these are superb numbers.

In 1990, the Reds met the Oakland A's in the World Series. The powerful A's were picked to win easily. In fact, many baseball experts predicted a sweep. Well, the experts were right. There was a 4 game sweep in the '90 World Series. But, the thing they got wrong was the ***team***. The Reds ended up sweeping the A's! Current Cub manager Lou Piniella was the skipper of that squad. It was Hal's first year with the Reds. He was solid defensively in that upset sweep, making no errors. In Game 4 he hit a sacrifice fly ball. That doesn't sound extremely important, but it really was. You see that particular sacrifice fly ball scored a run which turned out to be the winning run in a 2 to 1 game and also (since it was Game 4) it turned out to be the winning run for the entire Series.

After baseball (he played an impressive thirteen years in Major League Ball), Hal (who had attended undergraduate school at the University of Michigan) went to Stanford to earn an MBA. So, we know the guy is smart. Now he works in business somewhere, I think out in California. Once again, it is easy to see how Hal's named ended up on the list of notables who have graduated as a Munster Mustang.

<>

The third person listed was Joe Mansueto. Before I checked the site, I had never heard of Mr. Mansueto. It turns out that when I was a Senior at MHS, Joe was a Sophomore, Have you heard of him? If you follow the business world you probably have. Joe Mansueto founded Morningstar Inc. They rate Investment funds and people pay for their reports. They have proven to be wildly successful. Joe got the idea for the firm's name from his reading of Henry David Thoreau's book, Walden. Here are the last three sentences from that fine book:

*Only that day dawns to which we are awake. There is more day to dawn. The sun is but a morning star.*

When he first read that last line he wondered what it meant.

Once he figured out what it meant, he thought it was good enough to name his business after. The rest, as they say, is history.

Well, you might say, *lots of people* start businesses. Of the thousands of people who have graduated from Munster High and trod down the business pathways, what makes ***this guy*** so special? You know how "Fortune" Magazine prints lists of the richest folks in our country? Well, Mr. Mansueto is on that list. You see, there are over 300,000,000 Americans now and according to "Fortune", Mr. Mansueto is one of the 400 most wealthy of them all. He tips the scale at a more than impressive 1.5 Billion Bucks. That's Billion with a ***B***. I remember once that I had a math teacher (at dear old MHS) who was trying to impress on our minds the difference between a million and a billion. He did this by explaining how high a stack of brand new one dollar bills would be if you had a million of them. Then, he explained how high that stack would be if you had a ***billion*** of them. Trust me, a billion is a LOT more. If you feel curious, you can look it up on the Internet. You'll certainly say, "Wow!

If you read up on Joe you'll find out that he has done some pretty good stuff with part of that dough. For instance, he and his wife are having Helmut Jahn design a brand new library on the campus of the University of Chicago. Since they are putting up a cool 25 million for this little project, they get to have their names put on it. There are a couple of really interesting stories available about his admiration for Warren Buffet and the interesting time in his youth when he sold some Christmas Trees. He seems like a good businessman, a good husband, a good father, and a good citizen. So, again I can understand how his name ended up on that list. I wonder who put it there?

<>

So, there you have it. Three people. An Intrepid Seeker of Cool Artifacts, a Major League Baseball Star, and a Billionaire. What must it be like to do the things they have done? How does it feel to unearth a Fossil and realize that the creature it once was roamed the Earth millions of years before you did?

What is it like to stand in the batter's box at the World Series, to see and hear screaming fans, to realize that millions are watching you on television? And then, you hit that one fly ball which turns out to be the sacrifice run that wins your teammates a World Series Ring!

How does a man react when the business he thinks up at the kitchen table ends up putting over a ***billion*** dollars on the bottom line? And how does it subsequently feel to take millions and give it back to the Institution which helped you become the man you are? They use the money to build a beautiful new library, where one day you hope another young man or woman will sit in a chair and read Walden the way you did many years before. And perhaps, he or she will be inspired to go out into the world and accomplish amazing things just the way you have done.

◇

I'd agree that all three of these individuals are admirable and that they have spent their time on this earth wisely and productively. But, as I leaf through Sue Livarchik's 1972 Munster High Paragon Yearbook, I can't help but think that the Wikipedia Editors still have ***a lot*** of work to do. I can think of several people who ought to be on that list of notables. For instance, Sue Livarchik (formerly Sue Resler), whose book I see before me now, has spent over three decades helping second graders learn to read, write, spell, do math problems, and behave like responsible citizens of the world. She went to Munster High School, graduating in 1973. She's raised three wonderful sons with her husband, George. She's a devout Catholic who makes decisions in her life based on her faith in God.

Are any of these things less important than finding amber or dinosaur bones, hitting fly balls, or helping individuals figure out how to invest their dough? I, for one, don't think so. In fact, in the grand scheme of things, I would venture to say that teaching a second grader is actually ***more*** important to society than anything Sue, Hal, or Joe has ever done. Not that what they've done isn't cool, exciting, and awe inspiring. It is. But really, next time you see a seven year old, look into his or her eyes and imagine that Mrs. Livarchik never taught them the spelling words, "Dinosaur", "Baseball", & "Money". See what I mean?

So, the Wikipedia Editors of the world might want to get busy. Oh, and Sue only has three letters in ***her name*** too.

*(So, that's your homework for tonight. When you have your answers you can turn in your assignment at: karashouse5@aol.com.)*

* * * * * * *

## "The Rakish Ones"

On Saturday, November 17th something really cool happened (at least it was cool if you are a member of the service organization known as Kiwanis International). Mrs. Hofer and Mrs. Frataccia (the sponsors of the Kiwanis Builders Club at Ben Franklin Middle School) organized their 9th annual Leaf Raking Day to assist members of the community who are physically unable to do this chore themselves.

An army of kids and adults hopped on two buses and spent the entire morning swooping down on a dozen houses all around Valpo.

Now, many of the residents stood out in the driveway with tears in their eyes telling the rakers how much they appreciated the assistance. If anybody had any doubt about whether or not this was a worthwhile activity, one glance at some of those faces would have swept that doubt right off the edge of the planet.

Here's what I thought was the really cool part of the whole experience. There are 7 Kiwanis Organizations in town. They are: The Valparaiso Noon Club, The Valparaiso Sunrise Kiwanis Club, The Valparaiso Aktion Kiwanis Club (this is a club for individuals who work at Opportunity Enterprises), The Valparaiso High School Key Club, The Thomas Jefferson Middle School Builders Club, The Ben Franklin Builders Club, and The Parkview Elementary K-Kids Club. **6 of these 7** clubs were represented at the activity. Except for the Aktion Club, members of every Kiwanis Organization in town were involved in the morning's festivities. 9 year olds, Middle Schoolers, High School kids, and even some Senior Citizens worked side by side to get the job done.

If you want to witness a living and powerful example of the word "**teamwork**", you should have seen what we saw on Saturday. The bus would pull up to a house with a huge yard and a dozen ancient trees. Millions of leaves were scattered throughout the yard. This was the kind of job that would take all weekend if you were to do it solo. Then, BOOM! A rush of youthful energy would descend upon the ground. Tarps were deployed to gather up leaves which were a long way from the street. Rake, rake, rake. Laugh, laugh, laugh. Carry, carry, carry.

Then Boom, again! The yard was clean as a whistle (in about 20 minutes). The best houses (as mentioned earlier) were the ones where the owners were out there watching. I saw an elderly couple talking to some 4th and 5th graders. They told the kids that they really appreciated their work and that they loved them for doing it!

Kudos to Mrs. Hofer and Mrs. Frataccia for organizing this fun and important event. Lots of people might have been concerned about "Turf" in an endeavor such as this. That is, they might have said, "Well, this is a ***Ben Franklin Builders' Club*** event. If you want to rake leaves, go organize your own day! Those ladies didn't do that at all. Everyone who showed up was welcome. Everyone who helped felt wanted and important. The snacks, drinks, and pizza were for everybody on the "Rake Squad". I hope that it is a model for more service club cooperation in the future. That would indeed be a great thing! Stellar work, ladies. Superb job, Kiwanians of all ages!

## "Fierce Joy"

When I was a child, I loved the game of basketball. Now, I loved football and baseball as well. I think my answer to the question, "What's your favorite sport?" always sort of depended upon which month was showing on the calendar. But, some of my greatest heroes strode the hardwood. Perhaps because many of them were tall, quick, and sleek (in decided contrast to my stubby, chubby, and clutzy presence in the world), I think I admired them all the more.

Let me just type the names. Some you will know because they reached national or even world wide prominence. Some were local high school heroes whose names will be unfamiliar to you, but still mean so very much to me. Bill Russell, Walt Frazier, "Hondo" Havlicek, Cornelius "Bootsy" White, Bob Stout, Gus Hagberg, Willis Reed. Just saying these names brings back a flood of memories about each and every player. I can still see Bootsy White leaping high into the air off the Hammond Civic Center floor. You may ask what I mean by "high". I'll explain. I was sitting in the front row the night of the Sectional Championship game. Bootsy dribbled down into the corner near my seat and launched into space… I looked ***up*** and could clearly see the pattern on the ***bottom*** of his sneakers! That's how high.

In the seventh grade I wrote a story about where thunder comes from for English class. I think it was called "An Etiological Myth" (a myth which explains things in nature). In my version the Greek or Roman gods were playing round ball up in the heavens.

Every dunk (like the ones I saw Bill Russell or Wilt Chamberlain hammer home) turned out to be the thunder we heard down on the Earth. I still remember that Miss Dodd (our English Teacher) read that story to the whole lecture hall class. That was so cool.

For years I loved the game. The eras of Magic, Bird, and

Michael enthralled me as they did millions of others throughout the globe. Recently however, I'd grown a little disenchanted with the sport. Too many punks making too many arrest reports, too little emphasis on teamwork, and a general weariness with selfishness, ridiculous fights, and the exorbitant amounts of cash which are thrown around have left me (especially as far as the professional game goes) feeling cold and distant. As someone in a movie once said, (or at least should have said if they haven't yet). "They're killin' the magic."

However, on April 13th, 2008 a group of folks I'd never met, reached right into my soul and relit all those magic basketball lanterns on a beautiful Sunday afternoon. These people were the **Chicago Wheelchair Bulls**. The Valparaiso High Key Club (sponsored by Olga Granat and Cyndi Svilar – President Taylor Granat) invited the Bulls to town for a series of exhibition games. The fund raising event was held to help the Bulls purchase new wheelchairs for team members, notably Valparaiso's own Ben Mortenson.

Here's the thing I loved about everybody on the CWB: Though every single person on the team had been dealt a bad blow of one sort or another in life, nobody ever mentioned it the entire day. We were there to watch athletes! Butt kicking, highly skilled, take no prisoner athletes who work out hard, sweat hard, play hard, and have a kind of fierce joy which somehow reminds one of ancient Viking warriors storming the beach of unsuspecting villagers long ago.

Early in the game, one of Bulls players got his chair upended and tumbled to the court. Nearly every person in the crowd (many of whom, like me had probably never been to a wheelchair game before) let out a concerned gasp as though someone had dropped a piece of Mom's antique china. The player shrugged, pushed his hands against the floor and bounced right back into playing position. The audience learned. That happened several times during the game. As the kids say, "No biggie."

Some of these players (like Alex Parra or "Sooze" Haddick) only had one leg. Some of them (like Ted Beck) had cerebral palsy. Others (like Ben) have learned to live with spinal cord injuries. I found out that one of the players was going through chemotherapy. But, really while you're watching them you don't think about that stuff. You think things like, "Oh, my gosh! That guy just dribbled behind his back (in a wheelchair)! Or, "That player just nailed a three pointer (sitting down, more than 20 feet from the basket)! Or, that girl "Sooze" just made it from one end of the court to the other faster than I could if I were riding on a Harley Davidson! Or, "Holy Smokes, that guy just hit a ***no look reverse layup!***

While I watched these people play I kept wishing that some of the professional athletes who've been such a disappointment lately (steroids, multiple arrests, no moral compass) could see the levels of effort, determination, and skill displayed by the CWB. All this, with adversity staring them in the face, 24/7. It was a great, great afternoon of entertainment. Many kids from my 4th grade class were there watching and back at school on Monday they too were filled with awe at the performances they had witnessed.
If you have a minute, check out their website:
http://www.wheelchairbulls.com/

Just read Don Vandello's profile. That ought to leave you in awe. Don was there that day to support the effort, but he had recently broken his hip and was talking about going into retirement. I had a chance to talk with him and a few of the other players Sunday. Talk about character. Talk about class. Talk about drive. Don, and every player I met from the Bulls had the market cornered in those qualities.

Every day God keeps us on this Earth, He gives us more

chances to learn stuff. At the game I've been inadequately trying to describe it was my pleasure to serve as the Public Address Announcer. Here is the first thing I learned that day. Prior to the game it was my duty to announce the playing of the National Anthem. I said, as I have heard the great John Knauff and dozens of other announcers say, that we'd like the crowd to stand, turn toward the flag and pay tribute to America through the playing of Our National Anthem. Then, I looked over at the Bulls. Guess how many of them were "standing"? That was lesson one.

There was a kid from Wheeler High School playing that day on the side of all the exhibition teams. His name was Jared Arambula. This young man was born with Spina Bifida. I know that the VHS gym only holds a few thousand people. But, I wish everybody in town (indeed, everybody in the state or country) could have seen that young man play. He would streak down the court at lightning speed (I almost just typed "break-neck" speed, which is the kind of word like "handicapped" that everyone should really think about before they use it), zig and zag between three opposing players' chairs, fire up a shot, scramble for a rebound, throw in the put-back, and generally do everything that Walt, Bootsy, and Bob used to do for the crowd many years ago.

Jared will be attending the University of Alabama where he has received a full scholarship to play on their Wheelchair Basketball team! Kudos to you, Jared. Several of the 4$^{th}$ grade students who were in the crowd that day came to the unanimous conclusion that "you rocked"!

So, how does one thank a group of people for restoring one's faith in an entire sport? I don't know, I'm working on it... If I figure it out I'll let you know.

I can tell you that the Key Club **REACHED THEIR GOAL OF RAISING $2,500.00 FOR BEN'S NEW CHAIR!**

P.S. I just have to mention one more amazing person. Special thanks to Karen Scheeringa-Parra. This is a person you need to find out about. Use your internet and type “Hearts in Motion”.  It will be worth your time.  Fierce joy,  indeed.

* * * * * * *

## "Play Pumps"

On Public Television awhile back there was a "FRONTLINE" story about a fellow named Trevor Field. He was thinking about the problem of potable drinking water in South Africa. Apparently, people (women, in the piece I viewed) spend an inordinate amount of time traipsing back and forth with water containers in order to help their families survive. The problem is that the water they are fetching is more often than not contaminated. Illnesses due to the contaminated well water (which in most cases is far too close to the surface) are at epidemic proportions. The number of people who don't have access to clean drinking water in the country is estimated to be 5 million. The contaminated water is cranked up by hand pumps which are difficult to operate and the water itself is loaded with harmful bacteria. Kids are constantly battling dysentery and other illnesses due to this situation. All in all, it constitutes a first class mess.

So, Mr. Field teamed up with an inventor and created the "Play Pump." It is sheer genius. A play pump is a child's merry ground connected to an underground well on one end and a small water tower on the other. Kids play on the merry go - round and water gets pumped to the tower where villagers can access it. That's it. The wells (which are always near schools) are sunk deep enough to insure that the water is fresh and pure. Kids have fun playing, the village avoids disease, clean water becomes available, and everybody wins. If you want to see exactly how this works, go to: http://www.pbs.org/frontlineworld/rough/2005/10/south_africa_th.html and watch the short video. It will take a little over 6 minutes for you to see what is going on.

Not only did Mr. Field think up and implement this whole plan, he also got the bright idea of putting HIV awareness billboards on the four sides of the square water towers. As most of you know, the young people in Africa are in the gravest danger regarding HIV. So, Mr. Field's plan works to bag two birds with one ingenious stone.

We showed the video to our K-Kids group. Someone noted that it costs $7,000.00 for one "Play Pump" system (and another $7,000.00 to install, educate the populace, and maintain the unit). Watching this reminded us of the great initiative Kiwanis undertook to solve the problems related to Iodine Deficiency Disorders. Remember that?

After talking about it for awhile the 4th and 5th graders in the K-Kids decided that they want to purchase a play pump system to help the children in South Africa. One of the students in K-Kids, Hannah J., researched Play Pumps for a report she's doing for a school related "Energy Museum". She is the official spokesperson for the "K-Kids" "Play Pump" initiative.

The President of K-Kids is Lauren R. She also gives the idea her full support. Vice President Jane T. is on board as well (along with the rest of the K-Kids). So, here's what the K-Kids figure. There are lots of math problems which add up to seven thousand dollars. We think that anyone who took the time to read the article (and look at the video) might think it would be a good thing to help. So, if seven thousand folks read the article and each one of them sends in one dollar, we can buy a "Play Pump". Or if one wealthy gal or guy reads the article and donates $7,000.00 to the cause, we can buy a "Play Pump". Of course, what we're hoping for is something in between those two extremes.

One of the best Kiwanis endeavors I've been involved with in the last year was the leaf raking project sponsored by the Ben Franklin Builders Club. The reason it was so rewarding was because lots of different clubs in towns pitched in. So, what would it be like if all the Kiwanis Clubs in the district were convinced to kick in money for Play Pumps? What if we asked the Deltas, the

Tri Kappas, the Rotarians, the Lions Club, the Exchange Club, the Elk, the Moose, or other organizations devoted to helping kids? Student Council groups could help as well. Churches may be inclined to assist. I think this is going to be fun. Please send the article around. Thanks. Remember, any donation between $1.00 and $7,000.00 will be welcome!

Please make checks to "Parkview School" ("K-Kids / Play Pumps" on the memo line) and sent to:

Parkview School K-Kids Club (Attn: Greg Karas)
Parkview Elementary School
1405 Wood St.
Valparaiso, Indiana 46385

* * * * * * *

## "K-Kids and Miss America"

This beautiful and intelligent young lady promoting a local Kiwanis organization for children is striking enough to be Miss America. Actually, she *is* Miss America. Deidre Downs, from the great state of Alabama, recently paid a visit to Porter Hospital in Valparaiso, Indiana and met with a group of 40 Kiwanis K-Kids from Parkview Elementary School.

**Miss America - Deidre Downs**

Ms. Downs plans on becoming a pediatrician after her tenure as Miss America is complete. Therefore, many of the visits on her year long tour of ambassadorial good will are to hospitals. She spoke with the 4th and 5th grade students extensively about the importance of having a dream and pursuing it with "everything they had." She talked about her love of baseball as a child. She signed autographs for every student and posed with anyone who wanted a photo with her. She also noted how nice it was to be greeted by a group of children who (at such a young age) were already interested in helping others.

K-Kids, that is Kiwanis Clubs designed for elementary age children, provide just such an opportunity. The particular club that Miss America visited was the brain-child of three high school students from Valparaiso. Alyssa Walter, Emily Longhi, and Tessa Meyer were already members of their high school Key Club when they heard about K-Kids at one of their conventions. They approached their sponsors (Cyndi Svilar and Olga Granat) about the possibility of forming a club at one of the local elementary schools.

In fact, it was the same elementary school that all three girls had attended from Kindergarten through 5th grade, Parkview. Svilar and Granat thought the idea was a tremendous one and gave the girls their full support.

**K-Kids President (5th Grader Molly Tullis) stands with Club Founders Alyssa Walter, Tessa Meyer, and Emily Longhi. Miss America is seated before them.**

Fifth grade teacher Cheryl Highlan agreed to be faculty sponsor and help from the Sunrise Kiwanis Club of Valpo was also procured. The club began meeting, elected officers, and were even given a bell and gavel by the Valparaiso Noon Kiwanis Club and their Past President, Jon Groth. Members served and cleaned up at the local Kiwanis

Pancake Breakfast, helped out at the Special Olympics track meet, wrote Valentines to service men and women fighting overseas, and helped the school's Student Council raise $963.00 for Riley Childrens' Hospital in Indianapolis in their initial year of operation.

Club founders Meyer, Longhi, and Walter were honored at the Kiwanis Key Club Convention with a special award for organizing the club and planning and holding all of the meetings. Then one day Parkview got a call from Porter Hospital. The person in charge of public relations for the hospital, Andrew Snyder, happens to have a sister (Amy Elliott) who works as an instructional assistant at the school. He asked if the school (which is only a few blocks from the hospital) could provide a welcoming committee for Miss America's arrival at the facility. Principal Doug Hollar (who happens to be a member of the Sunrise Club) immediately thought of the K-Kids as the perfect greeting crew.
The kids were elated that he did. The chance to meet with "The Real Miss America" was a highlight of the year that many of the kids said they would remember for the rest of their lives. Hopefully, the chance to serve others as part of Kiwanis will also be something that stays with them for the remainder of their lives as well.

Miss America 2005 Deidre Downs

* * * * * * *

## "Manalive: The Thousand Dollar Proposal"

Some sneer; some snigger; some simper;
In the youth where we laughed, and sang.
And ***they*** may end with a whimper,
But ***we*** will end with a bang.

The brilliant G.K. Chesterton wrote a book once about a man named Innocent Smith entitled, Manalive. The premise of the book was this: Innocent would encounter people who were complaining about the monotony and boredom of modern life. Then, he would pull out a pistol and tell that person that he was about to die. The change in behavior for these people was instantaneous and dramatic. When faced with the prospect of having no life at all, the thrill of living which had somehow abandoned them returned with a roar.

Today you will go out into the world and have an impact on the people you come in contact with. For some reason, I am always keenly (perhaps overly) aware of the effect my presence might be having on others. Once, I was making a presentation at our school Open House. There was a woman in the second row with an expression on her face that made it seem like she was sitting in a patch of hot tar. It was obvious that this woman was feeling something beyond boredom. It was revulsion of the highest magnitude. I almost stopped the talk about homework and field trips to ask her if I had done something to inadvertently offend her. But, I didn't. I really to this day have no idea what was wrong with that person that evening. Actually, it could have had absolutely nothing whatever to do with my presentation.

Since that Open House I've daydreamed about what would have happened if I had pulled out a weapon (maybe a bow and arrow), pointed it squarely at her forehead, and told her that since she was so bored and disgusted with life (or at least my presentation) that I was going to put her out of her misery. Now, besides being instantly fired, perhaps there would have been other effects. The woman might have realized that body language, facial expressions, and the general "vibe" we put out **does** have an impact on others in the room.

In any event, I suppose that there might be a way to make people realize the joy and value of being alive without actually threatening their lives. I mean, if one thought about an alternative to pulling out an instrument of destruction, one might pull out, for instance, a checkbook.

In fact, here's an idea for creating a really positive, life affirming moment for at least one person in the world this week:

How about if we (the members of Sunrise Kiwanis) read today's paper and just decide to give $1,000.00 to some individual or family in there who seems to need it or deserve it? Doesn't that sound like fun? There wouldn't be a formal discussion at the Board meeting. The board is probably right here and could decide to do this ***right on the spot***.

As you've read this idea so far, people are probably lining up on either side of the fence. Some are saying, "Well, that's a stupid idea. We have a board so that we can wisely and prudently decide how to use our resources." Others might be thinking, "Why not? I'd love to read a story about somebody in the paper and decide ***on the spot*** that giving that person a thousand dollars would be an incredibly fun and rewarding thing to do. Why, it would be the kind of thing that the person would remember for the rest of his or her life." This would be a one time deal. Read the paper, find a worthy recipient, talk it over, write a check, and really make someone's day. It would be Immediate Service! Immediate and profound!

I know that our club is always engaging in thoughtful expressions of goodwill in the community. But, the thing about these acts of kindness is that they are always ***planned out*** and we often do the same thing year after year. It has been several years since I've served as Club President or even been on the board. But, if my memory serves me correctly we always have a nice surplus of funds which seem to be burning a hole in the bottom of the bank vault.

I am realistic enough to know that this idea might (probably will) be shot down. If it is, you won't wear hear me whining. But, if we somehow decide to do this, I'd like to ride over in the car with President Biff and Treasurer Ron (and whoever else would like to squeeze in the vehicle with us). I would like to see the person's face (maybe a Grandma who spends her time assisting orphans, or a teenager who is attempting to make a positive difference in our world, or a Vet who just returned from overseas, who knows?). Wouldn't that be a great moment, when President Biff says, "Well, we read about your situation in the newspaper and we just decided to give you a thousand dollars today. Please use it in good health and have a nice day!" Then, we'd walk back out to the driveway, get in the car and cruise away. Personally, I can't imagine doing anything more fun than that this week!

What do you think?

* * * * * * *

## "I Don't Think We've Rightly Understood..."

I think that being in Kiwanis (especially this particular club) is one of the best decisions that I've made in my entire life. I can still recall when my boss asked me to join (this was more than 20 years back). He explained to me that a group of individuals (led by Lonnie Steele) had been looking into the possibility of starting up a second Kiwanis club in Valparaiso. The first club met at noon, but apparently there were people who could not make a lunch time meeting.

My initial response was one of utter skepticism. The first two people who popped into my mind were Ralph Kramden (played by Jackie Gleason in "The Honeymooners") and Fred Flintstone. You might recall that Ralph was a member of a social club known as "The Raccoon Lodge". They (Ralph, Ed Norton, and their pals) wore big funny Raccoon hats and if I remember correctly, had a secret handshake. Fred and Barney belonged to a troop known as "The Royal Order of the Water Buffalo". They too had hilarious head gear which made them look totally ridiculous. My immediate problem was trying to figure out how to say, "No", without alienating my new boss ( I had only been working for him for one year). I hemmed and hawed, but in the end there was no real way to turn him down without feeling like a heel.

So, I agreed to give the whole thing a shot. My parents, aunts or uncles, and neighbors were not (as far as I knew) involved in anything remotely resembling a service club. I had been to a few Kiwanis Pancake Breakfasts and I had often wondered who those people were. What in the world could they get out of wearing those shirts, hats, or aprons which were emblazoned with that little blue "K"? How much were they getting paid to flip those pancakes? Why were they sometimes seen standing out in the hot summertime selling peanuts, when they could be at the beach lying in the sun, enjoying themselves? The whole thing was just a mystery to me. I dreaded the idea of wearing pins and badges, or funny shirts. I didn't want to learn a secret slogan, or a confusing and embarrassing handshake. Pretty much I wanted to be left alone (I hope that everyone has read the riveting account of C.S. Lewis wanting to be "left alone" in his excellent autobiography entitled, Surprised by Joy).

But, I had also noticed something else about many of these people. They seemed happy in a way that I often was not. I remember reading about that same time an account of the great Dr. Albert Schweitzer, who had one day received a visitor in Africa. The good Doctor insisted on carrying the gent's luggage all the way back to the lodging upon his arrival. The man protested. He thought that there were certainly servants available to do such menial labor. Dr. Schweitzer contradicted him gently by explaining that one of the greatest things we can do on this earth is to be of service to our fellow man, ***in any way*** that presents itself. As our club began doing work around the community, I learned just how much truth there was in this statement.

As we helped young children, students, elderly individuals, and people with disabilities through a variety of projects, I found that there was a terrific satisfaction in doing such tasks. I enjoyed the camaraderie, I looked forward to our weekly meetings, and I learned a lot from the vast array of speakers which we were treated to each week. But, the actual ***service to others*** was the part of being in the club which I enjoyed the most.

One thing which totally impressed me was how our club (at the International level) was not afraid to take on a HUGE problem like Iodine Deficiency Disorders. Though it took several years, and though it had a price tag of over 75 million dollars, the leaders of the club persevered. Now, the goal of iodizing the world's salt supply (and thereby eliminating the largest preventable cause of mental retardation world wide) has been largely achieved. When one realizes that millions of babies have been born who have ***been saved*** from having IDD because of this effort, it can do nothing except fill a Kiwanian with pride.

At the other end of the spectrum, we do small, meaningful things right here in the community. A college scholarship, free books for a classroom full of Head Start Preschoolers, manning our town's "Live Nativity" scene, helping wash dishes at the Cafe Manna Soup Kitchen, sponsoring youth organizations in our schools, cleaning up the highway, collecting food, mittens, and hats for people who have not been as fortunate as ourselves, are all ways that we've served. All these things have brought an extra level of meaning into the lives of our members.

One of my favorite parts in the great book, The Lord of the Rings, is when Barliman Butterbur is talking to the returning travelers after they have pretty much helped to save the world. Butterbur (who lives far from where the ***real*** problems have been) mentions that the Rangers (who were previously occupied in the secret protection of his little land until the war began) have been missed. All kinds of local troubles had popped up when the Rangers were off helping in the larger battle. He said, "I don't think we've rightly understood ***till now*** what they did for us." You see, it was not until they were ***gone*** that they were appreciated.

That is what I think it would be like if Kiwanis Clubs (and Rotary, Exchange, and Lions Clubs as well) all over the world suddenly disappeared. People would notice gaps that were not there before. Then, someone somewhere would say that wonderful sentence, "I don't think we've rightly understood ***till now*** what they did for us." As the New Year begins and we look to expand our membership, perhaps that is one thing we could tell people about; how individuals maybe don't notice us too much in their day to day lives, but how much folks would miss us if we were gone!

* * * * * * *

## "Lepanto, and the Mighty G.K. Chesterton"

"Journalism consists mainly of people writing, 'Lord Jones Dead', for readers who never knew Lord Jones was alive". This quote, from my favorite writer, Gilbert Keith Chesterton is representative of his wit. In scholarly works such as The Everlasting Man, and Orthodoxy, he sheds light on why our lives are only given meaning when we follow in the steps of our Creator. His Father Brown detective stories are well known among devotees of the mystery genre. His weekly columns in the London Illustrated News entertained readers with his signature brand of paradoxical whimsy and political acumen. His novels (including The Man Who was Thursday, The Napoleon of Notting Hill, and Manalive) never fail to delight readers with their sparkling prose, unique characterizations, and sense of joy and wonder. His biographies of men like St. Francis and Charles Dickens are acclaimed by experts throughout the literary world. His own modest autobiography is a joy to read and reread. Several different authors have written books *about* him (Joseph Pearce's is a relatively recent one and Maisie Ward , who wrote what is considered the definitive life of GKC, was one of his contemporaries). He died in 1936. Every book by and about Chesterton has provided me with hours and hours of unblemished joy. C.S. Lewis lists Chesterton as the main writer who led him back to God. Gandhi translated one of Chesterton's articles and cited it when he began his quest to free India from British Colonial Rule.

However, the thing I wish to write about today is his poetry. It fills a couple of volumes. Some of the poems are funny. Some of them beautifully shed light on religious themes. Some are love poems. Some are about his dogs (Winkle and Quoodle). But, the greatest poem he ever wrote is without a doubt, "Lepanto". Several critics have called it the greatest poem of the twentieth century. Odds are, many of the people reading today's newsletter don't know what Lepanto was and have never heard of or read this poem.

Lepanto was a sea battle which took place off the Gulf of Patras near Greece in October of 1571. The poem describes an epic battle between the naval forces of the Christians and the Muslims. It is as hard to describe this poem as it is to describe fireworks to a man who has been blind since birth. Let us just say that the poetry roars, shouts, exults, and paints an almost unbelievably vivid picture. The more one learns about the history of the battle, the more beautiful and compelling the poem becomes. The Admiral who leads the Christians into battle is the 24 year old Don John of Austria. The Christian ships are arrayed in the shape of The Cross. The Muslim Armada is spread throughout the Gulf in the shape of a Crescent.

There are close to seven hundred ships and over 180,000 men involved in this battle. The Pope blesses the Christian combatants who remain silent prior to the battle while the Islamic forces scream, bang metal noise makers, and generally attempt to strike fear in the hearts of their foes. Miracles occur and the Pope has a vision of the Christian Victory before it is even reported to him. Miguel Cervantes (author of Don Quixote) was one of the participants. The power and beauty of the poem shine through to an even greater extent when one reads it *aloud.*

According to historians, this battle was the pivotal moment which helped decide which religion would control Europe. The story is a true one and Chesterton tells it in such a compelling fashion that one wishes to read it again and again.

If you go to G.K. Chesterton's works on the web (a website maintained by a person named Martin Lawrence) you will easily find this poem (and hundreds of other Chesterton gems). It will be well worth the effort! There is also an excellent annotated edition of the poem in a book which has been edited by Dale Ahlquist and published by the American Chesterton Society.

* * * * * * *

## "Well Done, Last of the Kings of Narnia"

For those of you who are admirers of C.S. Lewis (as I most certainly am) the Chronicles of Narnia will be (as he might put it) part of your mental furniture. Anyone who remembers Digory and Polly stepping into Uncle Andrew's forbidden study and hearing that strange humming noise knows what a master of suspense Lewis was. Anybody who can recall Eustace getting the dragon skins peeled off him is aware of how Lewis could simultaneously entertain us and show us how our own lives ought to be improved. If you can remember Reepicheep the Mouse sailing over the standing wave at the end of the world and then going down, down, down into the great unknown you know how much Lewis loved adventure and what a genius he was at creating it for us.

There are a hundred more scenes one could recall. Lucy standing in Coriakin's study reading from his book of Magic Spells. Prince Rilian being freed from the Silver Chair and destroying it because it was a "vile engine of sorcery". Seeing Lucy step through the Wardrobe door for the first time and encountering a magical world filled with trees, snow, treachery, and beauty. Jill Pole watching helplessly as Eustace falls off the cliff, but suddenly a Lion rushes up to her side and starts to blow. Edmund betraying his brother and sisters and ultimately being forgiven for his sin as Aslan steps in and receives the death penalty in his place. Puddleglum the Marshwiggle stamping out the enchanted fire of the Lady of the Green Kirtle.

The Dawn Treader sailing into the eerie darkness where dreams came true. Lucy and Susan hearing a tremendous crashing sound "Like a giant breaking a giant's plate" and seeing that Aslan had come to life again.

These books have so many vivid adventures and such

a collection of enchanting characters that I hope everyone who has never had a chance to read them will give them a try. If you have children, they will love them (I read all 7 to my own kids when they were young). If you have grandchildren these seven stories would be a terrific gift. I have read them to my classes for 32 years in a row (and have never once grown tired of them). Many times, when former students get in touch, those books are one of the first things mentioned. A very great thing happened when one former student told me that she had read the books to *her own* children. That made me figure that the lessons and adventures in those stories had made a pretty big impact on her life.

In the seventh story, The Last Battle, one of the greatest encounters takes place between the young King of Narnia, Tirian, and the Great Lion, Aslan. Up until this point in the book Tirian has had a miserable time. He remains steadfast to Narnia, Truth, and Aslan, and during a furious battle he passes through a grim stable door where the strangest and most wonderful things begin to happen.

"A brightness flashed behind them. All turned. Tirian turned last because he was afraid. There stood his heart's desire, huge and real, the golden Lion, Aslan himself, and already the others were kneeling in a circle round his forepaws and burying their hands and faces in his mane as he stooped his great head to touch them with his tongue. Then he fixed his eyes upon Tirian, and Tirian came near, trembling, and flung himself at the Lion's feet, and the Lion kissed him and said, 'Well done, last of the Kings of Narnia who stood firm at the darkest hour.'"

I hope that each of us can receive such a message from the Golden Lion in the hour when we pass through our own Stable Door.

* * * * * * *

## "All that Money"

When lots of my friends at work were all excited recently about their chances of winning the record $365 Million Power Ball Jackpot, I had to express an opinion that was decidedly against the grain. I noted that I wouldn't want to **win** that money for all the "Anti-Oxidant Tea in China". I gave a variety of reasons for my reluctance. Here they are:

1. If I had ***earned*** a cool 365 million (probably about a week's income for Mr. Gates), I think I could more easily assimilate that into my day to day existence. See, if I had earned it, then there would be no weird feelings associated with having it. If I got it just because of blind, dumb luck, then the feeling that it really belonged to somebody else would probably haunt me for the rest of my days.

2. If I ***inherited*** $365,000,000.00 it would be a slightly different story too. First of all, my picture (and my family's) would not be plastered all over the TV and the newspapers. If I ***won*** the money, it would be, and that would make me uneasy because neighbors, old high school friends, and relatives who haven't seen fit to talk to me since Kennedy was in the White House, would all certainly come creeping out of the woodwork. How jerky would it seem when I told these people that I couldn't give them each a million, because I would then only have 36**4** million left for myself? Huge sums of money attached to large piles of guilt are not my idea of a fun time. So, I'd prefer earning the cash to inheriting it, but I'd have to graciously accept inherited funds, because after all, somebody did write my name on their will.

3. It would make the last 30+ years of my Professional Life into a lie. I spend a great deal of each year teaching kids about the value of hard work.
I tell them how important it is to **earn** their way through

their existence. Cheating, taking shortcuts, attempting to find the "easy way out" of situations are all completely frowned upon in the picture of reality I attempt to paint for them. How would it be then, if one day I showed up to tell the kids that I had won a bunch of money and Mrs. Fitzgibbons (or some such person) was going to be their new teacher until the end of the year? I would like my life to have stood for something at the end. Free money would certainly make that harder to accomplish.

4. I would be afraid that it would ruin my family. I remember seeing Michael Jordan on television discussing how much money he planned to give his children as they grew up. His view was unequivocal: "None! Not one penny!" The interviewer expressed dismay, "But Michael, you're a Multi-Millionaire. Don't you feel compelled to help your children through this life?" He expressed the opinion that **giving** money to your children was a certain path to messing up their lives. If they have it given to them, he reasoned, there will be no incentive for them to **earn** anything on their own. This would make them into financially dependent cripples. They would really never come to understand the value of money. He made the assumption that drug or alcohol abuse would be a very likely result of such a financial pipeline. Everything he said in that interview made perfect sense to me. I wonder if Michael has stuck to his guns as his kids have grown?

I know that many readers at this point will be thinking, "Sheesh! What a dud! Why doesn't that Stiff lighten up and just **enjoy the money**? Think of it, NO MORE WORK! Lots of fast cars, vacations to any place in the world, extra homes in Aspen, Florida, and California, maybe even the South of France. Horses, yachts, a private plane stocked with Tempur-pedic beds and a state of the art home theatre system, wonderful meals in any restaurant in the world, champagne, anything one's heart could ever desire! You could make your friends and family happy! You can make your life easy! How can you say you wouldn't want those things? Are you an idiot?"

You see, the implication in those statements is that our lives **now** (without all that money) are narrow, limited, and unexciting. If I go into Beef Mart and buy 2 good steaks, take them home, throw 'em on the sizzling grill, cook them to perfection (without the aid of a private chef), come into the house, turn on some beautiful music, sit down with my lovely wife, have a nice drink, and enjoy the meal, then I feel like it ***means something***, because I (actually, we) earned the house, the grill, the steaks, the drink, and everything else associated with that pleasant experience. Right now, I'm reading two very good books. If I had 365 million dollars burning a hole in my pocket, would I still make time to read? Would I feel the urge to make every moment "memorable"? Because after all, why would a person just be sitting here in plain old Valparaiso? Why aren't you basking on the seashore in Hawaii? Why aren't you climbing mountains in Europe? Why aren't you busy getting a facelift and having your hair dyed? To tell you the truth, I think I'd prefer just taking my bike up to the Northern part of the county and riding along that path up there for a couple of hours. My bike is pretty old. It doesn't even have any gears. But, it's **my** bike (and **my** funky lightning bolt helmet), thank you very much.

So yeah, I can live without all that dough. I'll still keep getting up 5 days a week and coming in to match wits with the 9 year olds. Some of them will be Doctors some day, and I will have played a small part in that. Some of them will own businesses in the future and every time they multiply numbers on a tax form, they might remember that some old coot with gray hair taught them how to multiply.

Some night when they read a book to their son or daughter, it might be one of the very same books which I have read to them.

Riches? My friends, they don't all necessarily come with dollar signs and decimal points attached.

Sincerely,

Captain Curmudgeon

* * * * * * *

## "The Man on the Corner"

One day in the fall of 1983 I was driving to my job teaching 4th grade at Morgan Township School. I was stopped at the light which is right on the corner of Route 30 near Valparaiso University. I was waiting to turn left. It was back then (as it is now) a long wait. There was a man standing on the corner. He was someone I had seen before. His appearance was disheveled, hair unkempt, jacket dirty, maybe stained with something which had recently been inside his nose. He was middle aged; definitely not one of the "beautiful people".

Imagine my surprise when this gentleman walked toward me, opened the passenger door of my Dodge Aspen, stuck his head inside and said, "Are you turning left? Can I have a ride to work, please?" My first impulse was to say, "No. No. Please, close the door. I can't be late for school." I also was repulsed. He was dirty. As I recall, he didn't smell too great either. But, he said, "Please." And he actually didn't look to be dangerous, so I said, "I can take you as far as Route 49, then I have to turn right to get to work."

The time we spent together was brief. He said a few words about his job at the Fiberglass place. I mentioned that I was a teacher. He thanked me for giving him a ride (even though I wasn't going to take him all the way to work). The whole thing was over in just a few minutes... I thought. But, almost 30 years later I'm still thinking about him.

That's because as soon as he left the car and thanked me, the thought came over me like a thunderbolt (as one came over Eustace Scrubb when he realized that *he* was the dragon), "That might have been Jesus." To some of you I know that might sound ridiculous. What in the world would Jesus be doing in Porter County, Indiana on a cold and cloudy October morning?

I guess the reason I thought that might have something to do with the 25th Chapter of Matthew. Do you remember the part that goes like this?

***"Then he will say to those at his left hand, 'Depart from me you cursed, into the eternal fire prepared for the Devil and his angels; for I was hungry and you gave me no food, I was thirsty and you gave me no drink, I was a stranger and you did not welcome me, naked and you did not clothe me, sick and in prison and you did not visit me. Then they will answer, 'Lord, when did we see thee hungry or thirsty or a stranger or naked or sick or in prison and did not minister to thee? Then he will answer them, 'Truly I say to you, as you did it not to one of the least of these you did it not to me' And they will go away into eternal punishment, but the righteous into eternal life."***

So the question has haunted me for close to 30 years, "How did I do?" The stranger had asked for a ride *to work*. I took him part of the way, but not all the way. Part of this was my desire to not be late, but part of it was my desire to not be bothered. I guess I helped him, but if it *was* Jesus, I can imagine that I probably scored about a B - or a C +. Does God grade on the "curve"? Was my half hearted effort good enough? I still don't know. What was in my heart? Whatever it was, it was pretty lukewarm.

I suppose being in this club is part of my effort to raise that grade if I possibly can. When we do projects to help the poor, or the weak, or any of the people in society who haven't had the breaks we've had, I guess it is a way of saying, "See, Lord, my friends and I are trying a little harder now."

And the guy on the corner? I've seen him around town from time to time. I always wonder. Every time I see him, I always wonder... Because, you never know.

* * * * * * *

## "The Expiration Date"

"The future for me is the same as it is for any other person; Unknown." This quote from Marine Kyle Price furnishes us with an opportunity to explore the nature of time, and especially *our* time here on Earth. Let's suppose for a moment that all of us were born with an expiration date. In other words, imagine that at birth there was a small bar code tattooed to your left wrist. If you traveled to the nearest Jewel Osco store and slid your hand along the checkout scanner, you would hear the familiar beeping sound. Then, up on the display screen there would be a digitally printed message which might appear as follows:

***Gregory J. Karas***
***D.O.B. - 12-15-54 (2:44 a.m. C.S.T.)***
***Chicago, Illinois - USA***
***Michael Reese Hospital***

***D.O.D. - 7-23-32 (7:14 p.m M.T.)***
***Phoenix, Arizona - USA***
***Willowcrest Gardens - Assisted Living Facility***

The key element would be that one would have to consciously go to the store and purposefully scan his or her wrist in order to get the information. Would you do it? If so, why? If not, why not?

Of course, this raises all sorts of little side ruminations as well. A person could take his or her baby into Jewel and scan the child's wrist before he or she was aware that the system existed. I had a debate once with a very intelligent woman who works at our school. She had had her two daughters' ears pierced when they were babies. My thought was that the kids owned their ears and they ought to be able to choose if and when someone was going to poke holes through them. She (obviously, since she did it) saw the whole situation in a completely different light. Her view was that they certainly would have them pierced one day; why wait? So, if the bar code existed when your own kids were born, would you scan 'em? Would you be tempted?

I once read a biography of the great folk singer Woody Guthrie. You might recall that he was afflicted with the terrible disease known as Huntington's Chorea, which causes one to lose neurological functioning, shake uncontrollably, and ultimately leads to a horrific death. In the story it mentioned that Woody's son, Arlo (who wrote the famous song, "Alice's Restaurant") was informed that a genetic test had been developed which would tell him conclusively whether or not he was going to get the disease as his life advanced. Point blank, Arlo refused.

In the great story by J.M. Barrie entitled Peter Pan, it is noted that the last great adventure of our lives will be death. Of all the thousands of days that we live here on this beautiful and sometimes heartbreaking rock, only one of them will be our very last one.

Once, the great British author C.S. Lewis was discussing *his* final day with some colleagues. He said that he hoped when he died that it wouldn't cause a big fuss (he knew that he had millions of readers worldwide who admired his works tremendously). Lewis indeed got his wish. He happened to die on November 22nd, 1963, the very same day that John F. Kennedy met his tragic demise.

Since I posed the question, I'll give you *my* answer. Nope. I'd be like old Arlo. No scanner for me because "Ignorance ***is*** bliss." Life has been in so many ways a wonderful adventure from where I'm sitting and the very best days have often been ones where things I didn't expect to happen, happened. So, I know it is waiting out there for me somewhere. And I agree with Mr. Barrie, it is going to be an awfully big adventure, whenever and wherever it takes place. My personal wish is that Jesus loves Golden Retrievers the same way that I do.

The important thing is that we're here right now. We're given 24 hours each and every day. We can choose to do productive and meaningful things *any time we want*. That's one reason many of us got up early this morning. So we could come down to the Kiwanis meeting, talk to some of our friends, and use that time to make this world a little bit better place than it was yesterday. Remember when Lou Gehrig said that he considered himself the luckiest man on the face of the earth (as we he was staring death in the eye)? I hope we all have that brand of courage when we see Joe Black ambling up the street in his tuxedo, with a smile on his face.

* * * * * * *

## " Mr. Smarty Boots and the Blue Mashed Potatoes"

This year will mark my 30th in an elementary classroom, and if I had a dollar for every time a child has asked me what my favorite color was, I would be in a financial position not to have to go back. But, if I didn't go back I wouldn't get to experience the sublime joy of being asked what my favorite color was (for the 7 millionth time). Let's think about that question for a minute. There are several people in this room and Diane has just handed you this newsletter. Some of you will glance through it now. Some of you will read all or part of it later. Some of you (of course, you won't know we're talking about you) don't read it all. If we were to ask everyone to name his or her favorite color and write it down on the provided line, most of you would have little problem with the task. Let's try it. If you can think of your favorite color, please take a moment to write it down on the line right now: ________________________________________. Thank you very much.

Now, for a moment let's consider ***why*** all those kids ask what our favorite color is. Do you think it is because they want our color to agree with their choice? That might be the case. Do you think they think they'll be able to tell something about your character if you reveal your choice? Hmmm. Let's say someone said his or her favorite color was pink. Is that suggestive of anything to you? Have you ever asked anyone what their favorite color was and had the answer be gray or brown? If someone says "black", do you tend to respond, "That's not a color. Black represents the absence of all light?" If someone says "white", do you say, "That's not fair. White is the combination of all the colors." How about people who choose weird color names like magenta or chartreuse? What if they mention a color which you really don't care for at all? Do you say, "Oh, yuck I hate that color."?

When a kid asks me what my favorite color is I usually say, "Most of the time, blue. But, if I'm thinking about kings or sunsets, then it is purple. But, if I'm thinking about the ocean then it is aquamarine. But, if I'm thinking about pine forests on top of beautiful mountains in Colorado or about Robin Hood, then it is a cool and dark green. But, if I'm thinking about buried treasure then it is a rich red for the rubies inside the battered oak chest, or shimmering gold for the pieces of eight, or sparkling green for the emeralds. Then, I'll ask the kid if he or she has ever seen a star sapphire. My dad had a ring when I was a kid which had a star sapphire in the setting. I used to look at that ring and marvel at the way the star inside the blue stone moved as you twisted it back and forth in the light. Then, I'll ask the kid if he or she has ever seen a kaleidoscope. If a prism is handy I might show them what that can do with light and color. Then, I end up by saying I guess I don't really have a favorite color. I just find ways and reasons to make all of them my favorite, depending on the situation.

Now, every once in a while I'll encounter an evil child who will say something like, "Well, pretend that all the other colors in the world except one were going to disappear and you just had to choose one. Which one would it be then, Mr. Smarty Boots?"

Beyond the shock of being called "Mr. Smarty Boots", this being forced into a corner always makes me say, "Okay. Blue." But, I really don't want to ever eat blue mashed potatoes!

Now, the same concept can apply to lots of other aspects of life. For instance, if people ask your favorite sport, doesn't it really depend on whether there are green or bright red and gold leaves on the trees; or a crisp layer of snow on the ground? Recently, I read a wonderful book about Willie Mays entitled, Willie's Time, by an author named Charles Einstein (no relation). Near the end of the book Einstein tells about a writer for the Sporting News who once referred to the Say Hey Kid as "The Soul of Spring Time".

Isn't that wonderful? Isn't that what baseball is supposed to be? Youth, power, hope, joy, and springtime? Isn't that what we felt as we saw Willie race to grab Vic Wertz's drive in the 1954 World Series (even though it was October)?

How about food? I can never answer the question, "What's your favorite food?" The reason is simply that there are just too many categories; too many wonderful things to enjoy. I remember going to Boston when I was a young child and for the first time in my life devouring *whole* deep fried clams. I thought I was going to die. If given the chance I would have probably eaten them until I exploded like a party balloon. But, what about Key Lime pie? Or Prime Rib? Or fresh Pineapple? Or how about some of that Ice Cream from Cold Stone? Sorry, I just can't pick one which rises above the others...

Music? What is your favorite song? That is impossible too! I saw Muddy Waters play live a couple of times before he died at a little club in Illinois called ***Harry Hope's***. "The Gypsy Woman told my mother, before I was born, 'You got a Boy Child's coming; Goin' be a Son of a Gun...'" To see the joy in Muddy's face and to hear the power in his voice was a rare treat that I'll never forget. But, I've also seen the otherworldly Derek Trucks play (both with the Allman Brothers and his own band). This person must be heard to be believed (and even then, it remains hard to believe that the sounds are really coming out of just a simple guitar attached to an amplifier). When I was in college we took a trip to Florida, and we stopped off in Macon, Georgia to visit the graves of Berry Oakley and Duane Allman. Have you ever listened to the tune, "In Memory of Elizabeth Reed"? If the evil kid told me that all the songs in the world except one had to disappear, I might choose that one. But, how about Beethoven's 5th Symphony? Or the wonderful "Eine Kleine Nachtmusik" of Mozart? Vivaldi's "Four Seasons"? How about the wonderful jazz numbers on "Kind of Blue" by Miles Davis? The beautiful cello work by Yo Yo Ma on a thousand different songs. Sorry, "favorite" for me is just too difficult a concept.

Books? Authors? Animals? Favorite athletes? What was your favorite class? Who was your favorite student? Who was your favorite teacher or coach? I can't even begin to narrow the lists down. Television programs? Remember "The Man from U.N.C.L.E."? Until "24" showed up I might have said that that was the greatest show. But, how about the old Johnny Carson show? Or Dick Van Dyke? Once again, I just can't do it! Favorite movies? Favorite actresses or actors? Favorite month? Favorite vacation destination? Favorite outdoor activities. Running? Biking? Swimming? Hiking? Canoeing? Fishing?

So, if there is a moral to the story I guess it would be this: Life is absolutely loaded with wonderful things. Be full of gratitude for all of them.

Remember in the movie "Elf" when the manager of the toy department tells Buddy the Elf (played with parallel universe brilliance by Will Ferrell) to make "work" his new favorite? Buddy has just told him that smiling is his favorite...

Just picture his face when he says that line, "Smiling's my favorite."

Well, enough rambling for now. I hope today is your favorite day of your entire life. If it isn't, can you remember the one which *was*? If you can, write it down here: ____________________________________________.

* * * * * * *

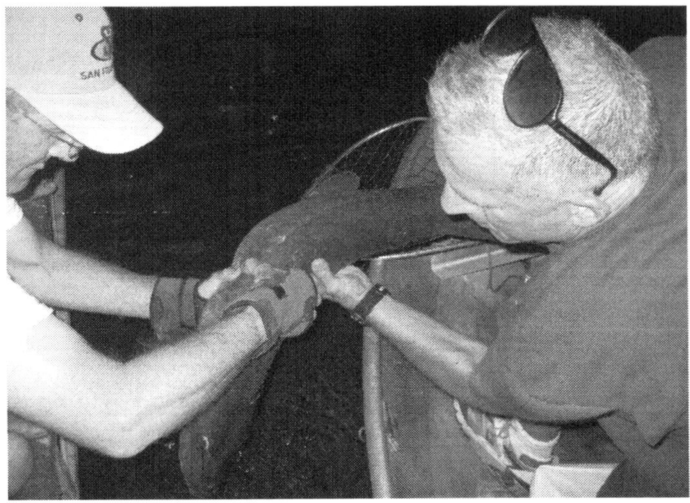

John Foelber and Mr. Smarty Boots enjoying life.

## "Extraordinary"

I once remember a boy in my class going up to the chalkboard and drawing what looked like it was going to be a smiley face on it. Large circle, two dots, but instead of giving the face a smile, he drew an absolutely straight line for the mouth. Beneath the figure he wrote the phrase, "Have an Ordinary Day." I remember how that phrase struck me. What do we mean by the term, "ordinary"?

Seeing the film, "The Passion of the Christ" recently made me think about the term "ordinary" in a variety of different ways. Certainly, torture and crucifixion were both ordinary events in the first Century A.D. No doubt, crowds in that city were used to seeing prisoners carrying their crosses out to that hill. Did you notice that a hole was dug, ready made in the rocky ground, so that the Cross would slide in and fit securely? That had certainly been used many times before Jesus was there. A large crowd followed for a form of cheap entertainment. The Romans who tortured Jesus were professionals. Remember the scene when the expert tells the neophytes to flip the cross over in order to gain access to the nails and secure them more thoroughly? This was a man who had plied his trade on numerous occasions. These were people who enjoyed seeing men suffer. It was an ordinary occurrence.

Things are only ordinary because other things are extraordinary. When we see clouds in the sky we often don't stop to point. Clouds are up there a lot. But, I remember one day when I was out at the Porter County Airport (some of us were working in one of the hangars) and we saw a double rainbow which stretched completely from horizon to horizon. We stopped and pointed and wished we had a camera because it was so special, so beautiful. And of course, none of us had a camera. That was an extraordinary event.

So, when Jesus is tortured and murdered there were

some extraordinary things to see. Remember the woman who stops in the street to help blot the blood off Christ's face? I wonder how many of you noticed something I did as the camera panned away from her? Did you see it?

Did you notice how the attitude of Simon of Cyrene changes as he helps Jesus to carry the Cross to the Place of the Skull? At first he is reluctant. Towards the end he seems to understand. He reassures Jesus that it is almost over. They are almost there. That transformation I found to be extraordinary. Remember the soldier who pierced Christ's side? As the blood and water flowed out of His body onto the soldier the posture of amazement which overtakes his entire being is nothing short of astounding. He realizes that whatever else has gone on today, the death of *this* Man, has been no ordinary thing.

The message for us? Two things Jesus said in the film I think pretty much sum up what we are supposed to do. They were, "Fear Not," and "Love one another as I have loved you." Short phrases. So easy to understand. So hard to do. I think it can only be accomplished if we accept some Extraordinary Help.

* * * * * * *

## "If we only have Love"

We were standing in the downstairs part of the Longbranch, one of the log cabin type buildings where kids stayed when visiting Hoofbeat Ridge Camp in Mazomanie, Wisconsin. I had a small tape recorder and there was a young lady with a guitar. Her first name was Mary and her last name was Meillier (I may be spelling that last name wrong – but, it was pronounced Mill - yay). This took place about 30 years ago. My memory may be fuzzy about exact names and dates. But, as far as what Mary did that morning, it is crystal clear.

The night before we'd heard Mary sing a song around the Hoofbeat Ridge Campfire. Now, lots of times the songs we sang at camp were funny, raucous, goofy, or sappy. I remember once on the bus heading to Devil's Lake to swim and hike, we offered up an improvisational version of the old Spiritual, "Amen"... That song, for those moments on the bus supplied one of the most transcendent experiences of my entire life on this planet.

I don't know why or how it happened, but ***every*** kid, and ***every*** counselor on that bus was singing with pure joy, at the top of his or her lungs. All hands were clapped in unbelievably vibrant unison, you know the four claps with the little hesitation in the middle, which come between the words "Amen"... Stop reading a minute and try it. It will come right back to you. Somebody in the bus would think up a phrase like, "Angels up in Heaven" – Then everybody else would chime in with 5 heartfelt "Amens". It went on and on. "Workin' in fields, now!" "Jesus standin' near us!" "Climbin' up to Heaven!" (I hope you have been singing those words – not just reading them).

At that moment, Blind Willie Johnson, Ray Charles, and Ella Fitzgerald had nothin' on us. It was as though God had said, "Okay, people you've got this gift for seven minutes. Let's hear what you do with it!" I don't think we let Him down.

Now, Hoofbeat Ridge was a horse riding camp, not a religious one. But, you would never know it from the spirit that was flowing around the bus during that song. When the number was over, everybody burst into spontaneous applause, then everybody laughed, then everybody got quiet for a moment and stopped to look at each other, like "Wow! What was that?" I have never forgotten the singing of that song or the pure sense of joy that washed over the people on that bus while it was being sung. I have never again tried to sing that song with other people. Ever.

In any case, back to Mary and her guitar in the basement of the Longbranch. The night before she'd been performing a number at the Campfire entitled, "If we only have Love". I had never heard this song before. Here are the lyrics in case you've never heard it either (they are by Jacques Brel):

If we only have love
Then tomorrow will dawn
And the days of our years
Will rise on that morn
If we only have love
To embrace without fears
We will kiss with our eyes
We will sleep without tears
If we only have love
With our arms open wide
Then the young and the old
Will stand at our side
If we only have love
Love that's falling like rain
Then the parched desert earth
Will grow green again
If we only have love
For the hymn that we shout
For the song that we sing
Then we'll have a way out
If we only have love
We can reach those in pain
We can heal all our wounds

We can use our own names
If we only have love
We can melt all the guns
And then give the new world
To our daughters and sons
If we only have love
Then Jerusalem stands
And then death has no shadow
There are no foreign lands
If we only have love
We will never bow down
We'll be tall as the pines
Neither heroes nor clowns
If we only have love
Then we'll only be men
And we'll drink from the Grail
To be born once again
Then with nothing at all
But the little we are
We'll have conquered all time
All space, the sun, and the stars.

Mary was a college age girl, with short, light hair and if I remember correctly a few freckles. She was pretty too. She sang in a beautiful soprano voice which I can only describe as belonging to an angel. When she sang the phrase, "And we'll drink from the Grail, to be born once again," I felt every inch of skin along the length of my spine tingling as though an electrical current had been inserted into the C5 vertebrae. When she'd finished singing the song at the campfire it was another one of those moments when everybody seemed to look around and think, "Well, ***that*** was the most beautiful set of sounds I have ever heard or will ever hear in my entire life."

After the campfire, I asked her if she'd mind recording the song. She looked at me kind of funny and said, "Why?" I told her it was the greatest thing I had ever heard in my life and I just wanted to have a copy of it. So the next morning, there we were standing in the basement of the Longbranch. I pushed the red button marked "Record" and Mary started strumming her guitar and singing that soul stirring number again. This version was even better than the one at the campfire. I sat there wondering how she could summon up so much emotion, so much grace, and so much love in a merely human voice. When she was finished I asked her what she was going to do when she finished college. I was thinking that she could be the next Joni Mitchell, traveling around the world and performing before sold out, adoring audiences. She said, "You know, I'm thinking about becoming a nun."

After I let the world finish completely flipping over I looked at Mary again and saw her for the first time the way I was supposed to have been seeing her all Summer. I don't know much about nuns, and I don't know if Mary M. became a nun or not. But, if she did become a nun, I hope she kept playing that song for the people she worked with for God. And if she didn't become a nun, I hope she had kids and I hope she sings that song to them from time to time. Either way, how could she lose?

I had that cassette tape for several years. Sometimes, driving around in my old beat up car I would play it. The best time to play it was around Christmas time. Mary's startlingly clear voice and her smooth and balanced guitar notes would come soaring out of the speakers. I'd look out the window and see snow covering the bleak Northwest Indiana countryside. Whenever I heard those words I would think about what we are supposed to be striving for in this world, and how we have come up short so many times. If the phrase "heartbreakingly beautiful" means anything at all to you, you would have loved that song too.

Then, one day I lost the tape. Now, if I lose my copy of "Louie Louie", or "Moondance", or "Little Martha" or any other song I love, I merely hop on I-Tunes and pay a dollar to download it again. But, I cannot do that with Mary M's rendition of, "If we only have Love". Memory will have to suffice. I wish I still had that tape, and I wish everybody reading this could have heard Mary sing that song too. What a gift! "And we'll drink from the Grail, to be born once again." Amen.

* * * * * * *

## "Clouds" *

In the late 1970's a friend of mine named Craig hopped on his motorcycle in the garage of his parents' Schererville home. He rode out onto the ever dangerous Route 30, had a horrific encounter with a semi-truck, and ended up never coming home again. I had only known Craig for about a year. We drove the "Hyster" high lift machines which traveled up and down the Wickes Furniture warehouse aisles in order to retrieve green Crestline plaid sofas, Bassett Coffee Tables, and Sealy Posture-pedic mattresses for the Northwest Indiana customers who filled our store. The Chief (this was Craig's nickname) was a big and burly guy. He had a full beard (we were in our late teens or early twenties) and a very full head of fuzzy hair which kind of looked like an "afro". I remember that he owned a dark green Dodge Charger which was his pride and joy. He laughed easily. He wore slightly tinted glasses. He was cool. Everybody in the warehouse admired the Chief greatly.

One night, we stopped over at the Chief's house after work. He lived with his parents. His brother was showing us all their shotgun which they used for hunting. He playfully pointed it right at my face and said, "Boom!" I kind of put my hand on the side of the barrel and gently moved it away from my face. I don't know too much about guns, but I knew enough to know that I didn't want to be staring at the "business end" of one of them.

The Chief shouted at his brother, "Hey, dummy! Don't ever a point a gun at somebody's face!"

His brother replied indignantly, "What do you think, I'm an idiot or something. The thing's not loaded."

The Chief was still livid. "It doesn't matter," he replied with spirit. "You just never point a gun at anybody!" He snatched the shotgun away from his brother and maneuvered the mechanism so that the gun "opened up". There, sitting in the right hand barrel, was a shiny red shotgun shell. Everybody in the room got deathly quiet.

I suppose we were all thinking about the previous thirty seconds and how they could have ended up ruining any number of people's lives (many of whom weren't even in that room). I'm guessing the Chief's brother (whose name escapes me) never pointed a gun playfully at anybody's head again. At least, I fervently hope so.

Anyway, shortly after that night the Chief died in the horrific motorcycle accident. One summer day, in the wake of that tragedy, I was driving down Route 30 myself. It was a beautiful evening, pretty close to sunset time. The sky was filled with huge, white, and incredibly beautiful clouds. I was heading west, seemingly straight into that ethereal panorama. It was the kind of sky which reminded one of Heaven, no doubt about it. There were huge shafts of light, coming down at an angle toward the Earth. The contrast between the clouds and the rest of the sky was so vivid that it appeared to be supernatural. Suddenly, close to the horizon I was startled to see a cloud which exactly replicated the profile of my friend, Craig, the Chief. His nose, an unmistakable round button nose, was there. His bushy beard protruded from the chin. The afro hair-do was there as well. It was so unexpected, and so startlingly life-like that I almost had to pull off onto the shoulder to collect myself. You could even see the outline of his tinted glasses. I couldn't help but think that the Chief was up there and he had asked God (or at least an Angel pretty high up the totem pole) if it was okay to send his friends down on Earth a message, letting them all know that he was fine and abiding in his Permanent Home.

Last week right here at the Kiwanis meeting, Dale Sonney, Reverend Jim, and I were discussing clouds. We talked about the famous "Peanuts" episode where Charlie Brown and two friends are explaining what pictures they can see in the clouds. Here is a little excerpt taken from "A Boy named Charlie Brown":

**Lucy Van Pelt**: Aren't the clouds beautiful? They look like big balls of cotton. I could just lie here all day and watch them drift by. If you use your imagination, you can see lots of things in the cloud's formations. What do you think you see, Linus?
**Linus Van Pelt**: Well, those clouds up there look to me look like the map of the British Honduras on the Caribbean.
[*points up*]
**Linus Van Pelt**: That cloud up there looks a little like the profile of Thomas Eakins, the famous painter and sculptor. And that group of clouds over there...
[*points*]
**Linus Van Pelt**: ...gives me the impression of the Stoning of Stephen. I can see the Apostle Paul standing there to one side.
**Lucy Van Pelt**: Uh huh. That's very good. What do you see in the clouds, Charlie Brown?
**Charlie Brown**: Well... I was going to say I saw a duckie and a horsie, but I changed my mind.

I love that emotion revealed by Charlie Brown, because I've felt it a thousand times when talking to people more intelligent or perceptive than myself. It also reminded me of lazy summer days in Munster when we did lie in the grass at 1535 Melbrook Drive, and we did stare up at the clouds to see what they looked like to us. Dale mentioned that his daughter was chastising him one day for not being able to think outside of the box and see pictures in the clouds.

I thought about the beautiful song by Joni Mitchell entitled, "Both Sides Now". One day I was in Chicago at the Borders book store killing time while my wife shopped in another store. When I got to the top floor there was a fairly large crowd of people sitting in chairs waiting for a guest speaker to arrive. That speaker was Judy Collins, who had performed a beautiful rendition of that song. When they introduced her she greeted the crowd and immediately

said, "Let me just take care of this right away."
Then, with no accompaniment whatsoever she sang,

***"Rows and floes of angel hair,***
***And ice cream castles in the air.***
***And feather canyons everywhere,***
***I've looked at clouds that way.***

***But now they only block the sun,***
***They rain and snow on everyone.***
***So many things I would have done,***
***But clouds got in my way.***

***I've looked at clouds from both sides now,***
***From up and down and still somehow,***
***It's cloud illusions I recall,***
***I really don't know clouds at all."***

Her voice was surreally beautiful. I was standing over in the "Blues" section of the CD department and she glanced in that direction (probably because the rest of her audience was politely seated in folding chairs and I was gawking at her like Eb from "Green Acres"). I thought, "Hey, that's Judy Collins. Millions of people around the world know her name. She is one of the most accomplished singers of her generation. And I'm just in here seeing her by accident."

Then, I thought about the lyrics of that song. At first, clouds represent angel hair and ice cream castles, and feathered canyons. When we're children, that is perhaps what we're more likely to see. As the singer continues, the other side of clouds gets revealed. They're raining on people. They're snowing on people. They ruin plans. They change outlooks. This of course, is bound to happen in the long run of our lives, but I think that it is important to keep the spirit of youth, and adventure, and optimism in the forefront of our minds as often as we can. It is something about having "The spirit of a little child..."

I remember another time, when I found myself hitch-hiking down Route 30 to get into work at Wickes. I think the old Pontiac Star Chief Executive had a flat tire or needed a new starter. In any event, I had to get to work. As I made my way down the highway, the sky grew ominously dark. The weather forecast had been for rain, so I was wearing my green rain poncho. During that time I was reading (for the first of many times in my life) Tolkien's classic, <u>The Lord of the Rings.</u>

As the sky changed to black, as lightning and thunder pounded the planet, the wind began to howl, and the sunset clouds became a tattered mass of ragged red and black cotton wool, I realized two things. It was dangerous to be outside at this particular moment. And, it was also an adventure to be outside. I thought about Gandalf, and Frodo, and Aragorn, and the rest of that Fellowship as they walked through the various dangers of Middle Earth. I thought about the cloaks that the elves of Lothlorien had given them. It seemed to me that my green poncho was exactly such a cloak (only green, not grey). I'm not too grown up to admit that I often pretend to be characters from the books I read. It was that day, and has been on many other days, an extraordinarily enjoyable way to pass the time.

So, bring on the clouds, and the thunder, and the rain. And bring on the ice cream castles. And bring on the wisdom to show us that all of it is leading down that highway, at the end of which waits the profile of the Chief, and a million other happy things we can only begin to imagine.

* Thanks to Mr. Dale Sonney, who suggested the topic of this article.

* * * * * * *

## "Muhammad Ali and the Scissors"

It was early January in 1980. I was sitting at one of the gates at O'Hare International Airport back in the days when you could wait for passengers to arrive and meet them right when they got off the plane. It was cold outside and it was dark. I was sitting in a black fake leather chair watching a kid play with a Matchbox car. I'm guessing that he was about 7 or 8 years old. He was rolling the car back and forth on a little piece of furniture. I'd like to be able to tell you that it was a metallic green 1971 Pontiac GTO with racing stripes and mag wheels, but my memory is not that good. I was waiting for a beautiful young nursing student to return to Valparaiso after visiting her family for Christmas. She was flying in from Long Beach, California.

Suddenly, the kid with the Matchbox car spoke to me. It was kind of a surprise because I had been watching him surreptitiously. He said, "Hey Mister. Look over there in the corner. That's Muhammad Ali." My immediate response was, "Yeah, right." I can't remember if I said that out loud or not, but I certainly thought it. But, then I looked up and sure enough, standing in the corner of the gate area, gazing out the window was indeed, "The Greatest".

He is a fairly big guy, but standing with him were two other men who actually made him look a little bit small. These guys were huge, I'm thinking maybe 6'7" or even 6'9". Now, there is no immediate explanation why the word, "Bodyguards" jumped into my mind when I saw these guys rather than the word, "Friends". Perhaps their long camel hair coats, dark glasses (even though it was night time) and imposing demeanors had something to do with it. But I distinctly remember wondering why the baddest dude on the planet (and at that time he was not yet quite done with fighting) would need bodyguards.

I was maybe twenty feet away from him. Inadvertently, I blurted out the word, "Champ!" Now, as I say he had been staring out the window and except for the little kid who had pointed him out to me, it seemed like nobody else in the gate area was aware of his presence. He turned straight toward me, lifted his index finger to his lips, slowly shook his head back and forth, and "shushed" me with a twinkle in his eye. I've read a few biographies about ultra famous people. The ones that come to mind right now were about Elvis Presley and Michael Jordan. Until I'd read these books I had not understood what the phrase, "Prisoner of Fame" really meant. When you read tales of how these two men were unable to eat a meal in restaurant, walk through a store and shop, or simply stroll down the street and enjoy the day, it makes a person happy to be one's regular, un-famous self.

Immediately, I felt guilty because he had obviously been attempting to maintain his anonymity. As soon as my wide trap had spilled the beans other folks in the vicinity picked up on the fact that they were in the presence of one of the most celebrated people on the planet. Immediately, a throng approached him like honey bees approach a hive. He didn't want to talk but he had a big smile on his face.

Here is the part of the adventure which surprised me the most. He reached into his pockets, took out some items, and started doing magic tricks. He did one trick with silk handkerchiefs. He did another one with some cards. But, the trick I remember most was the one he did with a length of rope. He took a piece of rope out of his pocket. It was probably about two feet long. Then, he produced a pair of scissors. He took the scissors and cut the rope into two equal halves. After that he rolled up both pieces in a ball and then, Voila! He whipped the rope up into the air and suddenly it had become merely one piece of rope again. It was a really good trick and to this very day I have no idea how he did it.

After each trick, the crowd would applaud. The bodyguards stood glowering at the growing mob, making sure nobody came too close to Mr. Ali. I noticed that the entire time he was performing, nobody spoke. He never spoke. He seemed to have cast a little spell over the crowd which said, “Entertainer at work. Please do not disturb.” And nobody did disturb him. I thought back to times I had seen this gentleman pummeling other human beings into submission on television. It was hard to grasp that this was the same person...He put the scissors back into his pocket.

Suddenly, I heard some noise over my shoulder. People were getting off the plane. That lovely young nursing student had arrived from California. What might have been a boring stretch of time waiting for her was turned into something very memorable by one of the greatest boxers in history. Apparently, Mr. Ali had also been waiting for someone on the same plane. The crowd kind of broke up as people went back to their everyday lives. I told the nursing student what had happened while I had been waiting for her. We glanced around to see if the Champ was still present, but he had disappeared with his party, and his two huge bodyguards into the Chicago night.

◇

Thinking about this story almost thirty years later I recalled something I had read about scissors which had been written by C.S. Lewis. Someone had asked the brilliant author and lecturer if faith or good works was more important to someone attempting to live the Christian life. I found his reply to be most interesting. He said, “That is like asking which blade of scissors is more important when cutting a piece of paper, the top or the bottom blade?” The easily discernible point is that both blades are essential. Therefore, a person attempting to live out his or her religious convictions cannot ignore one blade of the scissors or the type of life being attempted won’t work.

I thought about Muhammad Ali, and the interesting path which his life has followed. Then, I thought about the beautiful young nursing student, who turned out to be my wife for these many years. And finally I thought about C.S. Lewis sitting at his desk in England, writing about how faith and good works can be compared to a pair of scissors. It occurred to me that the whole episode had started with that little kid and the (possibly) metallic green 1971 GTO Matchbox car. That little kid who told me where to look to see something amazing.

So let's see, scissors, a little kid with a favorite toy, a beautiful woman, the Heavyweight Champion of the World, magic tricks, and the cold, and bold, and beautiful city of Chicago on a clear and frosty winter night. There we were all were, with large metallic birds full of people, swooping down onto the runways, delivering them to other people who loved them. I can never understand it when I meet people who try to tell me that there is no wonder left in this world. I guess it has something to do with having faith "like a little child".

* * * * * * *

## "Expert Child Care in the 1960's"

The Old Man walked into the backyard and handed my brother a box. Tom was a couple of years older than me and so I guess that put him "in charge". The box was shaped like a rectangular prism, probably about 7 or 8 inches high and 4 or 5 inches wide in either horizontal direction. The box was white and fairly heavy, but not unusually so. The Old Man did not (to the best of my recollection) say anything beyond "Here you go." He just handed us the box in that backyard at 1535 Melbrook Drive (did you notice that the address rhymed?) and walked up the concrete porch stairs into the kitchen. Green mint leaves grew outside along the back of our home. I remember the fragrance of them as the Old Man retreated from view.

I'd like the reader to guess what was in the box. We'll make it a multiple choice question:

A. Several packages of Topps Baseball cards.
B. Donuts from the famous Schweitzer Bakery on Kennedy Ave.
C. Dozens of dangerous M-80's (a highly explosive device).
D. A wonderful box of chocolate coated Malted Milk Balls.

Now, at some time or other my Dad did procure items A, B, and D for us. And let me assure you, those things did provide an unbelievable amount of pleasure. But, on this day and many other days I can recall the Old Man really did hand us a box of highly dangerous explosives, capable of blinding us, blowing off our hands, seriously scarring our fat little Greek faces, or if we had been extremely careless, taking our lives. I have no idea where he procured these dangerous treasures. The Old Man was seriously involved in the barter system, but the spoils we were usually most concerned with were the box seat tickets to White Sox games periodically provided by the legendary Nick Angel.

We were pretty young kids at the time, certainly not old enough to drive, probably still in Little League.

Our job then became clear: Get matches and blow 'em up. When we excitedly lit the dark green fuse and threw an M-80 down onto the grass it would explode with a deafening boom and leave a smoking divot the size of a pie plate on the ground. Sometimes, we would grab a big metal garbage can, fill it 3 quarters of the way up with water, and toss the bombs into the cans. M-80's had water proof fuses. The submarine explosion had a completely different timbre than one out in the open air. I guess I would describe it as a "***Ka-Schploom"!!*** A cylindrical plume of water would rise up out of the can in an elegant and profound fashion. Sometimes we would put little plastic model ships in the water and have our own private version of the sinking of the Bismarck.

Years later, when I read the awe inspiring Arthur C. Clarke science fiction classic, Rendezvous with Rama the cylindrical shape of the M-80 bombs would come back to me in my dreams. On some occasions, the Old Man would spring for "Cherry Bombs" rather than M - 80's. They too were powerful explosives. They were round, bright red (just like cherries), and had the same rigid little fuse protruding from the interior. We loved them equally. Working as I do with 9 and 10 year old children each day, I remain bewildered that he thought these were appropriate playthings for young boys.

Once, I remember taking some M-80's with a boy named Rodney Clark (I think Terry Lavery may have been on hand as well) and traveling over to the vicinity of Munster High. Rodney had a highly sophisticated slingshot device known as a "Wrist Rocket". He said, "Watch this."

He took a bomb, put it in the "cradle" part of the slingshot and pulled the surgical tubing all the way back. For some reason,

Rodney knew when a Cop Car was scheduled to drive down Columbia Avenue the same way other boys knew what time "Gilligan's Island" was going to be on TV. Sure enough after waiting less than a minute, the car came into view. He ordered me to light the fuse. I did so. He shot that M- 80 so far into the air, I could barely believe it. It traveled in a long lazy arc through the azure Munster, Indiana sky until it was about 75 feet above the cruiser. When it exploded the sound was unbelievable. The dizzying, reverberating "KABOOM" echoed off the exterior walls of Munster High and momentarily shattered the calm of that peaceful residential neighborhood.

I was actually afraid that the bomb was going to drop all the way down onto the car before it went off. But, like the bombs our country dropped on Hiroshima and Nagasaki, it detonated in the sky. The Cop stopped, got out of his car, and scanned all points of the compass for the culprits. Rodney however, knew his business, having been trained by his older brother, Dave. If you are old enough to remember the "Dave Clark 5", I can assure you that the song "Bits and Pieces" came into my mind as I thought about writing this tale. Also, the two Daves were not related…

In any event, we were close to the chain link fence behind the football field and another large open field separated us from the Cop. Long before he thought about coming after us on foot, Rodney had scrambled up over that fence, dropped to the other side, and melted into the tree filled neighborhood which waited as sanctuary to the East. Lave and I followed suit. Pursuit from the Cop was half-hearted and that was the one and only time I was involved in such a stunt.

I have in subsequent years pondered my Old Man's repeated purchase of those bombs and the nonchalant way in which he handed them over to us. Then the thought occurs to me, "Where was my Mom?" Did they think that the danger from such playthings was minimal? Were they hoping that we would grow up and become Navy Seal demolition experts? My Mom's Brother-

In-Law was an Insurance Agent… Had they secretly taken out a huge policy on both of us? As a teacher, I often shake my head at questionable choices I see adults making on behalf of their kids… ("Oh, you watched which "Slasher" film with your First Grader? How nice, did you have popcorn?"). How would I have reacted to my own parents' strategy of giving kids who spilled their milk at least once a week, a box full of bombs which (if you dropped a lit match into it) was capable of blowing up the entire backyard?

In their defense, it was a different time. Kids in those days would stand up in the backseat of the family Rambler as it rolled down the highway. Bike helmets? I not only never saw one, we'd never ***heard*** of such a thing. When I was born my Mom bragged about the fact that she took me straight from the hospital to the family drycleaners, where she smoked cigarette after cigarette with me cradled in her arms. When tobacco smoke was not filling my lungs, it was sure to be the dangerous chemical cleaning agent, Percoethylene. Even if we took a walk down the East Chicago street outside, the thick brown air from the local steel mills would be there filling up everybody's lungs, even if the tobacco smoke or dry cleaning chemical was not.

Yet, here I sit 54 years later…(I've never smoked cigarettes, and most of my clothes are "Wash and Wear"). So, I still don't know what they were thinking. Whenever I count my fingers, the total is still 10. When our kids were growing up, Tracker the Wonder Dog was mortally afraid of detonations, so we did what we could to avoid loud sounds during the 4th of July. But, I can still smell that mint. And I can still see the Old Man handing us that box. And I can still see that bomb floating through the sky, descending toward that cop car… KABOOM!!

* * * * * * *

## "Tracker the Wonder Dog"

We pulled out of the long driveway of "Golden Arrow Kennels" and I glanced over at my wife, Liz. Five year old Nick was strapped into the backseat and the baby Natalie was likewise secured in her car seat next to him. Everybody was excited because we were brining home a new member of the family. Tracker was a Golden Retriever, one of 8 puppies in the litter. His mother was named Daisy Mae, and his dad had some high falutin' name which escapes me more than two decades later. Supposedly, this father had "champion bloodlines". I wish I could remember that name now, but of course the harder I try to think of it, the more it escapes me. As soon as I head to the fridge for a glass of cranberry juice and forget thinking about it, it will probably come right to me. Maybe it was something like "Arbuthnot of Crippendale". It still isn't coming to me.

Tracker was a splendid family pet, from the very first moment he came into our lives. We read a book by a woman named Barbara Woodhouse called **No Bad Dogs** before we picked Tracker up and we pretty much did everything she said to do in regard to raising a dog. We crate trained old Tracker. At first I thought that it was confining and cruel to have a puppy sleep in the crate. However, Barbara explained that the crate actually mimicked the ancient dens wolves and other wild canines were used to. Indeed, the security of the crate had a calming effect on the little guy. And when we were ***right there*** he was perfectly happy to lie inside and look at us through the grate happily wagging his tail.

However, on the first night when everyone was going to bed and Tracker was put into his "den", he started whining. The book told us to take a Dixie cup ½ full of water and immediately toss it into his face when this whining started. I thought it was a little bit mean, but this Barbara person had trained and worked with thousands of dogs, so I did what you're supposed to do, I deferred to the expert. Don't you know, he IMMEDIATELY stopped whining and went to bed next to the socks we had stuffed with a ticking alarm clock inside the den.

It is hard for me to describe the kind of joy Tracker brought into our lives. After he got past the crate stage of training, he had a wonderful way of greeting me each morning. He would trot upstairs to our bedroom and stick his cold, wet nose right into my sleeping eye. If my face was buried into the pillow and an eye unavailable, my ear would do. Then, he would wait until I rolled over and grabbed his floppy ears. "Good morning, Trackie! You're my best friend!"

One of the things that dog loved to do was go for a run. If he saw me reaching for his green leash, he would immediately start the "Tornado Dance" (I'll let your imagination paint that picture for you). If things or people were in the way, too bad for them. Tracker topped 100 pounds and once his big body got moving, few forces of nature were able to resist it. I actually taught him how to spell. If I was sitting in a recliner and said, "Tracker, how would you like to go R-U-N-N-I-N-G?" - he would go instantly nutty. If I spelled a different word like "Painting" or "Bird Watching" there was no response. But, as soon as he heard those letters "R-U-N...", it was (literally) off to the races.

One bright and freezing winter day when we were living in a house on the shore of Flint Lake we took Tracker outside and hooked him up to a wooden sled. This was a sled with a curved back which could accommodate a little kid like Natalie. She was bundled up in a big blue snowsuit. Liz held onto Tracker after we got Natalie situated in the sled and I ran across the frozen top of Flint Lake until I was hundreds of yards away. Then, I removed my gloves and did the echoing "Hand Whistle" which I can demonstrate for you any time you wish. Tracker took off like a streak of golden lightning across the frozen surface of Flint Lake. Liz tried to keep up running along behind him, but that was an effort in futility. That dog had wheels. Suddenly, the sled hit a little ripple of ice and went soaring up into the air, Natalie flew out and went tumbling over and over onto the snow and ice. Liz and I ran toward her fearing the worst. Tracker swung around and sprinted in her direction as well, dragging the upended sled behind him. When we both got there she was lying on her back in her big blue snowsuit, Tracker was licking her face and we thought she was crying hysterically. Actually, she was *laughing* hysterically.

There are probably a thousand more stories I could tell you about Tracker. There was that time he brought home a muskrat that I think he thought we might like to throw on the grill for dinner. There was the time our friend Paul Diaz was taking care of him for us and he absolutely refused to go outside with Paul under any circumstances. Paul ended up carrying that big old hound dog out into the yard every time they had to go outside (it is a good thing that Paul is a strong and burly dude). One Christmas Tracker chewed up a little fuzzy "Honey Bear" ornament we had on our tree. We've still got that ornament and each time I hang it on the tree, I think about that beautiful, loyal, happy, friendly dog that God blessed us with for 13 memorable years.

I think God gives us pets for lots of reasons. They give joy and happiness. They make us responsible for a living creature's health and well being. I believe there is a mystical connection between the world of animals and the world of humans that we'll not fully understand until we cross over that very last bridge. I hope when that day comes that I'll see my dad, and my friend from Wickes, "The Chief" who died in that horrible motorcycle accident so long ago, and I hope to see a large and happy golden canine bounding up to me with his tongue hanging out and his ears sailing back in the wind because of the speed at which he's running. When I see him, I'll kneel down and close my eye, so he's got someplace to stick that wet, cold, and leathery nose. Tracker the Wonder Dog; just one more great and glorious and gift from God! Oh, how many of those there are!

* * * * * * *

## "Unbridled Joy"

One day Walter Payton died,
And Michael went away.
The men who once inspired us,
No longer came to play.
And Baseball? Well, the Yankees win,
Or else some brand new team.
In this town baseball is the surest way to kill a Dream.

The Northside had a Billy Goat,
Black Cat, a guy named Steve.
Some people thought these were the reasons,
They did not achieve.
You think about Jack Brickhouse,
Billy, Ron, and Ernie too.
You know these fellows always did,
The best that they could do.

When was it? 1959?
And that was measured joy.
You know that was so long ago,
Mayor Daley was a boy.
Ah, Luis Aparicio, the music of that name!
Would there ever be a shortstop,
Who could make us feel the same?

So really, 1917, that's how far back it stretched.
To folks who live in other towns,
That must sound so far fetched!
Except perhaps in Boston,
Where the Carmines shared that fate,
Until they showed the baseball world,
That others could be great.

When Shoeless Joe and his pals,
Won so very long ago,

I think it didn't cross their minds,
There's no way they could know...
That two World Wars would come and go,
And we'd land on the Moon,
And radio, jet planes, and television would come soon.

That all those things would come to pass,
Before we'd cheer anew,
My father lived past eighty years,
And died 'fore it came true.

So people in the streets today,
They cheered, and hugged, and cried.
Because the Sox this season,
Were a team no one denied.

Four pitchers with an Iron Will,
Were steadfast on that mound.
Jose and Jon, with Mark and Freddy,
Always stood their ground.

The men who roamed the Bullpen,
Had ice water in their veins,
And Cora watched the third baseline,
The other side had Raines.

Crede, Juan, and Tadahito
Always passed the test.
Paulie smashed that Grand slam in Game 2,
That was the best!

And what about Podsednik?
How he stood there in the rain,
And launched a ball into the seats,
Which took away our pain.

Remember that Geoff Blum?
You know you couldn't write that story,
The dad of triplets, 14th inning, helps cement the glory.
And A.J. on that dropped third strike,
He kept presence of mind,
Then Crede drove him in so we no longer were behind!

Jermaine was voted MVP, he hit in every game,
The RBI in Game 4 was the final key to fame.
And Rowand's glove, and Crede's dives,
Konerko's digs in dirt,
The leather Juan flashed in the 9th,
Made all of Texas hurt.

These guys just played baseball,
That's all they really did,
It made me think of Willie Mays,
Back when I was a kid.
I used to watch Brooks Robinson,
And marvel at his style,
The new White Sox who won this crown,
Bring back that childhood smile.

Jerry Reinsdorf showed some class,
He sent 8 busses in,
That helped to cleanse the city,
Of that ancient Black Sox sin.

And Kenny Williams built the team,
With Ozzie by his side,
Together, those guys had a plan,
To bring back baseball pride.

Ozzie, Ozzie Guillen,
What can anybody say?

He kept 'em loose, he took the heat,
So they could just go play.

He made the calls, the calls were right,
He made our dreams come true,
He proved to all those "experts"
That he knows more than they do.

So now we have 'Unbridled Joy',
And that sensation's real,
It's taken 88 years, but now,
That's the thing we feel.

Say it, say it slowly,
"**White Sox, Champions of the World**."
And watch as that great banner,
Comes to town and gets unfurled.

And cheer as that bright trophy,
With those pennants in a ring,
Comes back here to Chicago,
So that all around might sing.

And Thank the Lord Almighty,
That this day has come at last,
That Ozzie and his White Sox slew the burden of the past.

***This poem is posted on the Baseball Almanac Website***
***http://www.baseball-almanac.com/teams/wsox.shtml***

* * * * * * *

## "Mother, Did you Know?"

Once, a friend contacted me and explained that she had been chosen to make a church presentation based on the beautiful Christmas Hymn, "Mary, did you know?" Those of you who have heard it are aware of what a poignant and beautiful song that is. If you have never heard it, it would certainly be worth your while to seek out a rendition of it somewhere. Our family has a version of it by Christopher Parkening and Kathleen Battle. It appears on the CD entitled, "Angel's Glory".

My friend's assignment was to slightly alter the lyrics, so that they reflected thoughts concerning an everyday Mom (as opposed to the Mother of the Son of God). She wondered if I could lend a hand to this project. The poem below is what I came up with. It is dedicated to every Mom, Dad, Son, or Daughter in our club. Happy New Year and God Bless you all!

***"Mother, did you Know?"***

***Mother, did you know,***
***That babe you bore, would one day leave your side?***
***Did you understand, the speed at which,***
***We take life's magic ride?***

***Did you know, that tiny babe,***
***Would soon be tall as you?***
***Did you know, that little child,***
***Would do the things you do?***

***Mother, have you seen those tiny shoes,***
***Packed in a box somewhere?***
***Have you saved, the little toys,***
***They once kept with such care?***

***Mother have you prayed,***
***That they'd be safe, out in the World so cold?***

*Have you cried, when they were late?*
*It made you feel so old.*

*Lord Above we seek,*
*Your Wisdom now, In all we do each hour.*
*Lord Above we pray, that you send Peace,*
*Down with your Awesome Power.*

*Keep us in Your Heart, Please watch us Lord,*
*We all belong to You.*
*Lord we need Your Love, The Only Love,*
*That truly sees us through...*

*Mother, can you say,*
*Your life's been full, for you have given birth?*
*Can you Praise Our God,*
*For all His Gifts, The Light, the Joy, The Earth!*
*Oh Mother did you know?*

* * * * * * *

## "The Difference Makers"

Imagine walking into a room and seeing a person whose heart has stopped beating lying on a bed. Instead of shifting into panic mode (as I know I would do), you quickly and calmly summon your colleagues. Equipment is rolled into place, procedures are followed, and then sometimes (I think with the Grace of the Almighty) the person is revived. Had you done nothing, death would have taken center stage. Sometimes, because it is time, it does. But, at times your efforts give that person another five birthdays, a chance to live to see a grandchild come into the world, or just the opportunity to see a beautiful sunset on a lovely winter evening.

A while ago I wrote this poem for my wife, Liz. For close to 30 years she has worked as a cardiac nurse at Porter Hospital. I stand in awe of the work she and her colleagues do each day.

If you know a nurse, or if one has ever helped you or one of your family members, you might want to show them this poem (I was fortunate enough to be able to read it aloud at the Porter Associate Awards banquet).

### "The Difference Makers"

Glance into a patient's eyes,
See some fear or sadness there.
Look into that patient's eyes,
Then you've shown them that you care.

Brush against a patient's hand,
Take a sample, read a chart.
Firmly grasp that patient's hand,
Now, you've touched a soul and heart.

Hear a patient say some words
While you're busy, rushing by.

Stop and listen to those words,
Then, you'll learn the reasons why.
Nurses do these things each day,
For ten or twenty, thirty years.
Wisdom, skill, compassion, smiles,
Guide our patients through their fears

People come to them in trouble,
Every hour, day and night.
Nurses stand through all the dark times,
They are always there to fight.

For this work we honor you,
And your devotion to the cause.
You have made us want to stand,
And give you all a loud applause.

*(Dedicated to Liz Karas)*

* * * * * * *

## "Mr. Lucas, The Crossing Guard"

For many years there was an ancient gentleman who stood on the corner of Roosevelt and Institute by our school (Parkview Elementary). He held a red sign with the unambiguous word STOP printed across it in stark white. His nose was very large, pitted and scarred so that you hardly knew it was a nose. It almost looked like a testing ground for miniature landmines. He looked like he might be kind of grumpy. I didn't really know him. He was our crossing guard, Mr. Lucas. Besides his advanced age he also walked with a pronounced limp. I actually wondered if he had a prosthetic limb because that limp was so bad.

In the mornings I used to drive by him and wave. He would hold up his sign and nod his head as if he was working on the most important job in the world. And really, when you think about it, what is more important than keeping our kids safe in dangerous traffic? I mean, is Donald Trump making a real estate deal in Downtown Manhattan more important to you than the man or woman who keeps your children or grandchildren safe on the way to school each day?

One day in the middle of a very cold winter Mr. Lucas fell down. Some of the kids helped him up. Others ran to the school and let our principal (Mr. Hollar) know what had happened. Like I said, he was pretty old, and it became apparent that he couldn't really stand out there and do that job in the cold and snow much longer.

So, when he retired the kids & staff invited him to school & we had a little party for him. They thanked him for his many years of devoted service. I penned a short poem for him and one of our teachers (Mrs. Highlan) read it to him at the party. Here it is:

***"The Crossing Guard"***

***Standing in the Rain and Cold,***
***A smile upon his face.***
***The Crossing Guard helps build a bridge***
***That leads to a Safe Place.***

***Biting Wind and Raging Snow,***
***And Skies of Steely Gray.***
***It didn't make a difference,***
***He would be there every day!***

***He'd help our children safely cross,***
***A small thing, you might say.***
***But, stop and think about how often***
***He has saved the day!***

***A skidding car, a speeding truck,***
***A kid who just didn't see.***
***Mr. Lucas kept them safe***
***From Traffic Tragedy!***

***Like an Ancient Knight in Armor,***
***With his Shield in the Air,***
***He patrolled the world for them,***
***So they would be safe there!***

***So thank you Mr. Lucas,***
***For all that you have done,***
***You've kept us safe, You'll always be***
***Crossing Guard Number ONE!***

God Bless You from the Students and Staff
of Parkview Elementary School

After she read the poem Mr. Lucas had tears in his eyes. He said, "Why, it seems like you know my life better than I know it myself." That was the nicest thing anybody had ever said to me about something I had written.

Mr. Lucas is retired now. Maybe this week you could say a little prayer for him, and for all the crossing guards who patrol the world to keep the most precious people in our land safe from the modern metallic dragons who could possibly do them harm.

* * * * * * *

## "Great Victory"

Odds stacked high against the father and his son,
Out in Oklahoma City as the clock is winding down.
Orange sphere resting in the baseball player's hands,
As the heart rates rise among the people in the stands.

Pump fakes once to get the defense in the air,
Pass is launched that has the feeling of a prayer.
Twin brother watches from the far end of the world,
Wonders if he has a chance to catch what's just been hurled

Leaps high to grab it as the clock begins to wind,
Familiar streak of gold is now approaching from behind.
For an instant only it remains within his grasp,
Then he tosses it behind him with the quickness of an asp.

Fate now guides the ball into the shooter's zone,
Back in the driveway he has practiced this alone.
Catch, step, gather, as the seconds disappear,
Shot now sails high into the stratosphere.

Arc travels downward, it is heading toward the rim,
All eyes everywhere, focused just on him.
Twine is fluttered as we hear the buzzer sound,
Mobbed by teammates as he falls unto the ground.

David slays Goliath and the Bible says it's true,
And Bryce has brought Great Victory to Valparaiso U.
Congratulations Valparaiso University Crusaders
NCAA Sweet Sixteen!

* * * * * * *

## "In That Place"

We saw this kid play football on some cold and frosty nights,
The things he did, well let's just say, one verb would be "***ignites***".
The way he ran, the hands he had, the moves that he laid down,
Ignites would be the verb, and so then ***"Star"*** must be the noun.

One time we saw a catch he made, he did it with one hand,
Our jaws fell down, we couldn't believe the power and command.
And that it came from one so young, we sat and rubbed our eyes,
"That's like a play the pros would make," we uttered in surprise.

Folks step inside, the ball turns round, the uniforms all change,
And you would think ***two*** gifts from God, might be a little strange.
The confidence with which he shot, or drove, or dogged his man,
The joy with which he played the game was all part of the plan.

He had no fear, that's what we saw each time he took the court,
He filled us all with hope each night he came to play his sport.
The greatest game we ever saw he won on the last shot,
That day in Mackey when he crossed the lane to find his spot.

Again, we're back outside, the sky is blue the grass is green,
The game of Willie Mays is where we'll watch another scene.
His talent drew the scouts to him, this kid was on the ball,
His bat, his speed, his glove, his arm... hey, this kid had it all.

And that's the sport he chose to follow with his soul and heart,
He joined the Mets and started down the path to chase his art.
For artfully was how he played - he said, "Baseball is life."
He strode the world in gladness, rose above the pain and strife.

Can one kid shine in all three sports, I mean throughout the state?
An All Star and an All State Man, oh wow, wouldn't that be great?
Well Tim did that and he did more, I wish you all had known,
He played each game in what the experts nowadays call, "The Zone".

And now he plays another game, in fields where we're not yet,
But someday we'll be there with him, (at least that's what I bet).
And I bet he'll have a ball with him, and a smile on his face,
It's going to be so cool to see Tim Bishop in That Place.

* * * * * * *

## "Ah, Baseball... Ah, Chicago!"

"I have more memories than if I were a thousand years old."

Charles Baudelaire

It is the summer of 1962. Kenny Hubbs, the promising 2nd baseman of the Chicago Cubs is still alive and on his way to being named National League Rookie of the Year. I am a chubby little suburban boy, seven years of age, with one older brother, one older sister, and a neighborhood full of pals on Melbrook Drive. When we are not out in the backyard playing whiffle ball, we're inside the house watching as Jack Brickhouse describes the Cubs (or White Sox) action on channel 9, WGN. One of the neighborhood guys, probably one of the Shapiro boys, asks one day if I know what "WGN" means. "It duzzen't mean nothin'," I reply with spirit. "That's just the 'nitials of their station. Every station gotta have a set of 'nitials, so they can put it in the TV Guide."

"No," he responds. "The 'nitials hafta mean somethin' too! My dad tol' me. WGN means ***World's Greatest Newspaper***, cause the Chicago Tribune owns that station and they think they're the world's greatest newspaper!"

Being seven years old causes me to stop and reflect on this arcane bit of knowledge. The moment doesn't linger for long. "Hey, lez play whiffle ball! Me and Richard 'gainst you and Jay. We're the Sox. I'm Aparicio. We got first bats. I called it."

So we charge outside and play for hours in the hot summer sunshine. We're in my backyard, which is the place we always play. If you hit the ball on *this* side of the Janke's garage roof, it is a triple. If the ball sails *over* the roof, it is a home run. If the ball gets stuck in the willow tree it is "Interference" and you do that particular play over. On a grounder it is "pitcher's hands" out because we only have two guys playing on each team. Right field is an "Automatic Out". In other areas our language skills are sloppy, but we pronounce "Interference" and "Automatic" impeccably. We keep track of the number of homers we hit all summer. We chew "Bazooka" bubble gum and spit out the juice like Nelson Fox would with his tobacco. We play when it rains. We slide into third base and then wear the grass stains on our dungarees like a Congressional Medal of Honor. We play all summer long and if Heaven is any better than this, than you're gonna have to prove it to me. After the game we hop on our Schwinn bikes and head down to "Mac and Ann's" for bottles of 10 cent pop (deposit included).

That night during dinner our mom tells us that (that is my brother Tom and me) that the next day our Uncle John wants to take us to a Cubs game at Wrigley Field. Tom is 10. We have an older sister named Toni who is 12, but she is not invited, and it is not until I sit down to write this that I actually wonder why. At the time I thought that being a female and almost a teenager would preclude her from having interest in any such event as a Major League Baseball game. Maybe that was true.

We have been to lots of baseball games with our old man. He owns a dry cleaning shop in Hessville, Indiana. It is called Royal Cleaners (I've often wondered if the Kings and Queens of England and France have a strong background in dry cleaning, or if they merely took it up as a hobby, like racing horses or collecting priceless art objects). In any event, one of his customers, Nick Angel (what a great name!), often gives him box seat tickets to White Sox games in exchange for free dry cleaning. That, we are told by the old man, is how the world works. We usually go to night games. And if we're lucky someone on the White Sox blasts a home run and the scoreboard erupts into a pyrotechnic display of unadulterated joy. And if we're really lucky, it is fireworks night *after* the game and we watch in rapture as deafening explosions pummel the South Side sky.

However, we've only visited Wrigley Field once. It was after we had to get rid of a family dog. Our dad took us to "The Friendly Confines" as a diversionary tactic. The dog's name was "Prince."

Uncle John shows up the next morning to take us on our second pilgrimage to the home of the North Siders. We live in Indiana, a suburban town called Munster, so he gets there bright and early. Tom and I pile into the big blue Oldsmobile. Uncle John is a bachelor, a smiling World War II hero who shakes your hand and then you notice that there is folded dollar bill in your palm when he lets go. As we cruise down the expressway into the city I spot a little device on his dashboard. I ask him what it is. He explains that it is an electric eye which automatically dims the bright lights when cars are approaching from the opposite direction. I wish out loud that it was night time so that I can view this little technological marvel in action. "Ah, but if it was night time," Uncle John responds in a sage like manner, "we wouldn't be going to a Cubs game, now would we?" (The Cubs did not get lights at Wrigley until 1988).

So this is my second sighting of Wrigley Field. The ivy is on the outfield walls, and Jack Brickhouse is up in the booth (we irreverently call him "Brickhead" and laugh ourselves silly at how brazen and witty we are). Out on the diamond Number 14, Mr. Cub, is in his first season as a first baseman. For as long as we have been aware, Ernie

Banks has always played shortstop. As we approach the turnstiles I can barely contain my enthusiasm.

Uncle John purchases three tickets for the left field bleachers. I look at my brother out of the corner of my eye. Nick Angel's White Sox tickets are always for box seats. Tom nudges me and shakes his head slightly. He's giving me the "Keep your big mouth shut" look. You know the one where the eyes get wide, the bottom of the face elongates, and the head shakes slightly back and forth. It is enough that we are here. It doesn't matter where we sit. But, there is something about the expression on my uncle's face that tells us that this day's adventure is yet to really begin.

We're walking in the tunnel beneath the stands. We think we're on our way to our seats in the left field bleachers. However, there is a large man dressed in blue who heads us off at the pass. He is a Chicago cop. He has the patented Chicago cop gut, and a face that looks like it was designed using a land mine field for inspiration. He sticks out a fleshy hand and greets my uncle. Apparently, they are old friends. Uncle John introduces us.

The cop asks if we are big Cub fans. "Yessir!" we lie in unison. Tom is an ardent San Francisco Giants fan. His patron saint is the "Say Hey Kid", Willie Mays. This very season ('62) Mays is leading the Giants to the National League Pennant. He will hit 49 home runs this year. I worship at the altar of Al Lopez and the American League team from the South Side. My mom and dad actually bought me a White Sox uniform that I wear around the neighborhood. It has the number "11" stenciled on the back and the name "Aparicio" printed in block letters on the back of the shoulders. Little Luis is on his way to stealing the most bases in the American League for the seventh consecutive season. Unbelievably, next year the Sox will trade him to the Baltimore Orioles where he will remain until he comes back to Chicago in 1968.

But today we have to be big Cub fans, and the events of the next half hour will make the lie twist itself into truth before all is through. "Well, dat's good boys, because I gotta coupla baseballs here, but dere only for Cub fans."

The cop says this and produces two shiny, sacred little boxes which contain "Official National League Baseballs." He could have handed us the Holy Grail and our sense of awe would not have been greater. "Oh Man! Thank you very much, sir!" Our mom has drilled this politeness into our heads for years. I remember her teaching us how to speak to people when first introduced. "How do you do, SIR. How do you do, MA'AM." She would chant these words in a rhythmic, staccato voice which emphasized the "SIR" and "MA'AM" terrifically.

Later on, during the pre-adolescent smart alec phase, we would add the tag phrase, "And then you KICK 'em, in the CAN." But we're not quite in that phase yet and our manners are passable.

Now the cop turns his attention to my uncle. "John, lemme see dose tickets ya got dere." My uncle hands him the tickets. He regards them as if they are slices of 17-day-old baloney which someone has left on a very hot radiator. "Ah, dese are no good," he opines. Then he rips them up, right in front of us. "Lessee if we can't do a little betterenat, eh boys?" He starts walking and we follow him through the underbelly of the most mystical of all the ballparks in the land. Uncle John, the cop, Tom, and I move with great purpose through the crowd. I am clutching at my new treasure and simultaneously wondering about the ripped up tickets. I have to almost run to keep pace with the others.

Where are we possibly headed now? These questions and thoughts tumble through my mind, clicking like the baseball cards we have strategically clothes-pinned on our bike wheels to make noisy contact with the spokes. This is more information than my seven year old mind has had to contend with all at once, ever.

As we come up the stairs and catch our first glimpse of the field, I am almost overpowered by the greenness of the grass, the blueness of the sky, and the beauty of the ivy covered outfield walls. It doesn't even matter that a game is going to be played here today. The otherworldly splendor of the place and the magic of the very air we are breathing is enough for me. There is no place in the known Universe I would rather be than where I am at this moment. The officer leads us to our seats. They are in the second row, just a few feet behind and to the left of the Philadelphia Phillies dugout. They are perfect.

"Oh, thanks a lot sir!" my brother says as the cop hands us the corresponding tickets. "These seats are great!" I am just staring with my mouth open. Even Nick Angel's White Sox tickets never got us this close to the action.

Uncle John takes his seat. We move to do the same. "Wait a minnit, fellas," says the cop. "Don't siddown yet. I wanya ta falla me." He walks down the steps toward the field and performs the single most astonishing feat that I have ever witnessed. He opens the little door in the wall which leads out onto the Wrigley Field grass. Now, in my mind that would be like calling President Kennedy up on the phone, or opening the hatch of Alan Shepard's Mercury spacecraft and asking if we can come in to sit and chat with him for a little while before the launch. But the cop does it; and he follows it up by uttering this holiest of holy phrases, "Come on in boys, and meet summada players."

I pinch my forearm very hard. I am indeed awake. This is actually happening. I once asked my dad what happened to people who went out onto the field at a Major League ballpark. He told me that big burly security guards come and grab you and throw you out of the place. Or, if you do something really bad, like interfere with the game, they might even throw you in prison!

Yet here we are, sauntering onto the grass like we're the offspring of Mayor Daley. The cop takes off his cap to scratch his head. I catch a glimpse of something circular, shimmering, and gold, but he puts it back on too quickly for me to verify a halo sighting.

It is still quite a while before game time. The Cubbies are taking batting practice. Other people along the first baseline notice our little excursion. "Hey, where ya goin'?" croaks an old man in a Cubs hat. He has probably dreamed of having a moment like ours for over sixty years. A kid about our own age has a look of envy and dismay plastered across his visage. "Howda you guys get to go out there?" he asks in bewildered tones. "Hey, c-can I come too?" sputters another. We shrug and smile and it is not until years later that I fully understand that pleasures like the one we are having are made keener because of their exclusivity. Only one championship team carries the trophy. Only one Prince kisses Sleeping Beauty. And today, only one pair of little Indiana brothers gets to stroll out on the diamond at Beautiful Wrigley Field.

The cop is walking into the Phillies dugout like it is his own back yard patio. We follow, zombies of amazement, in his wake. The team from the City of Brotherly Love will finish in 7th place in 1962. Clay Dalrymple is their catcher. He will lead the majors with a .987 fielding average. Roy (Squirrel) Sievers plays first base; Tony Taylor at second;

Bobby Wine at shortstop; Don Demeter is at third. Johnny Callison, Tony Gonzales, and Wes Covington are in the outfield. All the players are cordial. They shake our hands and sign the baseball. Wes Covington is the last to sign. I stare at the huge bicep beneath the sleeve of his Phillies uniform. I've never seen such muscle. As we leave the dugout I reach out and touch a red Phillies batting helmet. Nobody yells at me.

The cop winks, "Come on boys. Let's go meet summada Cubs." One of the boys back in the neighborhood, Shezzy (real name, David Shapiro), is the quintessential Cub fan. His dad is a doctor and they have lots of money. When you go into their house it is air-conditioned. There is (or will soon be) a large color TV in their basement. The boys (there are four of them) will receive Fender electric guitars for their birthdays. In short, they have lots and lots of cool material things which the sons of a drycleaner won't see for years to come. That's okay though, because they don't have this moment.

I keep nudging my brother as we walk around the field. Several times I repeat the phrase, "Shezzy's gonna burn when he finds out about this." I'm hoping that the pre-game show, "The Lead Off Man", comes on soon so that as he tunes in he can see us striding boldly about the field, calmly engaging in small talk with his heroes. What will his reaction be? What will the reaction of any of the kids at Ernest R. Elliott Elementary School be next fall? Perhaps they will elect me Emperor of the school; at the very least, King. I try on different gloating strategies as we approach the Cubs.

The first Cub we meet is Billy Williams, a future Hall of Fame player. He is in the midst of only his second season with the Cubs. Last year in 1961 he was the National League Rookie of the Year. Next year (1963) Billy will begin an Iron Man streak which will last for 1,117 games.

For his career he will bat .290 and blast 426 home runs. We shake hands and exchange pleasantries. For him this is nothing new. For us, the moment is indescribable, something which only happens to other people.

Behind the plate is Dick Bertell. He toils daily in the sun, wearing the "tools of ignorance" for a club that will finish in 9th place behind the Colt .45's (later the Astros). Only the lowly Mets, with a mere 40 victories, will fare worse than the Cubbies. The Mets will be an American joke for quite a few years. However in 1969, they will be the laughing champions as the season comes to a close and the Cubs take a prolonged and painful nosedive. Mr. Bertell greets us, signs the ball, snaps on his catcher's mask, and trots away.

George Altman is starting in the outfield today. Next year the Cubs will trade him to the Cardinals. The Cardinals will ship him to the Mets. The Mets will send him back to the Cubs in 1965. If I remember correctly, George gets so used to packing and moving, that one season he packs up and goes all the way over to Japan to complete his career.

Andy Rodgers is taking over for Ernie Banks at shortstop this season. I can honestly remember nothing about this man. I see in a book years later that he was born in the Bahamas. He will bat .278 this season and make 28 errors. Poor guy. What mortal could hope to fill the shoes that Ernie vacated by moving over to first base? Who, besides Frazier Thomas, could be the host of "Garfield Goose" or "Family Classics"?

Now the cop wants to take us over to meet Ron Santo. We see him standing there behind the cage. He has just finished up his batting practice cuts. As we start in his direction he turns and jogs into the clubhouse. He disappears, and does not return again while our moment of magic is still in progress. Maybe he hates little kids. Maybe he signed ten thousand autographs already and he said to himself, "I'm not gonna sign another one as long as I live." Years later I hear on the radio that Santo is a diabetic. For quite a while he had concealed that fact from the fans. I flash back to that moment and all is forgiven. Ron was merely checking into the clubhouse for his pre-game insulin fix. My admiration for him swells as he reclaims his rightful place in the pantheon of my heroes.

The center fielder we are introduced to now is a young man with sharp eyes who looks fast. He is just a rookie. His name is Lou Brock. He hails from El Dorado, Arkansas. This year he'll bat .263. Next year he'll hit just .258. Not much of a prospect, I guess. The Cubs will decide to trade him to the '64 Cardinals for a pitcher named Ernest Gilbert Broglio. Brock will team up with Bob Gibson and others to bring the World Championship to St. Louis in 1964 and 1967. The Tigers will barely squeak by them in 1968. Broglio's earned run average for 1964 will be 20.25.

Thinking about this blunder in later years makes the crumpled fenders, ripped tuxedo flies, and financial foh-pahs of my own lifetime seem insignificant by comparison. Thank you Chicago Cubs. I have yet to goof things up as badly as you did in the Brock for Broglio fiasco. It is the yardstick by which all bad decisions are measured.

The second baseman is another rookie; only twenty years of age. That's just ten years older than my brother is on this day. He is a slick fielding shy kid who seems to have a great future ahead of him. In fact, this year he will win the Rookie of the Year award for the National League. His name is Kenny Hubbs. I should walk right up to him and say, "Nice to meet you, Mr. Hubbs. Thanks for signing the ball. By the way, two years from now, please don't get on any airplanes in February. It was bad for Buddy Holly when he was 22. It is going to be just as bad for you as it was for him."

In the time to come I picture three men sitting around a table, laughing and playing cards (probably, they're playing hearts). Their names are Roberto Clemente, Thurman Munson, and Kenny Hubbs. They are in Heaven and they all have two things in common. All of them perished in plane crashes, and all of them were baseball heroes. There is a little plaque on the wall which explains why God chose to take these three men off America's diamonds and up into Paradise in the same fashion. I see myself walking up to read that plaque. I notice Knute Rockne at another table in a different corner of the room. He's sitting with some young men wearing purple jackets, but I don't have time to investigate further.

In 1966 the Topps trading card company will print a Dick Ellsworth baseball card, and mistakenly use an old photograph of Hubbs. When I see the card, I get goosebumps. But, being eleven years old, I will refuse to cry.

This episode however, is not allowed to end on a sad note. The cop takes us over in the vicinity of first base. There he stands, tall and slender, with incandescent brown skin. Number 14. He is blessed with possibly the most optimistic face which God has ever created. I'm not sure how others feel, but whenever I meet a celebrity (which has been rare indeed if one does not consider the day being reviewed), my greatest fear is that he or she will not live up to the advanced billing. We have seen Ernie Banks on television a thousand times. Knocking one out onto Waveland Avenue; smiling and chatting with Jack Brickhouse on "The Tenth Inning" post game show; playfully bantering with Cubs and non-Cubs as he revels in the joy that is Big League Baseball. What if he snaps and tells the cop that it is too close to game time? What if the charm turns out to be made for TV only? My juvenile paranoia proves to be unfounded and the opposite is true. Ernie's eyes are brighter, his smile more genuine, his courtesy more sincere than any human I have ever encountered. I've memorized the conversation and have replayed it in my brain a thousand times.

"Ernie," says the cop. "I'd like you to meet two friends of mine, Tom and Greg Karas."

"Well, hello Tom. Hello, Greg. Did you boys come out to see the Cubs win one today?"

"We sure did Ernie."

"Well, that's fine. It's certainly a pleasure to meet you boys. Enjoy the game now."

"We will Ernie. Thanks. Thanks a lot for signing the ball."

"You're welcome, boys. So long, now."

Before we leave the field, I stand on first base with both feet. I stare down at my shoes, wondering if my mom will let me get them bronzed. I know this is a memory I will carry with me until I am an old, old man. I return to my seat in a daze. I have no idea who wins the game. I spend much of the afternoon staring at the baseball. Miracles, I now know, do occur. One has just happened to my brother and me.

◇

Well, in the eyes of a kid who is seven, I am an old man now. I have traveled from the idyllic fields of childhood into the more weather-beaten pastures of the adult experience.

Yet, I have managed to keep at least one of my feet anchored in the past. Since I am an elementary school teacher I get to see a little of the optimism and wonder which are still present in a child's life each day. To be sure, the explosion of technology and a creeping national cynicism have conspired to make that innocence shrink a little more each year. But the innocence is still there. Kids are still kids and their eyes still do widen occasionally in surprise and delight.

In addition to being a teacher I'm also a married father of two kids. My beautiful wife Liz and I have tried when possible to provide some of those magic moments for both of them. My son's name is Nick and my daughter is Natalie, and they are both adults themselves now. But, in September of 1990 when we take them to a ball game at Comiskey Park (to the old Comiskey, the *real* Comiskey, before corporate moguls re-christened the new stadium, U.S. Cellular Field), we have an experience which has echoes of that magical summer day in 1962. It is during the waning days of the campaign and also the final moments in the life of the old stadium, just days before it goes under the wrecking ball.

The season will end tomorrow night. It is the second to the last game of Reggie Jackson's remarkable career. His incredible hitting feats in the World Series have earned him the moniker, "Mr. October". There was even at one point a "Reggie" candy bar. Jose Canseco is also with the club at the time.

We arrive early to see batting practice. After parking we notice an old gentleman getting out of his car a row away from us. He looks vaguely familiar. I glance down at his license plate to see if it gives any clue who he is. It reads "MINOSO" (followed by a single digit). "That's Minnie Minoso," I say to my wife and kids. "He was an outfielder on the White Sox when I was a boy. He's one of the coolest guys the Sox ever had! His real name is Orestes!" Minnie, nods, smiles, and waves when we greet him.

The Minoso sighting turns out to be a good omen. We camp out early in left field and enjoy batting practice. We have no connections like those which allowed Uncle John to get my brother and me out onto the actual field in '62.

But, it doesn't matter. We are in the seats looking down on the ground where Babe Ruth, Mickey Mantle, Ted Williams, Nelson Fox, and Luis Aparicio have all trod. That is magic a plenty.

Nick and I have brought our baseball gloves. During batting practice Canseco is especially impressive. He blasts ten or twelve balls into the outfield seats. None of them are close to us. Batting practice ends and the A's take some fielding practice. Canseco is now out in left field catching fly balls. A corpulent coach with a fungo bat (who is standing in the vicinity of where the shortstop would normally play) is hitting them to him. Some of the shots travel all the way to the warning track. Canseco handles most of them effortlessly. We are standing in the front row, very close to the place where the famous "cup of spilled beer ready to hit outfielder Al Smith's head" photograph was taken.

The chubby coach cracks another fungo shot to left field. This one is traveling a little deeper than the others. Amazingly, it is soaring in a long lazy arc through the early evening sky right toward the spot we are occupying along the green left field wall. Canseco jogs back and prepares to make the catch. He is on the warning track. Nick and I follow the path of the ball, but are vaguely aware of his presence below us. He is near the picnic area now as the ball makes its final descent. Canseco reaches up and jumps to haul it in. Nick and I reach down. It is a matter of mere inches. Having the high ground enables me to get above Canseco's gloved hand. The ball pops into my glove and for one brief instant all three mitts smack together. An old man in a checkered shirt behind us with a cigar and a beer croaks, "Sign him up."

It is at that moment that I remember I had my glove with me (of course, a different one) on the day that I met Kenny Hubbs, Lou Brock, and Ernie Banks. Adults can basically be divided into two categories. There are those who would be too embarrassed to bring their baseball gloves to a game. Then there are those who know the true meaning of the phrase, "Luck is what happens when preparation meets opportunity." The two have just met.

Canseco whirls around and glares at us. We have interfered with his practice time and he is not amused. The difference between Ernie Banks and Jose Canseco is instantly emblazoned upon my mind. Ernie realized that one of the things he was there to do was to give joy to people. And what better joy for a kid than getting a baseball at a major league game? Jose, on the other hand, is ticked off because his rehearsal has been interrupted. I hand the ball over to my son Nick, and see him smile a very familiar smile. It was the same smile my brother and I gave the cop back in '62.

After the game Nick and I hustle down with the ball toward the visitors' dugout. It is on the first base side. Reggie Jackson is standing nearby, signing autographs. It would be a real coup to have this "Canseco Ball" signed by Reggie. We wait, but there are hundreds of people with gloves, photos, and programs, who all have the same idea. Before we are even close to the front of the mob, Reggie has smiled, waved and headed back into the dugout.

I look down (one last time) at the wall which separates the fans from the field. I see a very old looking man, standing right near the first base dugout. He is a large man, and somehow he has the look of a retired cop. His face is heavily pockmarked, and he is sporting a mysterious, twinkling eyed smile. He glances wistfully around the stadium. It is as though he is saying with his eyes, "Take a good look around. Pretty soon da only thing dat's gonna be left of dis place is da memories." Then, he turns back in our direction. For one odd moment I feel like he might be looking directly at us. It is cool out and he is wearing a cap. He momentarily removes it and I think I see a glint of circular gold. He replaces the hat quickly after shoving back his gray hair. Nick and I rejoin his sister, Natalie and my wife, Liz. We walk out through the stadium underbelly, out into the crisp and magical South Side night.

◇

As the generational wheels spin a part of us can only sit and watch the change. My dad passed away in October of 2002 at the age of 82. He lived his *entire life* without ever seeing a World Series Champion in Chicago. I never once heard him complain about that. At games on the South Side he would sit quietly and watch while my brother and I hooped and hollered for Little Luis, Jim Landis, Minnie Minoso, and Nellie Fox. Every few innings he'd ask if we wanted a Frosty Malt, a hot dog, a Coke, or a bag of peanuts. When October rolled around and the Yankees or the Cardinals would win the World Series, he seemed to not even notice, or at least accept it in the same way that people in Northwest Indiana inevitably accept snowstorms, corrupt politicians, and air pollution. That's just life. Some good things happen, some bad things happen, and then one day, you die. If people are looking for joy in this world, the last place they'd better be is inside a ball park as the baseball season comes to a close. Nostalgia? Yes. But, it is almost always a nostalgia tinged with sadness. Baseball happiness was for other people in different cities.

What if "Shoeless" Joe Jackson and the seven others had not chosen to accept gamblers' money in the 1919 Series? Why did Charles Comiskey (the "Old Roman") have to be such an unremitting skin flint? What if Al Lopez and his "Go Go" Sox had fulfilled the tremendous promise they showed by thrashing the Dodgers in Game One of the 1959 World Series? After all, they had won that first game, 11 - 0. Someone suggested that the games out in Los Angeles threw the Sox for a loop. Do you realize that over 90 thousand people were in attendance at the Coliseum for those west coast games? Who plays baseball in front of 90 thousand fans? Have you ever seen photographs of the weird configuration that stadium had to have in order to squeeze the game in? Baseball in Chicago was just one series of "What ifs" after another. Several times the champagne was right there inside the bottle, but no one (on either the South *or* the North side of town) had ever figured out how to pull up that cork.

Indeed, on the North Side, people had a bag full of superstitious explanations for the shortcomings of the Cubs. People could point at the Billy Goat, the Black Cat, and a guy named Steve Bartman, in order to explain why Cubbie Blue had not truly been in baseball fashion since Theodore Roosevelt was at 1600 Pennsylvania Avenue. My word, that was an entire *century* ago! Yankee fans are upset when they have to wait over a year for a World Series trophy.

In this new millennium however, the laws of the baseball universe seem to have been reversed. The first sign was when the Red Sox found themselves down to the Yankees 3 games to none in the American League Championship Series of 2004. Boston fans found themselves in a familiar position. They were ready to lose. They were ***conditioned*** to lose. They too, had experienced frustration which had stretched back until the era of the First World War. If anything, their sense of futility was even more pronounced because on many occasions they had been right on the brink of winning it all. But (and needless to say it just might be the largest "but" in the entire history of baseball), they miraculously beat the Yankees four straight and went on to sweep the Cardinals. Beantown became delirious. People in Chicago paid attention. If the curse of the Bambino could be reversed, maybe the cloud which had blocked the sun since the Black Sox scandal could be blown away as well.

Ozzie Guillen had come back to town in 2004. He didn't believe in curses or omens (on second thought, I guess Ozzie did believe in curses, but just as a part of his vocabulary). He mainly believed in good, aggressive baseball, supported by stellar pitching. In 2005 the Sox won 99 games in the regular season and then scorched their way through the first two rounds of the playoffs with a 7 - 1 record. I got out to a couple of games that year. One against the Cubs and one against the Red Sox. My wife and I watched most of the games on the local channels in Chicago and when the playoffs rolled around, the contests appeared on Fox. One of the ironic things about baseball is that the more important the games become, the less and less an average fan can be in attendance. We heard stories of people paying over $7,000.00 for tickets to games in the World Series.

Obviously, nobody in our family was going to attend. TV would have to suffice.

One of my responsibilities as a teacher is supervising field trips for students from time to time. Each year we take our school's fifth graders to Indianapolis for a tour of the State Capital, the State Museum, and the Indianapolis Zoo. I teach the fourth grade, but we get substitutes for our classes and gladly help shepherd the kids around the Hoosier Capital for two days. This trip always takes place in October and in most years that had never presented a scheduling problem. However, during the playoffs I was checking the calendar and noticed that Game 4 of the World Series was going to take place during the trip. One day I mentioned to the fifth grade teachers the potential scheduling conflict. Sure enough, as the trip and the playoffs developed, that turned out to be exactly the case.

Now, the journey we take is unique in many regards. The kids get to walk right through the Governor's office in the beautiful and cavernous State Capitol Building, they climb around on the huge Soldiers and Sailors monument which is smack dab in the middle of the city, and at night they get to sleep next to the dolphins at the Indianapolis Zoo. There is a large and beautiful glass domed room built into the facility which allows visitors to stand beneath the dolphins and gaze up in awe as they gracefully and silently swim past. It is the last place in the world which would normally bring thoughts of baseball to someone's mind. But on that night, October 26th, 2005, there are a couple of us in the building who can think of nothing else. Mrs. Lute and myself.

I have brought along a tiny black and white television set with about a four inch screen. Other than an odd cell phone or two, it is our only link to the outside world. The aforementioned Monica Lute, one of our school's teacher's aides, has grown up with the same love of White Sox baseball that I have. Monica's daughter (she has four of them) was with her at a game once and the Great Konerko tossed her a game ball as he trotted off the field between innings. But Monica also shares the same sense of perpetually impending doom which tells her that it really can't be possible that it is the end of October *and* the White Sox are one game away from becoming Champions of the Baseball World. This hasn't happened in the universe which we've inhabited for the last half century. I had assured Monica before the trip that I would be bringing along the TV. It is the only reason she agreed to attend. After an entire lifetime of waiting, one field trip was not going to ruin her chance to see the impossible occur. The 5th grade kids are gone on a three hour, behind the scenes tour of the zoo (which other adults in attendance and on the zoo staff have graciously agreed to supervise).

My teaching partner, Bryan Benke (who really is not a big baseball fan, but who is perceptive enough to realize what this moment might mean to us), Monica, and I are all lying on sleeping bags spread out a short distance from the "Dolphin Dome". The television is propped up on a duffel bag and we watch in agonizing suspense, for a couple of different reasons. You see, we all remember the monumental collapse of the Yankees a year before. If something like that could happen to them, it could *certainly* happen to a team from Chicago. When a fifth grade teacher (Mrs. Highlan) suggested that we might want the Sox to lose a game so that the winning contest could be viewed in the comfort and privacy of our own homes, Monica replied, "Oh, my gosh! Don't say that! Never hope they lose! Never. NEVER!" Monica understands (deep inside her bones) just how difficult it is to win, and just how contagious and insidious losing baseball *can* be (always *has* been) in Chicago. But, there is something oddly different about these White Sox. They have been, throughout the entire playoffs, the team which has ***received*** all the lucky breaks. They have been the beneficiaries of (almost) all the questionable umpire calls. The air itself has just smelled different this season. It is as though angels had flipped the entire Universe over with one of Nellie Fox's thick handled bats.

The other thing we worry about is that the kids (over 50 of them) are going to come storming back into the Dolphin facility at any moment and destroy the "baseball mood". You see, there are only a few children nowadays who have an affinity for baseball the way that virtually every kid did in the long ago past. Video games, skateboards, I-Pods, and weird television programs about things I can't begin to fathom (like huge, yellow, square talking sponges), take up lots of their attention. Only a couple (C.J. and Spencer come to mind) really have an emotional investment in the game, from what I can discern. I jokingly suggest that the worst thing that can happen is that when the kids return, one of them will run into the lobby, trip over Monica, fracture his leg, knock the TV off the duffel bag and break it. His injury will force us to drive him to a local hospital with the antenna from the set still lodged somewhere in his body. The radio in our school van will catch on fire and the cell phone batteries will all die simultaneously. We will stop a homeless person on the street to ask if he knows the outcome of the game. The man, his overcoat covered in dirt and slime, will pull out a handgun and say, "Yeah, I know who won." Then, he'll pull the trigger twice...

The game is unbelievably suspenseful. Seven drama filled innings come and go without either team scoring a single run. In the middle of the fifth inning I trot out into the dolphin dome to pray during the commercial break. From my time as a high school and college athlete I know that we are never supposed to pray for victory. Coaches would tell you that you were allowed to pray for strength and you could petition God so that no one would get hurt during the contest. But really, on the night of the last game of the World Series I find myself breaking the rule without a second thought. I think of an ancient man in Tampa, Florida, lying in his bed. He is 97 years old. He was the manager of the White Sox back in 1959. People called him "The Senor". I remember him wearing his glasses in the dugout when we attended games back in the 1960's. His name is Al Lopez. I pray that the White Sox can win so that he can truly rest in peace.

I think of men like Myron Knauff, a former principal and assistant superintendent from our school district, who was personal friends with Dr. Bobby Brown, the President of the American League. Dr. Brown would often get tickets for his friend Myron. In fact, at the famous World Series game in 1959 when the cup of beer was photographed in the act of falling on left fielder Al Smith's head, Myron was in the very same bleachers, six rows back. Myron is still around, he recently turned 90, and he is probably the greatest sports fan that lives in the entire state of Indiana (or the whole country for all I know). Even at his advanced age, people can still spot Mr. Knauff at high school football games, junior high track meets, soccer games, cross country meets, volleyball matches, and basketball games. His attendance at these events has approached a legendary status. People will nod and say, "There's Myron." His integrity and spirit are as strong as they were at the last White Sox World Series, when I was four years old. I pray that the White Sox can win for him.

I think about my old man, Anthony T. Karas, the drycleaner from East Chicago who took us to Comiskey Park so many times, so many years ago. As mentioned earlier, he died in 2002 in October and I remember thinking that it was ironic that he left the earth during the month in which the World Series takes place, without ever seeing a victorious one happen close to where he lived. He was not a huge baseball fan, but he knew that his kids were. I remember walking with him to the hardware store in East Chicago when I was about 5 or 6. There was a huge, rotating spool of twine on the counter positioned next to a horizontally mounted razor blade. The clerk would expertly spin the twine around and snap off a piece to help wrap up customer orders in crisp brown paper. On the shelves behind the counter, there were boxes and boxes of Topps Baseball Cards. Each box contained several packs of cards and each pack had that magical, rectangular pink bubble gum waiting inside with the even more wonderful cardboard icons. If I close my eyes right now and inhale I can smell the twine and the pink dust which mystically adhered to the gum and cards. Nearly, but not every time we'd go into that store, our Old Man would spring for two boxes of cards. One for my brother, Tom. And one for me. Good Lord, don't tell me there is no magic in this world.

Back at the dry cleaning shop we would open up the cards, gobble multiple pieces of gum, and wildly exclaim as the contents of each pack revealed themselves to us. "Billy Williams! Oh, look! Look! Minoso! Ah, I got Juan Marichal! Oh, man, Willie Mays! Willie Mays! I can't believe it!" And then finally, to bring the most sublime joy into my juvenile existence, there would be the card with number 11 wearing a White Sox uniform, Luis Aparicio... ah, the music of that name!

I open up my eyes and I'm still inside the dolphin dome. A sleek and beautiful mammal glides above my head in the darkened, surrealistic setting. I gaze at him and recognize the vast gulf which lies between our worlds. With all of his beauty, power, and intelligence the thought occurs to me that this creature of the deep could well be an angel in his own right. What if mankind had done that? Captured aquatic angels and put them inside million gallon tanks for our entertainment and amusement. If that could be true, then I know they would forgive us, because as we've shown again and again, "We know not what we do." But, if he is an angel, he may very well be there to answer my prayers, in spite of the way we have treated him and his kind. "Please," I whisper as he swims by, "Please let the White Sox win this one game."

Back in the lobby, the game continues to be a nail biting affair. The eighth inning comes and Jermaine Dye is at bat with a man on second. The contest is still scoreless. Suddenly, the doors to the dolphin facility fly open and all 52 kids come storming in shouting, asking questions, and noticing us sprawled on the ground in front of a *television set!* One boy, Tom, does almost exactly what I had dreaded earlier in the evening. He flies into the room, leaps over the duffel bag and TV set, missing the outstretched antenna by less than an inch. When he lands the cord of the set gets wrapped around his left leg. Bryan sticks out a hand to grab him and I steady the set and the duffel bag. "Tom, NO!" I shout as if he were a wayward puppy, "BE CAREFUL!"

Luckily, the disaster is averted and we tell the kids to get their sleeping bags ready in the adjoining room and we'll send in reports to them regarding the outcome of the game. Dye cracks a shot to center field and the Sox score what turns out to be the lone run of the entire ball game! In the bottom of the 9th, shortstop Juan Uribe makes an unbelievable diving catch into the stands on a foul ball and then ends the game with another dazzling play of a ground ball right up the middle. The Houston fans are stunned. The White Sox are filled with the type of elation that can only be experienced after 88 years of waiting. The television set cuts to a bar called Jimbo's on the Southside and people are shouting, crying, and shaking their beer bottles as if they were in the locker room with the team and those bottles were filled with champagne. The phrase that immediately enters my mind is “Unbridled Joy”.

I am drained and in nearly utter disbelief. Inside my traveling cooler I have brought along a bottle which looks like champagne, but actually contains sparkling pear juice (after all, we are on a field trip supervising kids). I open up the bottle and we pour the bubbly into small plastic cups, for all the adults present; third grade teacher, Mrs. Deb Wolf, Student Teacher, Miss Jamie Dodaro, Fifth Grade Teacher, Mrs. Cheryl Highlan, my teaching partner, Bryan Benke, Monica Lute, and myself. I just wanted to drink the victory drink, but Mrs. Highlan looks at me and says, "Wait, wait! You brought this. We have to have a Toast!" So I say, "A Toast to my Dad, who was born in 1920 and died in 2002, and never once got to see this happen!" We all drain our glasses. Bryan walks into the room with the kids (who are settling down into their sleeping bags) and announces, "Ladies and Gentlemen, the 2005 World Series Champions, The Chicago White Sox!" The room filled with 5th graders explodes in wild cheers.

After we settle the students down (no minor task) I sleep fitfully for a couple of hours, but realize that it will not last. I walk again into the dolphin dome, but all is quiet there. We are locked into the facility and have been told by zoo officials not to open the doors under any circumstances during the night. I stroll to the front of the lobby in the darkness. Zoo security is on duty 24/7. Periodically, we have seen them drive by the door in carts, or sometimes walk by with flashlights. I am standing by the doors gazing up into the October sky when an ambulatory guard comes by. Like many security people he seems to be a retiree, but still hale and hearty. This large gentleman is wearing a dark blue jacket. He stops for a moment and shines his flashlight into the lobby to see that all is well in dolphin land.

When I see his face through the glass my jaw inadvertently drops. He is indeed quite old, far older than I had at first imagined. His nose is huge and gnarled. His frame and hands are large. His entire face is peppered with pockmarks. His smile is broader than the largest jack - o - lantern I have ever carved. He grabs his two way radio off of his belt, lifts it to his mouth, and pushes the button. I can just barely hear his voice through the glass. "Kenny, dis is me. Tell 'em to get tings ready for da Senor. Everyting's been taken caruv down here now. And, hey, remember dat kid from '62? Da one wid his brudder who came ta get da ball signed when youse played da Phillies. Dat one who I tolya I was his G.A. too? He's here, Yeah. Right here at da zoo! Yeah, he’s 50! Can ya bleeve it?" He replaces the radio into his belt, adjusts his trousers, and walks off in the direction of the giraffe enclosure. As he leaves, he gives me the quickest wink as he tips his cap.

I walk back to my sleeping bag and lie down. As I drift into slumber my dreams are as sweet as they were when I was seven years old. Ernie Banks shakes my brother's hand and turns toward me. Minnie Minoso nods his head and smiles. Nellie Fox is up to bat against the Yankees with a man on first base. Comiskey Park is full of screaming fans. The third baseman charges in as Fox squares around to bunt. The shortstop sprints to cover second base. The runner on first breaks as the ball is delivered. Fox punches the pitch sharply *over* the head of the charging infielder with the bat still in bunting position. The runner from first sprints like a rocket around the diamond and ends up streaking toward home plate. The ball spins toward the foul line in shallow left field. Fox slides into second with a double. The left fielder retrieves the spinning sphere and rifles it toward the plate. The stadium erupts as the runner from first slides safely into home. He springs to his feet and dusts himself off, then trots back to the 3rd base dugout. He glances up and makes eye contact with us as we leap into the air, cheering ourselves hoarse, right in front of Nick Angel's perfect box seats. He's wearing Number 11.

Ah, Baseball. Ah, Chicago!

* * * * * * *

## Acknowledgements

I would like to thank my middle school English Teacher, Miss Dodd. One day she chose to read a story I had written to the entire lecture hall full of 7th grade students. The story was about how the gods up on Mount Olympus played a rough brand of basketball which was responsible for our thunder down on Earth. I can still remember the astonishment with which I watched her read that little story to the packed lecture hall. They actually listened. It was the ***first*** time I had any idea that I could write things which other people might enjoy reading. Anyone who doubts the importance of teachers in this world should have been sitting in the lecture hall that day to see the look on my face. It is something I try to remember every day when I walk into my fourth grade classroom.

I would also like to thank the great and greatly talented Barbara Pedersen. Barbara runs the educational training organization known as C.L.A.S.S. (Connected Learning Assures Successful Students). It has been one of the supreme pleasures of my life to know and work with Barbara. Individuals who have attended her workshops and seminars will know exactly what I'm talking about. It is safe to say that the book you are holding in your hands right now would never have existed without Barbara's encouragement and never ending optimism.. I've seen lots of people speak to groups of teachers and learners in my time. Barbara is without question the very best.

Many of the pieces in this collection are essays or stories I wrote for the Sunrise Kiwanis Club of Valparaiso, Indiana. The newsletter of that fine organization is called the "**Sunrise Snews**" because of a warm and funny gentleman named Dale Sonney. Dale thought up that clever name two decades ago. The editor of the **Snews** is Diane Price. One of the stories in this collection is about her brave son, Kyle. It would probably take another entire book to tell you about all the good things Diane has performed on this planet. In fact, I wish that you all could meet the entire Sunrise Kiwanis Club. They were the original audience for this work. Many were the times that I'd sit and think, "Will the good

Reverend, Jim Mitchell, get this joke or appreciate this point?" It was a great guide.

There are four people I sometimes bounce these pieces off before sending them to the newsletter. Cheryl Highlan, a teaching buddy for many years at Parkview Elementary, Aunt Joan Bryant, a retired school teacher in Coronado, California, the aforementioned Barbara Pedersen, and Doris Johnson, a former teacher from long ago in Munster. They are all too nice, because they invariably report that they love the pieces. I would probably be better off with more critical friends. But, none of them would be so kind, supportive, and encouraging as these four remarkable ladies.

I also want to thank my family. My beautiful wife, Liz, my wonderful son, Nick, and my radiant daughter, Natalie have all filled my life with adventure and joy. Sharing the years with my wife and raising our kids has been a richly rewarding experience. The only moment I would change in the last three decades would be the salt, water, and mattress incident of 1987. And even that one can still make me laugh. As Nick gets set to marry his beautiful fiancée, Emily, and Natalie begins her law career in Washington D.C., the tapestry of our lives continues to unfold.

Oh, yes. I'd also like to thank Tracker the Wonder Dog. J.R.R. Tolkien created a dog named Huan, who was given (three times in his life) the gift of speech. Tracker may have been "just a dog". But, sometimes when I looked into his eyes I was reminded of Chesterton writing about God simply being Dog spelled backwards. May you all be blessed with such a canine friend...

I would also like to thank the photographers who gave their kind permission to include their work in this book. Cheryl Highlan, Olga Granat, and (I think) Becky Clover all took snapshots which helped to tell some of the stories with a bit more clarity.

And finally, I'd like to thank anyone who purchased this book and is now holding it in your hands. I hope that some of the pieces have given you enjoyment, made you think, or provided you with a few moments of diversion in your day. If you've made it all the way to the end and you're still wondering about the title, **The Hummingbird Defenders**, then your patience has finally been rewarded. For the longest time, I wrestled with what to call this collection. As usual, the Good Lord (or at least His Angel in Charge of Important Dreams) stepped up when time was running out.

As I was completing the project I had a dream one night that I was running along the top of the old Munster High School Fieldhouse, just like the characters in the film, **"Crouching Tiger, Hidden Dragon"**. I was trying to get into the building, but was frustrated at every turn. I stopped and opened up a little porthole high in the roof. I looked down (sort of like Jill and Eustace did from inside the snow covered hill near the end of **The Silver Chair**), to a group of people far below. One of them (maybe it was Coach Robertson) shouted up to me, "Call it **The Hummingbird Defenders**!" At that exact moment I woke up, at last certain of the book's title. I have a few guesses what it means, but it is probably better to just keep them to myself. Thanks again for reading, and thanks finally and most importantly to Him from whom all blessings flow.

◇

August 27, 2009 - Valparaiso, Indiana
Greg Karas

Made in the USA